CRACKPROOF YOUR SOFTWARE
The Best Ways to Protect Your Software Against Crackers

CRACKPROOF
YOUR SOFTWARE

THE *BEST* WAYS TO *PROTECT* YOUR SOFTWARE
AGAINST CRACKERS

Pavol Červeň

**NO STARCH
PRESS**

San Francisco

Printed in the United States of America on recycled paper

1 2 3 4 5 6 7 8 9 10–05 04 03 02

Crackproof Your Software is an English version of *Cracking a jak se proti nemů bránit*, by Pavol Červeň, the original Czech version (80-7226-382-X), copyright ©2001 by Computer Press. English translation prepared by Skrivanek Translation Services.

Trademarked names are used throughout this book. Rather than use a trademark symbol with every occurrence of a trademarked name, we are using the names only in an editorial fashion and to the benefit of the trademark owner, with no intention of infringement of the trademark.

Publisher: William Pollock
Editorial Director: Karol Jurado
Cover and Interior Design: Octopod Studios
Composition: 1106 Design, LLC
Copyeditor: Andy Carroll
Indexer: Broccoli Information Management

G.J. SAVERNO

Distributed to the book trade in the United States by Publishers Group West, 1700 Fourth Street, Berkeley, CA 94710; phone: 800-788-3123; fax: 510-658-1834.

Distributed to the book trade in Canada by Jacqueline Gross & Associates, Inc., One Atlantic Avenue, Suite 105, Toronto, Ontario M6K 3E7 Canada; phone: 416-531-6737; fax 416-531-4259.

For information on translations or book distributors outside the United States and Canada, please see our distributors list in the back of this book or contact No Starch Press, Inc. directly:

No Starch Press, Inc.
555 De Haro Street, Suite 250, San Francisco, CA 94107
phone: 415-863-9900; fax: 415-863-9950; info@nostarch.com; http://www.nostarch.com

Library of Congress Cataloging-in-Publication Data

Červeň, Pavol.
  [Cracking a jak se proti nemů bránit. English]
  Crackproof your software / Pavol Červeň.
              p. cm.
      Includes index.
      ISBN 1-886411-79-4
         1. Software protection. 2. Computer security. 3. Data protection. 4. Computer crimes. I. Title.
QA76.76.P76 C47 2002
005.8--dc21
                                    2002012207

ABOUT THE AUTHOR

I started programming on 8-bit computers and the only good programming language for them was assembler. My father bought a PC about four years ago, and if not for that PC, this book probably would not exist. (When I finished this book, I was 23 years old.)

I have tried several programming languages but have remained faithful to assembly because I think it is the clearest and the most beautiful programming language. What you write in assembly is exactly what you will find in the compiled version — nothing less and nothing more.

In the days of DOS I dealt with the problems closest to assembly — viruses, and even dreamt about working for an antivirus software company. When Windows 9x appeared, assembler was used less and less and there were also fewer viruses (at least fewer assembly viruses). That's when I discovered something new, unexplored and often mysterious: protecting software against illegal copying. As I explored this challenge, I became so preoccupied with it that I quit the virus field (though I still enjoy the protection field and think I will stick with it for some time to come).

My page at www.anticracking.sk will give you a bit more information about what I do and our product, SVK - Protector: a powerful tool for securing software against unauthorized copying, use, and distribution. SVKP was designed with ease of use and high speed as a priority without sacrificing high levels of protection. It offers three different methods of securing: It uses RSA algorithm, API functions, and new anti-debug tricks.

Pavol Červeň

BRIEF CONTENTS

CONTENTS IN DETAIL

INTRODUCTION

1
BASICS

2
CRACKING TOOLS

3
THE BASIC TYPES OF SOFTWARE PROTECTION

4

CD PROTECTION TRICKS

5

PROGRAM COMPRESSION AND ENCODING:
FREEWARE AND SHAREWARE

6

COMMERCIAL SOFTWARE PROTECTION PROGRAMS

7

ANTI-DEBUGGING, ANTI-DISASSEMBLING, AND OTHER TRICKS
FOR PROTECTING AGAINST SOFTICE AND TRW

8

DETECTING BREAKPOINTS, TRACERS, AND DEBUGGERS

9

OTHER PROTECTION TRICKS

10

IMPORTANT STRUCTURES IN WINDOWS

11

SUGGESTIONS FOR BETTER SOFTWARE PROTECTION

Glossary
231

About the CD
232

Index
233

INTRODUCTION

This book is designed to help all programmers who have ever written their own software to better protect their software from illegal copying. It will also be useful to programmers creating freeware who wish to protect their source code.

The idea to write a book like this came to me some time ago when I realized how poorly the topic is covered and how difficult it is to acquire the information necessary to adequately protect software. When I was involved with game production in the Czech and Slovak Republics, I was astonished at how simple their protection was, and that very often they had no protection at all—yet it is so easy to protect software, at least at a basic level.

The problem lies in the lack of information and experience in this field. That's why I wrote this book, which will present many previously unaddressed topics concerning software protection.

Protection as a Deterrent

My experience tells me that there is no protection that cannot be easily removed and, as such, much of the work you will put into protecting your software is simply a deterrent, delaying the inevitable. It's only a matter of time, possibilities, and patience before a cracker cracks your software.

Of course, the better your deterrent, the more time you'll have to sell your software before you find it available (or crackable) for free, online. What creators of a program or game would want to find their product, whether shareware or commercial software, pirated on the Internet the very day of the release? That would definitely result in reduced sales.

Good software protection prevents the cracker from removing the protection correctly. With such protection, the program won't work, or won't work correctly, and more people will buy an original copy. Of course, a successful crack will appear in the course of time, but the time you buy is money earned. Really good protection will buy a considerable amount of time and will engender several versions of the crack, some of which will not work properly. In such a case, even many hardcore pirates will buy an original copy rather than try to crack one, just to avoid the hassle.

Working with Assembler

In later chapters you'll find many examples of applications protected from debugging, disassembling, or possible decompiling. The examples are all in assembler, but they are written as comprehensibly as possible and are accompanied by footnotes in a source code. Even a mediocre assembler programmer should be able to understand them. I chose not to use a higher-level language like C++ code because it wouldn't be understandable to programmers who work in Delphi, and vice versa. I chose not to use Visual Basic because most examples cannot be written in it. Assembler is the best choice because even code written in C++ will have some parts written in assembler.

Another advantage of assembler is that it can be directly inserted both into C++ and Delphi code, so assembler examples are universal for both languages. Visual Basic programmers can also insert the code into a library created in another programming language (assembler, C++, or Delphi) and then call the library from the application code. This is certainly not a perfect solution, but it is better than no protection at all.

Publishing Cracker Tricks

This book took considerable effort to write. I had to do a good bit of research, and most of what I present here comes from the web pages of crackers. There are plenty of them, and it is sad that there is almost nothing comparable for developers.

Some people argue that information like that presented in this book should not be freely accessible to everyone. However, keeping it secret would be counterproductive. The fact is, crackers are very well informed, while developers have virtually no resources. When a cracker learns how to remove a certain kind of protection, it is only a matter of time before detailed information on how to do so is published on specialized web pages. On the other hand, developers who don't follow the field of cracking carefully will not be aware of how easily their protection can be cracked and will continue to use this protection, even though it may be removed in a matter of minutes.

It is no surprise that crackers create the best software protection, since they are often the best informed and have the most experience. This situation will hopefully change in the future, and I will be very glad if this book helps in this effort.

My thanks go to all the people without whom this book would never have been written.

First, my special thanks to my friend **Linda** and my family, who tolerated my late-night sessions and my bad mood in the mornings when I had to go to work.

Thanks to my Internet friends:

EliCZ   Thanks for all the help and for your faultless source code. There is hardly a better system programmer than you, really.

Ivan Bartek   Thanks for everything; I look forward to our future cooperation.

Miroslav Bamboušek   You helped me a lot with your keen observations and your help with C examples. I would probably be unable to manage SafeDisc without you.

Ice   Thanks for everything, especially for your inspiration.

Stone   Your wonderful source code helped me in many cases.

The Owl   You are a real master of anti-debugging tricks and other hidden secrets of Windows 9x.

Liquid   Thanks for the anti-FrogsICE tricks.

Pet'o Somora   You are a wonderful mathematician and an even better friend. Thanks for your patience in explaining those problems.

Further, thanks to the following people: Hoe, Doom, Hňup, Brbla, Slask, Lorian, Christopher Gabler, Nihil, Iceman, Maxx, Ender, Alfo, Sadman, Crow, Rainman, Saňo, Momo, Dugi, Ivan, Maroš, Mikie, Kremeň, Neuron, Daemon, SAC, Light Druid, and Vladimir Gneushev. And to everyone whose names I have forgotten to list here but who helped with this book, thank you.

1

BASICS

Before you can protect your software well, you must first understand the methods crackers use to crack your software. *Crackers* are the people who try to remove the protection from your software so that it can be illegally distributed.

Why Crackers Crack

The first mistake developers often make is in underestimating the power and number of crackers, and that's the worst mistake any developer of protection can make. Mostly, crackers are very smart people who will work on removing software protection for days at a time, and in extreme cases even for weeks, for the challenge of it. The cracker's success almost always depends on his motivation.

It may surprise you to learn that most of the cracker's motivation is not financial. Crackers post their cracks and information for free, after all. They're not making money off your software, though the people who use their cracks are saving money. Rather than crack software for financial gain, crackers are taking part in a sort of informal competition. A cracker who can remove a new and very complicated protection scheme becomes a highly regarded and respected person within the cracker community.

How Crackers Crack: Debuggers and Disassemblers

Protection developers often presume that without source code, crackers will not be able to understand the software's protection. This is a huge mistake. Crackers use two kinds of utilities for breaking software protection—debuggers and disassemblers.

Debuggers

Debuggers allow crackers to trace an application, instruction by instruction, and to stop it at any point and follow its important sections. It is true that applications written in higher-level languages (like C++, Visual Basic, or Delphi) may be traced only in assembler, but crackers understand what is happening in the application code amazingly well—probably better than most people can imagine.

The truth is, the higher the level of the programming language, the more difficult it is to trace. But on the other hand, higher-level programming languages offer fewer possibilities for creating really good protection. Everything has its bright and dark sides.

Disassemblers

Disassemblers can translate application code back into assembler. One advantage that disassemblers offer over decompilers is that they always translate into assembler, so the cracker has to know only that one language. The quality of the resulting translated code depends on the quality of the disassembler. The best disassemblers even comment on the translated code, which makes the code that much easier to understand. For example, if the cracker finds a "Wrong serial number" string and locates its place in the code, he will be able to find the part of the code that protects the application. At that point, nothing can prevent him from studying the protection and breaking it.

Decompilers

Decompilers can translate application code back to source code. A decompiler can only translate applications that were written in the language for which the particular decompiler was created. There are, for example, decompilers for Delphi, Visual Basic, and Java. A good decompiler can do a good job of translating the application. Once an application is translated, it's easy for the cracker (if he knows the particular language) to find the sections of interest and determine how they work.

The Most Frequent Protection Failures

There are several reasons why a program may not be well protected against illegal copying:

- No program protection: It is very common for programs to contain no protection at all, and yet their authors require users to purchase the program. When a program is unprotected against copying, developers should not be surprised when their profits are small.

- Weak program protection: Approximately 70 percent of all programs have very weak protection, which crackers can remove very quickly.

- Program protection causing program failures: Many programmers protect their products weakly or not at all because they are afraid that incorrectly programmed protection will create problems with their programs.

It's better to use weaker protection code than none at all, but you will not stop the better crackers this way. Fine-tuning the protection scheme is the most important part of any protection strategy. Once the protection is created, the programmer should become a cracker for a while and, using the crackers' programs, test whether anything has been forgotten.

2

CRACKING TOOLS

If you don't know your enemy's weapons, you cannot defeat him. Let's take a look at the programs most commonly used by crackers.

SoftICE SoftICE from Compuware (www.compuware.com) is one of the best debuggers in the DOS environment. You will not find anything better for Windows 9x and NT. Many crackers therefore say that NuMega (the producer of SoftICE) is their favorite company. Since SoftICE is probably the best debugger, we will use it too, and we'll look at it more closely later in this chapter.

TRW2000 This is a debugger for Windows 9x. It isn't as good as SoftICE, but its price is acceptable considering the high quality. You'll find shareware versions online.

WinDasm Together with IDA (discussed below), WinDasm (shown in Figure 2.1) is the best disassembler in the Windows environment. Compared to IDA, WinDasm's disassembled code is shorter and easier to understand. It's a great loss that, unlike IDA, WinDasm is no longer in development. You can find shareware versions online.

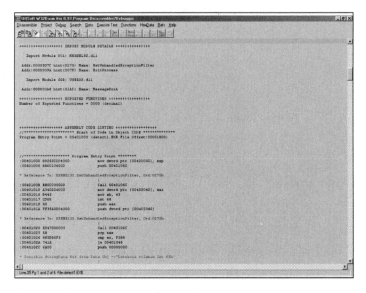

Figure 2.1: It is really easy to disassemble a program in WinDasm

SmartCheck   SmartCheck from Compuware is an IDE tune-up tool for programs written in Visual Basic. It is better than SoftICE for debugging Visual Basic applications.

IDA Pro (Interactive DisAssembler Pro)   IDA (shown in Figure 2.2), by Ilfak Guilfanov, is a wonderful disassembler for DOS and Windows programs. It is not a static disassembler like WinDasm, and it even lets you manage the translation manually. (This is a great feature to have when a program that you want to study uses various tricks to protect it from disassembly.) IDA has many other great features. You can request a demo of IDA Pro from www.ccso.com.

Sourcer   Sourcer, from VCOM, is a wonderful disassembler for DOS programs, but it is not widely used for Windows. You can get it at www.v-com.com.

Hex Workshop   Hex Workshop, from BreakPoint Software (www.bpsoft.com) is a hex editor for the Windows environment.

Hiew (Hacker's View)   Probably the best HEX editor for the DOS environment.

SoftICE Basics

As mentioned earlier, we will be using SoftICE in this book, so we'll take a closer look at it here. The SoftICE manual is an excellent and comprehensive resource (see Figure 2.3), so we'll just have a look at some of the basics of working with the program.

Before you can work with SoftICE, you must enable Windows API calls. You can do so in SoftICE's winice.dat file where you will see the following text:

```
;      *****Examples of export symbols that can be included for Windows 95*****
;      Change the path to the appropriate drive and directory
```

Figure 2.2: IDA looks like a DOS program, but it is a fully 32-bit application

Figure 2.3: SoftICE contains wonderful and detailed documentation

You'll see various libraries listed below the preceding text, from which you can export symbols into SoftICE. Remove the semicolon (;) characters from in front of the kernel32.dll and user32.dll libraries. The text will then look like this:

```
EXP=c:\windows\system\kernel32.dll
EXP=c:\windows\system\user32.dll
```

You have just permitted functions to be exported to SoftICE from kernel32.dll and user32.dll and from their Windows API calls. Now you can set breakpoints for these calls in SoftICE. For example, you can directly use the command bpx MessageBoxA to set a breakpoint for this API call.

Another way to export to SoftICE is through the SoftICE loader menu, where you select Edit and SoftICE initialization settings. Select Exports in this menu and use the self-explanatory Add to add further exports and Remove to remove them.

Once you have made these changes, you must restart your computer so that SoftICE can be reinitialized.

In the following sections I will explain the basics of using SoftICE.

Key Commands

To get into SoftICE, you can use the key combination CTRL+D. This combination always works, whether you are at the Windows desktop or running a program or game. (Figure 2.4 shows what SoftICE looks like when it's running.)

If you press F10, the program you are debugging will be traced, one instruction after another, and the trace will not nest into call procedures. If you press F8 or entering the T (Trace) command, the program will be traced, one instruction after another, and the trace will nest into call procedures.

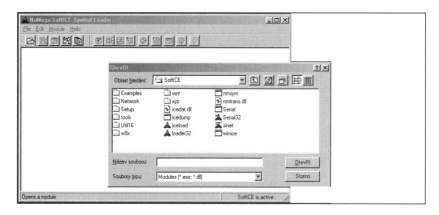

Figure 2.4: Running SoftICE during a program tune-up

The F11 key is very important. If a breakpoint is set to an API call, SoftICE will stop at the beginning of this call. Pressing F11 again is like calling the RET function, though the API call will be performed before SoftICE stops. The advantage to this is that you don't have to perform manual call tracing, which can be time-consuming.

The BPX Command

The BPX [API call or an ADDRESS] command sets the breakpoint to that API call or address in the program. For example, BPX GETDRIVETYPEA would set the breakpoint to the Windows API GetDriveTypeA function. (You don't have to worry about lowercase or capital letters.) When using the BPX ADDRESS command, you enter a program address where the breakpoint should be set, and if the running program encounters this address, it will be stopped and you will be switched back into SoftICE.

The BPR Switch

The BPR [address1 address2] switch sets the breakpoint within a memory range, specified from address1 to address2. When anything reads from this range or writes to it, the program will be stopped and you will be switched into SoftICE. The switch has three options: r (read), w (write), and rw (read or write).

The BPM Switch

The BPM [address] command sets the breakpoint to a certain memory location. If anything reads from this location or writes to it, the program will be stopped and you will be switched into SoftICE. Like the BPR switch, this switch has three options: r (read), w (write), and rw (read or write).

If you use an x value as the switch, the so-called *debug breakpoint* will be set. This breakpoint will be written directly into the processor debug registers, and an INT 3h will not be set at the address, as with normal breakpoints. This kind of a breakpoint is much more difficult to discover.

Display Commands

The display commands are as follows:

d [address]   This command will show the memory contents in DWORD (4 bytes) beginning at the location defined by the address.

ed [address]   This command will let you edit memory contents in DWORD (4 bytes), beginning at the location defined by the address.

r [register value]   This command will change the register value. You can use it with conditional jumps.

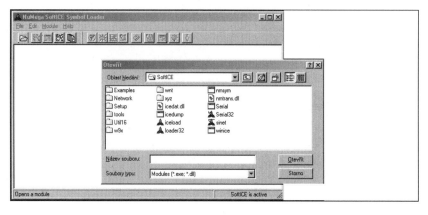

Figure 2.5: SoftICE Symbol Loader

You can also change special register values.

s [address1 address2 string or byte1, byte2 and so on] This command will search the memory for a string or bytes from address1 to address2. For example, s 400000 401000 "test" will search for a "test" string from address 400000 to address 401000.

s This command will continue searching for a string or bytes from the last found one.

code on This command will show instruction prefixes.

wf This command will show coprocessor register values.

exp This command will show exports.

rs This command will show the program window in the actual state, and will return to SoftICE when you press any key.

address This command will let you insert program code in assembler directly from the entered address.

hboot This command will reset the computer. It is useful in case of a system crash.

Of course, SoftICE also contains many other commands. You can find all of them in the SoftICE documentation.

3

THE BASIC TYPES OF SOFTWARE PROTECTION

In this chapter I will describe most types of contemporary software-protection programs, all of which have their pros and cons. Which is best depends only on your opinion of the program code and the creators' preferences.

Registration-Number (Serial-Number) Protection

Programs that use registration-number protection require the user to enter a registration number to register the program. The registration number depends on specific criteria.

Programmers use different types of registration-number protection, including the following:

- Registration number is always the same.
- Registration number changes in accordance with entered information (company, name, and so on).
- Registration number changes in accordance with the user's computer.

- Registration-number protection in Visual Basic or Delphi programs.
- Registration number is checked online.

Registration Number Is Always the Same

A program protected with this method requires the user to enter a registration number (see Figure 3.1). However, because the registration number is always the same, the cracker only has to find the correct registration number, post it online, and the program can then be registered by anyone.

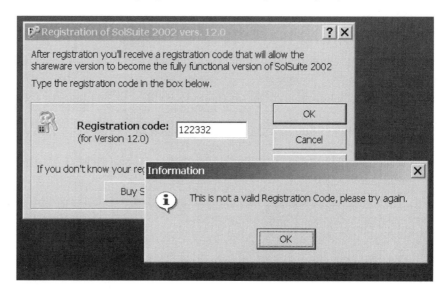

Figure 3.1: Registration number is always the same

One advantage of this method of protection, when compared with other registration-number protection techniques, is that the correct registration number doesn't have to be saved in memory to be compared with the entered number, which will often be XORed or recalculated in some other way. The correct registration number will then also be recalculated and both results compared. Naturally you can use more complicated calculations that are not easy for the cracker to understand, making it difficult to get from the result back to the correct registration number.

You can make excellent use of this protection method by encoding several program sections, such as a Save function, with the correct registration number value. If a cracker uses the patch method (directly adjusting conditions in the program code) and the correct registration number hasn't been entered, the originally blocked functions will still not work correctly.

It isn't a good idea to decode the blocked sections right after the correct registration number has been entered. It is safer to decode these sections only when the program has been started, or better still, only after the blocked function has been called. If the function is encoded again after use, and the program contains many encoded sections, the program will never be decoded in the memory as a whole, which means that a dump from memory will not help the cracker very much.

This software protection should be combined with other types that will be described later on.

Registration Number Changes in Accordance with Entered Information

This is the most frequently used type of protection. In this case, before you enter the registration number, you have to enter a user name, company, or other information, and the correct registration number changes according to the information you enter (see Figure 3.2). If you enter a registration number that doesn't match the information entered, the registration won't succeed (see Figure 3.3). The more skilled the programmer, the more difficult he can make it for the cracker to break this protection. However, even though the calculation algorithm may be very complex, once the user has entered the registration number, it is compared with the calculated one, and the cracker only has to trace the program to find the correct registration number.

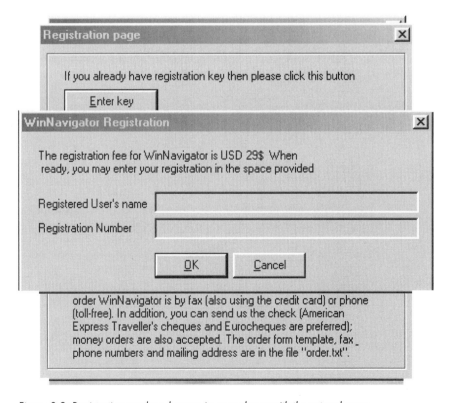

Figure 3.2: Registration number changes in accordance with the entered name

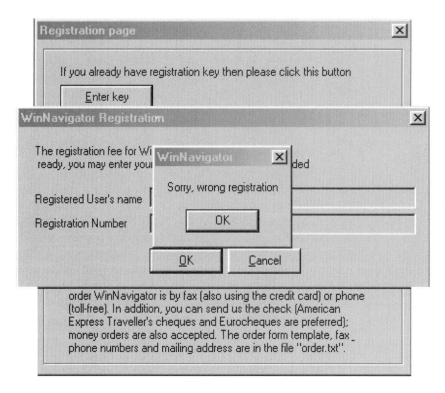

Figure 3.3: When an incorrect registration number is entered, the registration is unsuccessful

To buttress this protection, it is a good idea to design the algorithm so that the entered name and registration number must produce a certain result. Most programs don't institute this control—the registration number doesn't have to be checked, and it can offer a range of results. The attacker may exploit this range and generate a registration number in accordance with his own wishes.

When this sort of protection is used, the program should contain another hidden algorithm to check whether the entered registration number was really the correct one. It shouldn't tell the user, though, if it finds any inconsistencies. It will be enough if the user is somehow punished. (I will leave this up to the programmer's imagination.)

You can also encode some parts of the program (as mentioned previously) so that they cannot be used in an unregistered version. Then, once you've verified part of the registration number, you can use the unverified part for decoding the parts of the program. If you use good scrambling and a sufficiently long code, it will be almost impossible for the cracker to find the correct value for decoding. ASProtect (described in Chapter 6) works in this way.

Registration Number Changes in Accordance with the User's Computer

This is an unpleasant type of protection for an attacker, and it may even fool an inattentive cracker because, although he will register the program at his computer, it will not be possible to register the pirate version anywhere else. The registration number may change, for example, in response to the hard drive serial number or according to some random sequence. (It is important to hide this registration number carefully, because if it is found, it could easily be changed into a uniform number and the program could be registered at any computer with the same registration number.) Naturally, the registration number should also change in accordance with other data (such as user name, company, and so on) so that it works for only one user (see Figure 3.4).

When using this type of protection, it is very important to hide both the code that detects the computer number and the checking code that assesses the correctness of the entered registration number. It is good to combine this method with other types of protection.

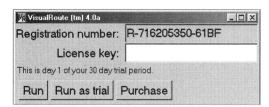

Figure 3.4: Every computer requires a different registration number

Registration-Number Protection in Visual Basic Programs

Protecting a program in Visual Basic (VB) isn't easy, since the programming language itself is a high-level language (the higher the language level, the further the compilation is from assembler). With high-level languages it is difficult to influence the compiled source code.

VB programs fall into the following groups:

- VB4
- VB5 and higher
- VB5 and higher, compiled in p-code

We'll look at each of these in turn.

VB4

Although it may not be obvious to most users, the VB4 family of programs has very inadequate protection, and the experienced cracker will find most registration numbers within five minutes (see Figure 3.5). The trouble is that VB4 programs mostly use the same VB40016.dll (VB40032.dll) library call for comparing the entered registration number to the correct registration number.

Even when a VB4 program uses some other comparison method, it is usually possible to find the correct registration number easily in memory. The registration number is usually placed close to the entered number, so all you need to do is search the memory for the entered registration number to find the correct one.

One advantage of VB4 programs is that they are hard to trace in SoftICE because their code isn't compiled into a machine code but only into pseudo-instructions that will be performed after the program is started. There are decompilers for VB4, but they are rarely used.

Figure 3.5: At first sight, a registration requirement programmed in Visual Basic isn't different from other languages

How VB4 Programs Are Cracked

How are VB4 programs cracked then? Even though VB4 is only rarely used for programming these days, it is good to know about it to avoid the mistakes in its use.

For a 16-bit VB4 program, the cracker has to find something like the following in memory and in the VB40016.dll code:

```
8BF88EC21EC5760E33C0F3A674051BC01DFFFF
```

He then sets a breakpoint to the address where the code was found, and he is able to see the following program instructions in the debugger:

Prefix	Instruction
.	
.	
.	
8BF8	mov di,ax
8EC2	mov es,dx
1E	push ds
C5760E	lds si,[bp+0E]
33C0	xor ax,ax
F3A6	repz cmpsb
7405	jz 2667
1BC0	sbb ax,ax
1DFFFF	sbb ax,ffff
.	
.	
.	

Now all the cracker needs to do is to see what he finds at the address where the repz cmpsb instruction compares the entered registration with the correct one. (You have only to look at the addresses es:di and ds:si to find the correct one.) This very simple tactic usually works, which probably isn't good news for most 16-bit VB4 programmers. Fortunately, 16-bit VB4 is used less and less. When it is, I recommend using a good DOS compressor or some other EXE protector for the program itself.

Most 32-bit VB4 programs use the MultiByteToWideChar function in the VB40032.dll library to compare two strings. During registration, all the cracker needs to do is set a breakpoint to the hmemcpy function before clicking OK, and then trace the program until he gets into VB40032.dll and finds the following bytes in the memory:

```
56578B7C24108B74240C8B4C2414
```

Then, he sets a breakpoint to the address found, and after repeatedly clicking OK, he will see the following code:

Prefix	Instruction	Explanation
.		
.		
.		
56	push esi	
57	push edi	
8B7C2410	mov edi, [esp + 10]	;es:edi --> registration number should be here
8B74240C	mov esi, [esp + 0C]	;esi --> correct registration number
813F70006300	cmp dword ptr [edi], 00630070	
7527	jne 0F79B381	
803E00	cmp byte ptr [esi], 00	
.		
.		
.		

VB5 and Higher

The software protection in VB5 and higher is slightly more difficult for crackers to tackle than that found in VB4. Many crackers are rather disappointed when they find out that they have a VB5 program in their hands, and they often leave it alone, but the experienced ones aren't scared off that easily.

Crackers aren't keen on cracking VB programs (or those written in Delphi) because the code is hard to read and understand, and it takes a lot of time to trace. To crack VB5, they usually use methods for generating a registration number for just one user, or modifying the program code to allow for any registration number. Only rarely does someone create a registration-number generator for a VB5 program, and then only the best crackers are able to do so because the code is so difficult to understand. (They may use SmartCheck, since it helps them understand the code.)

The fact that VB5 programs are so unpopular among crackers, and that it's difficult to create registration-number generators for them, is one advantage of using VB5. When a good compression program or protector is used, VB5 programs can be a challenge for any cracker.

It is a good idea to use a registration number that changes on different computers. This involves heavy interference with the program code, but the result is that it is almost impossible to use anti-debugging tricks.

VB5 and Higher, Compiled in P-Code

Programs compiled in *p-code* (short for packed code) are probably the VB programs least liked by crackers. Unlike VB4 programs, p-code programs are translated into pseudo-instructions, not machine code, and these instructions are performed when the program runs. Programs in p-code can be traced in SmartCheck, but not easily. The most experienced crackers will try to trace such programs in SoftICE, but only a small group of them will be able to do so.

VB programs compiled in p-code combine well with other software protection, and when they are used with a good compression program or protector, they are a challenge for any cracker. As a programmer, you should use registration numbers that change with different computers. Doing so will heavily interfere with the program code, but it will make it nearly impossible to use anti-debugging tricks.

Registration Number Is Checked Online

Some newer programs use the latest in modern technology for testing the correctness of a registration number (see Figure 3.6). Once the registration number is entered, the program sends it via the Internet for verification. A server then tests the number and returns a report which tells the program whether the number is correct (see Figure 3.7). The program processes this report to determine whether the program was properly registered. Despite this online exchange, though, most of these protection programs are very simple, and an experienced cracker can get rid of them quickly and reliably.

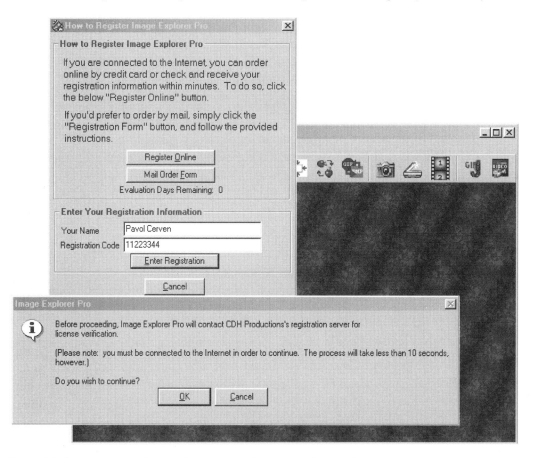

Figure 3.6: A program is ready to send registration information to the control server via the Internet

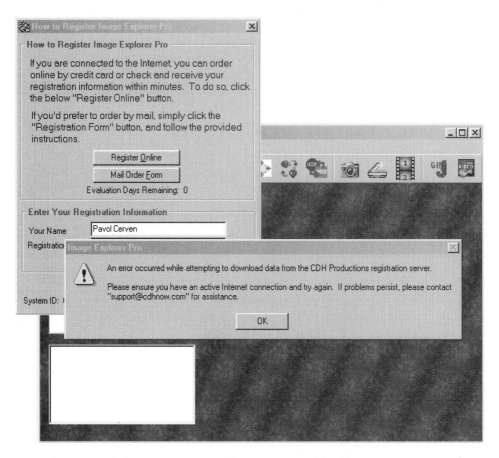

Figure 3.7: The program displays an error message if an error occurs while connecting to the server

Several of these programs do have slightly better protection because they contain random checking routines in their code. When such a program finds out that it was illegally registered, it will send a message to the producer via the Internet containing information about the user. I don't think this is a good approach—a better approach would be to have the program cause some trouble, or to simply delete itself, or something along these lines. Again, I'll leave that up to the programmer's imagination.

Online verification of registration numbers is done more and more often, but it's not appropriate for all software. Before deciding to use it, consider the audience for your program. For example, if your program always uses an Internet connection, the user will have to be connected to the Internet to use the program, and online verification is a reasonable option.

Most current software protection based on the principle of online verification isn't very good and is easy to remove, though there are several very good exceptions. For example, online verification is ideal for sending data to a program that is necessary for the program to function correctly.

Consider a program that has the Save function disabled in the unregistered version. When a user enters a registration number, that number is sent to a checking server. If the registration number is correct, the server will send a report confirming program registration, together with a short data bundle that could unblock the Save function. The server might, for example, send a parameter to decode a previously encoded function.

With this protection scheme in use, it would not be enough for a cracker to fool the program into thinking that the server confirmed a registration number. Even if the cracker were to succeed at fooling the server, the Save function would not function.

For this protection to work properly, the decoding key must be rather long so that it can withstand an attack. Also, the problem of a cracker using a correct registration number from a legally registered copy still remains, since with a correct registration number in hand, a cracker could decode the Save function correctly. Therefore, when using this protection scheme, it's very important to make the registration number different for each computer, thus making its illegal use difficult.

NOTE *It is also possible to allow only one use of the registration number, or to limit its future use to the IP address of the computer where the program was originally registered.*

Time-Limited Programs

Time-limited programs try to ensure that a program will not be used once the trial period has expired (see Figure 3.8). This is not usually a very effective method of protection, though, because once the time limit is cracked, the entire program is available to the cracker. It is much better to disable some functions in a program's unregistered version, thus forcing the user to buy the registered version if they want to use all of the program's features.

Time-limits are implemented in various ways. The various possibilities are:

- The time limit is removed once the correct registration number is entered.

- The time limit is removed once a registration file is entered.

- The time limit cannot be removed; the user's only option is to buy the full program without the time limit.

- The time limit is contained in a Visual Basic program.

- The time limit applies to a certain number of starts, after which the program can no longer be used.

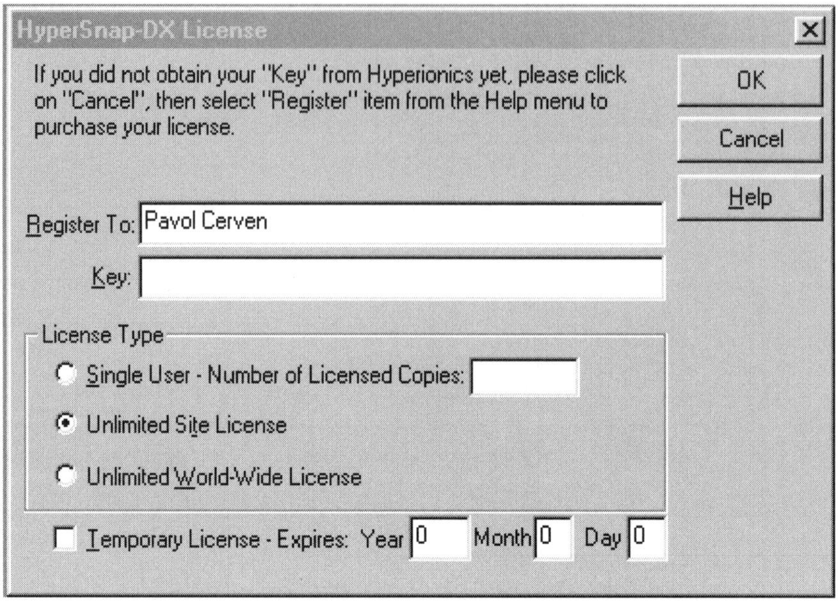

Figure 3.8: This program may be used for 30 days. Once this period expires, the correct registration number must be entered.

Time Limit Is Removed Once the
Correct Registration Number Is Entered

This approach has the same problem as registration-number techniques described previously in this chapter. The only difference is that if the correct registration number isn't entered, the program will not be registered, and it will refuse to run after a certain period of time.

When adopting this approach, the quality of the registration number must be high, since crackers do not focus on the time limit when removing this protection. Your program should use only a simple check when testing to see how long the program will be allowed to run. The program might, for example, detect a date during its first use and write that date into registers or a file. The program could then check after each start to see whether the time limit has been exceeded and, if so, refuse to run (see Figure 3.9).

Time Limit Is Removed Once a Registration Key File (.REG) Is Entered

This is a wonderful type of protection that isn't used very often. When using this protection, you might consider sending the registration file via the Internet. The registration file could, for example, contain a substantial part of the program code, which would unblock the time limit.

But beware: Crackers will focus on the routine that tests whether the time limit has already expired, so you must secure this routine against an attack. A cracker will rarely create a correct registration file to counter this protection

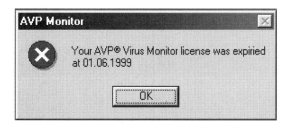

Figure 3.9: The time limit has expired. Now the user must register to receive a registration file.

because it is rather difficult to do so; it's much easier for him to cancel the time limit right in the program.

Do not use a checking method that tests to see whether a registration file is in the program directory and whether it contains correct data. It is much more effective to place the protected application's code right into the registration file. Of course, this isn't easy to do, and it's a method reserved for good programmers only.

Should you decide to use this type of protection, take the time to carefully test the result and make sure that the time limit test is as inconspicuous as possible. Consider using several separate tests together that will cause errors if the protection is not removed correctly. (Many antivirus programs use this kind of protection—see Figure 3.10.) And, as is often the case, it is a good idea to combine this protection with other types.

```
AVP 3.0 Key File███████████████████AD.8██p█ÐÂ<███w███CŤX█ũaúb90ö█dxñyĕr~ĕĕ2█ĕç
í█ĕá██áÜî%Û;%Kunh%█blzfSŢ█ĔĔ9ď68Ć:;██
```

Figure 3.10: This is a registration key file for Kaspersky's antivirus program, AVP

Time Limit Cannot Be Removed; User Must Buy the Full Program

Program demos often use this type of protection, which prevents the program from being starting once the time limit expires. There is no registration code to be entered (see Figure 3.11).

Crackers who encounter this type of protection will probably focus on the routine that checks to see whether the time limit has expired, and they may make a direct change to that program code. As such, it is a good idea to add a protective program that checks the file's checksum; it is important to protect the routine that tests the time limit. One approach is to use several separate tests together that will cause errors once the protection has been removed, and to combine them with other types of protection.

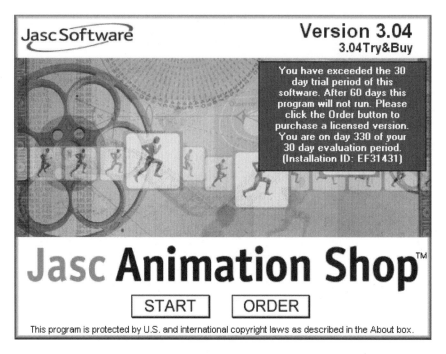

Jasc Software

Version 3.04
3.04 Try&Buy

You have exceeded the 30 day trial period of this software. After 60 days this program will not run. Please click the Order button to purchase a licensed version. You are on day 330 of your 30 day evaluation period. (Installation ID: EF31431)

Jasc **Animation Shop**™

START   ORDER

This program is protected by U.S. and international copyright laws as described in the About box.

Figure 3.11: This program cannot be registered directly; the user must buy a registered version without protection

Time Limit Is Contained in a Visual Basic Program

This kind of protection isn't widely used, and it's also not popular among crackers because it is difficult to remove. As was mentioned earlier in the discussion of registration numbers, a VB program is hard to trace (or nearly impossible if it's a VB4 program) and it is hard to understand.

NOTE *If your program prints a message once the time limit expires, you will make the cracker's job easier.*

The more experienced crackers will overcome this type of protection easily, since the method used doesn't vary much. As with other methods, it's a good idea to use several separate, interwoven tests. For example, if the first test is removed, the program might use a hidden test after, say, ten minutes to check whether the time limit has expired, and, if so, close without warning.

It is extremely difficult to locate this kind of protection—if the protection has been made well, it is a very time-consuming job. As always, it's a good idea to combine this method with other protection methods.

Time Limit Applies to a Certain Number of Starts

This is basically the same as other time-limit methods, except that it limits the number of starts rather than a number of days. This can create many problems for a cracker, since the program doesn't have to detect a date but just has to save the actual number of runs somewhere (in registers or a file). Otherwise, the issues are generally the same as those for other time limits.

Registration-File (KEY File) Protection

This sort of software protection creates a registration file, usually in the same directory where the program is installed. The program checks the contents of this file and, if the file is correct, the program will behave like a registered one. If the file is missing or it is not correct, the program will behave like an unregistered version or will not run at all. The registration file may contain information about the user, or constants for decoding encoded program parts that are accessible only in a registered version.

There are two general types of registration-file protection:

- Some program functions are blocked without the correct registration file.
- The program is time-limited without the correct registration file.

Some Program Functions Are Blocked
Without the Correct Registration File

This is a very good type of software protection, and crackers don't like it. Still, like all protection, it can be removed. When this protection is used, some of the program's functions are blocked without the correct registration file. As soon as the registration file is placed into the program directory, the program becomes registered and it functions normally.

There are several ways to implement this protection. The worst, and the one most easily removed, uses a routine that tests to see whether the correct registration file is present. If the program finds the correct file, it will unblock previously blocked functions. In such a case, the cracker need only find this routine and either "persuade" the program (by changing the code so that it believes the registration file is in place) or deduce the registration file's structure through the routine and then generate it.

If you choose to use this method, encode the registration file so that it won't be easy for a cracker to generate (see Figure 3.12). You might also consider inserting additional testing routines into the program that start randomly once an unblocked function has been used. If a routine finds that the registration file isn't in place, the program reacts as the programmer wishes.

Another possibility that is more difficult to program is to insert a part of the unblocked function's code into the registration file, or to insert a constant there that will unblock those functions. This trick makes crackers helpless, but its disadvantage is that if someone acquires one registration file, it will run on all computers.

```
 * WhereIsIt Key File *██Pavol Cerven██Skuska██6280██2.03██2.6.1999████████████
 ████████████████████████████████████████████████████«&█§"██j\H±-Ü¸č██đ▌÷ý˙
 ô¸Ł█y∎ťĊA·|h█]█_¬Î<ä█wíźĕ◎ę-?bą śpäĒáV0˙█…&úb-ë͟|óÑy▪tIłⱦX)O█ü{čDt„5ÑĘâš»Bú
 Ɪˊ<█OrhDAŞ█Áé█;█ ū(Ć´█*██±pÂ/█dŚdₚⁱĨμ\ w█éⱦLk<¸D>|ŸŽⱦ68x███Âₚ˞Ⱡ7Q█/ⱦ…ÂɪŸsG
 EⱦÉo2A%bů¸Ô¬█şźí█ä1;: ██ý÷*█?Pô█ék"śⱦT§ũ█ĕ+█wH%█Í3ã,)█HđÂ2"?M˙█Ôĕ@*˙˙¸ą*,˙Û█
 ŘÒqO█4ⱦRí█Á"śt█ÎⱦⱦÎô˝V1ECj█í█k0,█;q█ĚqEμ█%Š█Öi█¬█;-v¸Ⱦ4·█Bśqî█Ô¸ä█*˝Ñ˝0>ě█ñ1
 /ÂⱦÔ·˙Žⱦ█ž"|¸5łźí1ć łⱦŽ¶BN‡ÍúoH¬˙ŘĕÄ·█GĊLůŝa˙█ñ«Â█CrqXÖü█>\█-]█4Ü█c˝Á=%đ"·đ˙
 █äⱡ¬1ⱬ-˙Eⱦ´źzGo·Ŝ█Óíe█š±¸|h1G;█Yⱦ;ú█3#K███H█°˙˙˝~…z█XÔesO◎ć█Â§p███-1˙3°ŽÕⁱ"eU
 e˝á<I█çŞNÕ=óⱦ█( Đ█č█b█ⱦFĔÄZw<éž|yⱦ zZh█_Ö čó5"Ż"PÁT"^-ⱡ█ş|Ic█ŃŚ…█¶Ő/)p˙LÓÛⱦ
 U█yE}Â█Ē=Ű˙██$"|-Ž]Ňđ5|vꯥž█1Ôżⱥj██;~˝M█»ñ˙˝w M█mŇ█°·ⱦîŝ█XÜąéÎ>˙<˙ć█·×íÝ-⅌(F
 █████████ü█Á˙1█sÚ˝»w˙ą˝äꯥ0}ÁRKÝ·˙█ⱦⱦú█WⱦLć›Ü>█Ÿ⅌{ⱦ°˙˙@"G6›ą˙||Ö4ŘÃU◎Iéⱦ‡Î>█đ
 █Cãoꯥe˝á»¸Ř,đęN4o<-Đ"█7K█út█ž█ŻÚ█¸+tꯥJⱥé-bčÍÝ█˝x1|żĕ˙ĕ█ž÷"˙Â e*ËF0¬9Â-»qA5
 &»█u{XU>˝E˙ F§÷ŻźÍHRýđ█"[T-█ⱦ«█ČÝ¸S9xꯥx7gąKĘa█ö(B█·H«č█ź˙█éⁱi¬2◎-Ô]Ş#Ⱡ/"đž˙
 A[h\=đôôⱦ˝@Yu█Ûęo-:˝Ő »AżØćâÚ█B█uñó^█íÂV˙SÔꯥotⱦ%`
```

Figure 3.12: A very complicated registration file

While this type of protection is good because it is hard to remove, it is bad for users who aren't connected to the Internet. If your users have to wait to receive their registered software by mail, they may be put off.

Program Is Time-Limited Without the Correct Registration File

Most antivirus companies use this type of protection. The program is unregistered and is time-limited without a correct registration file, as was discussed earlier in the "Time-Limited Programs" section. As with all the software protection in this chapter, the time limit is cancelled once the registration file is loaded.

Hardware-Key (Dongle) Protection

Protecting software with hardware keys is another, less-used alternative for software protection. In this protection scheme, a copy-protection device, called a *dongle*, is connected to an I/O port on the computer and must be present for the protected program to run.

There are two types of hardware-key protection:

- The program cannot be started without the hardware key.
- Some functions of the program are limited without the hardware key.

HASP and Sentinel are two of the most widely used hardware keys and are probably the best, so I will describe both of them.

Program Cannot Be Started Without the Hardware Key

Most hardware keys are very simple. The program sends data to the port where the hardware key is supposed to be, and waits for a reply. If the program doesn't receive a reply, it refuses to run and gives an error message (see Figure 3.13).

More advanced hardware keys encode the data sent to the port. Or the hardware key could include an EPROM, with important parts of the program built into the hardware key itself. In this case, if the cracker has only the program and not the hardware key, it is almost impossible to remove the protection.

There are several ways to locate the routine that tests for the presence of the hardware key. For one, an API hook that tests for the key's presence during each API call is often used. Another method that's commonly used is to call the API by means of a function specific to the particular key. Some more advanced hardware keys use their own drivers.

If a cracker learns to remove a certain type of hardware-key protection, it's often not a problem for him to remove such protection at any time in the future. Of course, companies are continually trying to improve their protection programs by writing better drivers, so removing hardware protection is not always a given. Still, it's easy enough to find software emulators for the most common hardware keys that try to emulate the key's presence.

It is very important when using a hardware key to manage the protection in the program code itself, and not to rely on drivers or API calls from the manufacturer. Crackers often know these drivers and API calls very well, and they don't have much of a problem overcoming them.

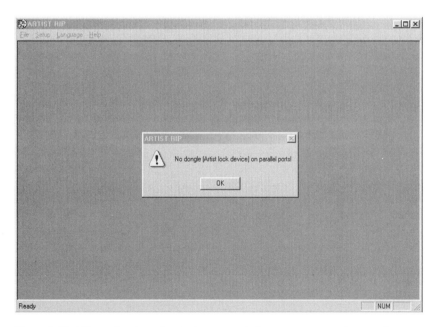

Figure 3.13: When a hardware key isn't connected, the program cannot be started

When a cracker can't find a suitable emulator for a particular key type, he will try to emulate its behavior directly in the program code. When doing so, he usually will not try to change the driver's code, because it's typically well protected against these attacks. Instead, he will insert the emulation code into the program. The best protection against this crack is to perform a multiple *cyclic redundancy check* (CRC) against program changes both in the file and in memory.

One major downside to using hardware keys is that because a dongle must be supplied with every copy of the program, the program's price and its cost to manufacture increase, and you may encounter distribution problems. Therefore, hardware keys are mostly used with very expensive programs and not with shareware.

A hardware key may be a good solution for smaller teams developing custom-made programs, but if you choose to go this route, buy the complete protection instead of trying to develop your own because it isn't easy or cheap to do.

Some Functions Are Limited Without the Hardware Key

The principle of this protection is very simple—when no hardware key is connected, some important functions of the program won't work (see Figure 3.15). Once a hardware key is connected, the program is fully functional. When these important functions are contained in the hardware key itself, this type of protection is very good. The key may also contain codes for decoding these functions right in the memory.

It is almost impossible to remove this protection without the key, especially when the encoding is good. However, if these functions are only blocked, and are unblocked once the hardware key is used, the cracker will have a much easier time removing the protection, and can probably do so even without the hardware key.

HASP Hardware Keys

The HASP series of hardware keys (see Figure 3.16), from Aladdin Knowledge Systems (www.ealaddin.com), offers several options. HASP installs its own drivers when the software is installed, and this software is used later for communicating with the hardware key. HASP has special drivers for DOS, Windows 9x/NT/2000/XP, and Mac OS X.

Figure 3.14: The program has just found out that the hardware key isn't connected

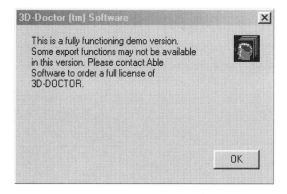

Figure 3.15: The application will start with some functions limited

Program developers wishing to protect their product with HASP must communicate with the hardware key by means of the installed drivers, because everything is secured by HASP API calls. To see where these calls are performed in a HASP-protected program, look for cmp bh, 32:

```
HASPCall:  ...
cmp bh, 32                                      ;test to see whether this
                                                ;is a higher HASP service
          jb    jump
          mov   esi, dword ptr [ebp+28]
          mov   eax, dword ptr [esi]
jump:     mov   esi, dword ptr [ebp+20]
          mov   esi, dword ptr [esi]
          push  ebp
          call  Hasp( )                         ;the basic HASP service is called here
          pop   ebp
          mov   edi, dword ptr [ebp+1C]
          mov   dword ptr [edi], eax            ;saves the return value
          mov   edi, dword ptr [ebp+20]
          mov   dword ptr [edi], ebx            ;saves the return value
          mov   edi, dword ptr [ebp+24]
          mov   dword ptr [edi], ecx            ;saves the return value
          mov   edi, dword ptr [ebp+28]
          mov   dword ptr [edi], edx            ;saves the return value
...
```

The basic HASP service always consists of the same call. The program makes decisions according to the parameters by which it was called, and then it decides which HASP service to call.

Figure 3.16: One version of the HASP hardware key

If you look one level higher in the program code, you will see code like the following:

```
...
push eax
push ecx
push 000047FE              ;password1
push 000015C9              ;password2
push ebx                   ;lptport
push edi
push 00000003              ;HASP service number 3
mov  [esp+38], 0000001A
                           ;address
call HASPCall              ;calls the ReadWord ( ) service
...
```

In this case, HASP function no. 3 was called: ReadWord(). All other services will be called in this way. Let's look at the most important and frequently used functions.

Function no. 1: IsHasp()

This function is always called first. It considers whether the hardware key is attached. Simply changing the return value of this service will absolutely not overcome HASP.

Input values:
BH = 01
BL = LPT port
Return values:
EAX = 0 — Hardware key wasn't found
or
EAX = 1 — Hardware key was found

Function no. 2: HaspCode ()

This function is usually called right after the IsHasp() function. password1 and password2 are codes that are used for communication with the hardware key. The seed code determines the return values.

Input values:
BH = 02
BL = LPT port
EAX = seed code
ECX = password1
EDX = password2
Return values:
EAX = code1
EBX = code2
ECX = code3
EDX = code4

Developers using HASP often make a mistake when testing the return values. Basically, it is enough to test two values or to perform the test using a more complex mathematical calculation. It is also possible to test more values for each return code, which makes the cracker's life more difficult.

Function no. 3: ReadWord()

This function reads dword (a word) from the HASP memory. The address from which the reading will be performed is located in EDI. You must multiply the address by two to find it.

Input values:
BH = 03
BL = LPT port
ECX = password1
EDX = password2
EDI = address
Return values:
EBX = Read data

ECX = status 0 — Correct, otherwise there was an error (you can find the error description in HASP documentation)

Function no. 4: WriteWord()

This function writes dword (a word) into the HASP memory. The address where the writing will be performed is located in EDI. To find out the address, you must multiply it by two, since it is a word.

Input values:
BH = 04
BL = LPT port
ECX = password1
EDX = password2
EDI = address

Return values:

ECX = status 0 — Correct, otherwise there was an error (you can find the error description in HASP documentation)

Function no. 5: HaspStatus()

Use this function to acquire the following information about HASP: memory size, HASP type, and LPT port.

Input values:
BH = 05
BL = LPT port
ECX = password1
EDX = password2
Return values:
EAX = memory size
EBX = HASP type
ECX = LPT port

Function no. 6: HaspID()

Use this function to learn the HASP ID. EAX contains the lower part of the ID, and EBX contains the higher part.

Input values:
BH = 06
BL = LPT port
ECX = password1
EDX = password2
Return values:
EAX = ID lower
EBX = ID higher
ECX = status 0 — Correct, otherwise there was an error (you can find the error description in HASP documentation)

Function no. 50: ReadBlock()

This function reads a memory block from HASP. The address from which the reading will be performed is located in EDI. The block length to be read is located in ESI, and the address where the read data will be saved is located in ES:EAX.

To learn the actual address from which the reading will be performed, multiply the address in EDI by two, since the data is read by words.

Input values:
BH = 50 or 32h
BL = LPT port
ECX = password1
EDX = password2
EDI = start address
ESI = data block length
ES = buffer segment

EAX = buffer offset

Return values:

ECX = status 0 — Correct, otherwise there was an error (you can find the error description in HASP documentation)

Function no. 51: WriteBlock()

This function writes a memory block into HASP. The address from which the reading will be performed is located in EDI. The block length to be written is located in ESI, and the address from which the data to be written will be read is located in ES:EAX.

To learn the actual address into which the writing will be performed, you must multiply the address in EDI by two, since the data is written by words.

Input values:

BH = 51 or 33
BL = LPT port
ECX = password1
EDX = password2
EDI = start address
ESI = data block length
ES = buffer segment
EAX = buffer offset

Return values:

ECX = status 0 — Correct, otherwise there was an error (you can find the error description in HASP documentation)

Naturally, HASP uses other functions besides the ones just discussed, including functions such as: SetTime(), GetTime(), SetDate(), GetDate(), Writebyte(), and Readbyte(). I will not describe these here, however, since they are easy to understand if you have the HASP documentation. The HASP documentation is really wonderful, and it is absolutely essential for all developers.

HASP needs only about 128 bytes of memory, and a skilled programmer can use even this small amount well. For example, he might use the read data to decode a certain part of the program.

To avoid testing to see whether each byte was read correctly, it is possible to use a CRC test for the read data. This will confirm that the data was read correctly without revealing to a cracker the data that was to be read.

Another good way to use HASP is to write important data into the hardware key to be read and used later. This works because, when dealing with HASP, crackers have to write an emulator that emulates HASP drivers. Probably the most difficult part is writing into HASP memory, because the emulator mostly runs in a code area where writing isn't allowed. Crackers, therefore, ignore this function and don't emulate writing at all; they only return a 0 value in ECX to show that the service was successful.

Finally I'm coming to the HASP Envelope treat. HASP Envelope is a PE file encoder that encodes the original EXE file. When started, it will decode the original EXE in real time and run it. I don't want to deprecate its functionality at all, but removing the HASP Envelope is no problem unless correct decoding depends upon the connected hardware key. In this case, the return values aren't tested but are decoded directly, which is a cracker's nightmare. Of course, this protection can also be removed with a correct key, though in most cases the HASP Envelope will not be removed because of possible related problems (CRC test).

HASP drivers, themselves, are well programmed, and it is difficult to debug them. They contain many anti-debugging tricks and other finesses against curious individuals. Still, even with all these measures in place, several crackers have managed to get through them to write an almost 100 percent functional emulator. Of course, this is the problem we continue to encounter with all commercial software protection. Naturally, a new version of HASP drivers appeared soon after that emulator was released, but you can be sure that it won't take long before a new emulator appears, too.

HASP is definitely an excellent protection program when correctly used. However, if program developers simply rely on HASP, and after calling a function only test the correctness of the return values, it won't really be difficult for a cracker to remove the protection from the program. HASP's biggest disadvantage comes from the added costs connected with selling a HASP-protected program. Therefore, HASP protection is really only worth considering for expensive programs that will not be distributed via the Internet.

Sentinel Hardware Keys

Sentinel, from Rainbow Technologies (www.rainbow.com), is the other popular hardware key option (see Figure 3.17). Because Sentinel is very similar to

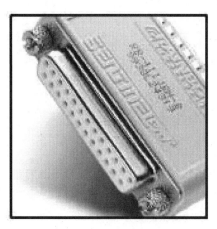

Figure 3.17: There are several kinds of Sentinel hardware keys

HASP, I will not describe it in detail. Sentinel documentation is as good and detailed as HASP documentation, making it easy to use.

There is, however, one particular aspect of Sentinel worth mentioning, and that is the fact that there is a test before each API call for the hardware key to see whether the packet communication was initialized correctly. It looks like this:

```
      ...
      cmp word ptr [esi], 7242
is correct
      mov ax, 0002              ;sets the error number
      pop edi
      pop esi
      ret 000C
      ...
```

Value 7242 is a packet marker. If it is not found at the beginning, error 2, Invalid Packet, will be set.

You can easily find each API call for the hardware key service simply by looking for this test. The protection essentials are the same as for HASP, and it is again necessary to prevent emulation in the program memory.

4

CD PROTECTION TRICKS

CD-checking software protection is used by almost all programs distributed on CD. The products in this category range from very simple defenses (that aren't real protection against crackers at all) to highly sophisticated protective software.

The simpler products only check to see whether a program started running without the correct CD, which would threaten the program's functionality. There are many ways to find out whether the original CD has been inserted into a CD-ROM drive. And, while most protective software is helpless against "burned" CDs, it can at least make it impossible to simply copy a program to a hard drive.

One reason to use such simple defenses is to protect against the so-called "ripping" of games. "Ripping" refers to the removal of large but unessential parts of the game, like animation, music, or DirectX. The shrunken game is then compressed so that people with slower connections can download it from the Internet, thus significantly increasing the number of pirated copies.

How CD-Checkers Work

The classic CD checkers have their place in the world, and when correctly programmed, can cause problems even for the better crackers. Still, this protection is often easy to find and remove.

Most checking routines use the GetDriveTypeA API call to find the CD drive, and all other checks are performed only after determining which drive is the CD-ROM. The simplest protective software only checks for the CD's name or label. If the CD's name has been changed, the program will not run, since the program has determined that the original CD isn't in the drive.

Some protection developers have tried to complicate CD copying by naming CDs in a way that causes an error during copying, often using a blank space in the CD name or some special character that appears as a blank space. Until recently, many burners couldn't copy such CDs.

Another common trick is to check for one or more selected files on the CD, especially those that are most commonly removed from ripped versions, such as DirectX, animation, music, and documentation. This technique was commonly used with 80-minute CDs because, in the past, the limited supply of 80-minute CD media meant that crackers had to remove something from the program in order to make their version fit on available CDs. Even today, crackers sometimes remove something to be able to copy the game to normal-length CD-Rs.

The most complicated protective software, like SecuROM or SafeDisc, can check errors on the CD.

Random checks that test for the presence of the original CD as the game is being played are very unpopular with crackers, and often result in the protection being incorrectly removed from a game and many subsequent repairs being required. This kind of protection has been successfully used with several games (see Figure 4.1).

Of course, as with almost all protection software, sooner or later the best crackers will learn how to remove the protection. The problem is that when they crack it the second time around, they do so much more quickly.

CD Protection Software

Let's take a look at the CD protection software available to you, and we'll consider what works and what doesn't work, and why.

CD-Cops

CD-Cops is commercial protection from Link Data Security (www.linkdata.com) that isn't very widely used. CD-Cops recognizes original CDs and rejects copies. CDs protected with CD-Cops can be identified by a window appearing on the screen once the program starts, as well as by the CDCOPS.DLL file and files with .GZ_ and .W_X extensions on the CD.

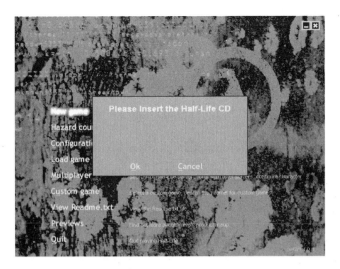

Figure 4.1: Protective software has just found out that the original CD wasn't inserted

The protection itself is a part of a protected executable file. When this file is started, it checks to see whether the original CD is present by testing the angle between the first and the last accessible CD blocks. The original CD contains an 8-byte code with the correct angle and a checking routine detects the angle on the CD and then compares it with the decoded correct angle. When a burned copy of the original CD is present, the angle will differ, and the program will not run. (One advantage of this protection scheme for the CD manufacturer is that it doesn't require a special CD copying machine.)

CD-Cops's testing routine is a truly sophisticated piece of programming. It also uses a clever trick: It sets a timer to see if the testing routine runs for a long time, which would mean it is being traced. If it finds that the routine is running for a long time, it causes an error in the program. CD-Cops also contains several checksums, which prevent changes to the program code—parts of the routine are decoded in memory when running.

But CD-Cops has a critical weakness: It can be decoded without the original CD. In fact, you can even find a decoder for it on the Internet. The reason is that the program's creators left the correct code in the program which, even though encoded, some clever crackers were able to decode. Had CD-Cops used a technique similar to SafeDisc, which decodes the program without checking it, and only after reading the angle from the CD, it would have been impossible to decode a CD-Cops–protected program without the original CD.

DiscGuard

DiscGuard from TTR Technologies (www.ttrtech.com) packs its protection with the executable files on the CD and encodes them; a digital code on the original CD is then used for decoding. When a user attempts to copy a CD protected with DiscGuard, the digital code is not copied correctly, and when the copied program is started, the decoding routine identifies it as a copy and runs it as a demo version or with other limitations, as the developers wish.

One distinct disadvantage for developers using DiscGuard is that they need to use either a special copying machine—a device called DG-Author—to produce DiscGuard-protected CDs.

As far as I know, DiscGuard has been used with only one popular program, the Colin McRae Rally game. While the cracker who removed the protection failed the first time, a corrected working version was posted the very next day. Given the fact that this was a completely new kind of protection, the speed with which it was cracked didn't reflect well on its developers. Their only salvation was that the cracker was Moelch, who later became famous for cracking Settlers 3.

One advantage of DiscGuard is that there is no universal decoder, probably because it is rarely used.

LaserLock

LaserLock is commercial protection from MLS LaserLock International (www.laserlock.com). The LaserLock-protected CD contains an invisible directory with files containing unreadable errors. The encoding software is used together with a laser mark when the CD is produced, which at first made it truly impossible to copy, but it can actually be gotten around quite easily. While there is no decoder for LaserLock, there is a program that can copy a LaserLocked CD to a hard drive. Alternatively, you can set a CD-burning program to ignore errors and copy the CD, and the error-containing files can even be saved with a hex editor, and all readable parts of the file can be copied into a file on the hard drive.

LaserLock has protected many programs and games, the most well known of which are Fallout 2, Shogo, and SpecOps. (LaserLock was massively upgraded in its last version. While it appears as though this protection may someday become obsolete, LaserLock is currently used quite fequently. However, there is a public decoder for this protection.)

SafeCast

SafeCast is commercial protection from C-Dilla (www.c-dilla.com), which also developed SafeDisc, described next. (C-Dilla is now a part of Macrovision, www.macrovision.com.) SafeCast is designed for development teams and is supposed to prevent program copying during development. It requires no special copying machines, and the protection is designed especially for burned CDs. When beta testers receive the encoded CDs, they must contact the company that encoded the CD to receive either by mail or email the code necessary to run the program.

SafeDisc

SafeDisc (often called C-Dilla because of the company that developed it) is today's most commonly used protection, so we'll take a detailed look at it. It is used by international game producers such as Ubi Soft Entertainment, GT Interactive, Interplay Entertainment, Microprose, Red Storm Entertainment, Take2 Interactive Software and TalonSoft, Electronic Arts, and Microsoft.

As with other commercial protection, SafeDisc's release was preceded by a huge campaign on the Internet claiming that its protection couldn't be removed and that it was unconquerable. Of course, a pirated version of the first SafeDisc-protected game appeared about one week after the release of the game. This certainly didn't make the people at C-Dilla happy, and it calls their protection into question, but because there is no adequate competition, SafeDisc continues to be the choice of more and more distributors.

The presence of these files on a CD signals the presence of SafeDisc:

- 00000001.tmp
- clcd16.dll
- clcd32.dll
- clokspl.exe
- dplayerx.dll

SafeDisc-protected CDs also contain both a main EXE file and a file with the same name as the main EXE, but with the .icd extension. The EXE contains the main protection, and the original EXE file is encoded in the ICD file. This encoded EXE uses anti-disassembling macros, which make it very difficult to trace.

SafeDisc also uses several anti-debugging tricks designed to thwart SoftICE, in particular. First, it divides the EXE into two parts. The first part contains only decoding information for the second part, but otherwise has no important code. The second part is encoded by the first one, which makes it impossible to change anything in the first part, even when attempting to do so in memory.

A protective device in the first part of the EXE uses the CreateFileA trick (described in Chapter 7) to check for the presence of SoftICE. If SoftICE is found, a message appears warning that a debugger must be removed from memory. If the cracker disregards the warning and tries to work around it, the program wrongly decodes the second part of the EXE as soon as the debugger is found again. The decoding routine itself then tests again for the presence of the debugger using CreateFileA.

SafeDisc also uses an INT 68h trick (also described in Chapter 7). If a debugger is found, the decoding constants will be set incorrectly, and the second part of the EXE will be incorrectly decoded.

An older version of SafeDisc used a trick with the debug register that could discover any active debugger. This trick had to be removed, though, because it was incompatible with Windows NT.

The second part of the EXE tests for the presence of the original EXE using a simple CD check, and tries to read errors from the original CD. If it finds an error, it displays a window requiring the user to insert an original CD. If the cracker tries to get around this warning, the program will simply crash rather than display an error message after the next incorrect decoding.

The second part of the EXE, behind the test for the original CD, contains a program that calculates the code necessary to decode the original EXE. The program first runs CLOKSPL.EXE, which shows only a picture during loading. Next, the program is fully engaged in calculating the decoding key according to various conditions. CD errors are read and, depending on the presence of or lack of errors, conditions are either true or false.

It is almost impossible to influence the program with a patch because it reads the errors with CLCD16.DLL and CLCD32.DLL. Eventually the calculation result is XORed with the actual date, which means that the code is different every day. (It would be interesting to run the program right before midnight, because the date change should trigger the decoding security device.)

Finally, the second part of the EXE file decodes a small routine found in memory, which contains addresses for calling DPLAYERX.DLL and the correct decoding key. It is difficult to stop the running program in this small decoding routine. Tracing is out of the question because it was started by creating a new thread, and the second part of the EXE calls it with Resume Thread API calls. One way to get into it, though, is to change the first instruction at the beginning to INT 3h, set a breakpoint in SoftICE at INT 3h, run the program, and then, once the program stops at the breakpoint, replace the INT 3h with the original value. In this routine, SafeDisc loads DPLAYERX.DLL into memory and then calls its procedure.

DPLAYERX.DLL works like the main EXE. While the library is loading into memory, the _DllMain@12 function is started, and it secures the decoding of the second part of the DLL. The function (Ox77F052CC) is called together with a key for decoding the original EXE, and the key is once again XORed with the date so that the correct key is used for decoding.

The _DllMain@12 function works like the first part of the EXE and contains the same anti-debugging tricks. Anti-debugging tricks are again used at the beginning of the second function, Oc77F052CC. When a debugger isn't found, the program decodes the original EXE, which is encoded in the file with an .icd extension. (Decoding is performed in memory, and the program is not saved to disk.) Once the EXE is correctly decoded, the original program is launched.

SafeDisc was a perfect piece of programming, but, as with all commercial protection, once it had been overcome once, it could easily be overcome again. You can find a decoder for SafeDisc on the Internet that allows a SafeDisc-protected program to be run from a one-to-one copy of the original

CD, including errors. The problem with these decoders is that it's difficult to create an exact one-to-one copy of the CD, because such a CD may contain more than 22,000 errors. Too, when copying, the CD must be read only at 1x speed so that the errors are read correctly and, moreover, not all CD-R or CD-ROM drives can read these errors correctly even at 1x.

Given the ease with which SafeDisc can be overcome, it would be ridiculously naive to use SafeDisc protection alone (remember Settlers 3). Still, SafeDisc is the best commercial protective software on the market, and it's not a bad investment for a company that doesn't want to develop their own protection. While SafeDisc will not stop the distribution of pirated software, it will dramatically reduce the copying of original CDs by average users.

NOTE *A program for decoding SafeDisc (unSafeDisc) without an original CD has appeared recently. R!SC clearly worked very hard and carefully analyzed the decoding. Because he found several serious failings in SafeDisc's design, he was able to create a program that may be able to decode all known versions of SafeDisc. The presence of this decoder could, of course, limit SafeDisc's commercial feasibility. The question now is whether the developers will make radical changes, completely rewrite the protection, or wait until their protection becomes essentially unnecessary. (At the present time, there is a new and improved version of SafeDisc, called SafeDisc2. Technology is better than in the previous version, but it has been broken and it is possible find a decoder for it.)*

SecuROM

SecuROM (www.securom.com) is commercial protection from Sony DADC. The similarities between SecuROM and SafeDisc suggest that SafeDisc is probably based on SecuROM, and that SafeDisc's creators simply improved SecuROM. This is suggested by the presence of the files CMS16.DLL, CMS_95.DLL, or CCMS_NT.DLL on the SecuROM-protected CDs. Like SafeDisc, SecuROM is in continuous development.

SecuROM's protection is based on the same principle as SafeDisc. Though it has been used to protect many games and programs, including Forsaken, Descent, FreeSpace, FIFA 99, Alpha Centauri, Machines, and the famous Diablo 2, I won't describe it in detail because it is being used less and less. The short story is that some SecuROM data is encoded in an EXE file, which is only correctly decoded once the original CD is inserted. Special copying equipment is required to produce a SecuROM-protected CD.

While it's not easy to crack SecuROM's protection, it's certainly not impossible. It's slightly easier to remove SecuROM than it is to remove SafeDisc because only some of the data is encoded, and because its decoding routine and protection system is somewhat simpler. Basically, the memory dumper that saves the EXE file to disc after correct decoding can be used for decoding, as with SafeDisc. (Naturally, this can also be done manually in a debugger, but it would be slightly more time-consuming.) Note that SecuROM, like SafeDisk, was upgraded in its latest versions.

You can find a SecuROM decoder on the Internet that is able to start programs from a one-to-one CD copy. On the other hand, it isn't easy to make such a copy: Its creation may take several hours, and the result is far from certain.

If you start a SecuROM-protected program from an original CD, you can dump it using the latest version of ProcDump. While developers should consider this cracking possibility, it would be even better if SecuROM itself concentrated on tackling this flaw.

VOB

VOB is the latest commercial protection in the SecuROM and SafeDisc family, and, in my opinion, also the best. Debugging VOB is a real pain because it uses anti-disassembling macros that prolong debugging terribly and make it very unpleasant. Otherwise it is nothing revolutionary. (See Figure 4.2.)

Figure 4.2: VOB is given away by the section name in the PE file header

As is common with this type of protection, the program checks for errors on the original CD, which differ on copies. Decoding values for a given product are calculated according to a certain algorithm, and these values are then used to decode the original PE file. Since this is really nothing new, crackers who have managed to remove SafeDisc find it easy to remove VOB as well (see Figure 4.3).

VOB isn't currently very widely used, though the Czech game Polda 2 and even Settlers 3 have been protected with it, and as far as I know it is no longer being revised.

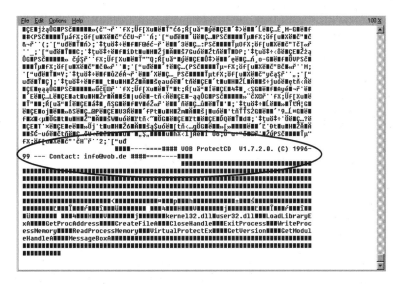

Figure 4.3: You can even find the version used at the end of the protected file

Other CD Protection Tricks

There are some other protection schemes used for CDs:

- CD contains more than 74 minutes of data
- Damaged TOC (table of contents)
- CD contains huge files
- CD contains physical errors
- CD contains one or more huge files
- Demo has selected program functions limited

CD Contains More Than 74 Minutes of Data

I first saw this type of protection in the game Commandos. It is based on a user's inability to copy the program to a typical 74-minute CD because the program is too big (larger than 660MB). The program's original CD is written at a higher than normal density, which makes it a higher capacity.

When this protection first appeared on the market, it was effective because it wasn't possible to buy 80-minute CD-Rs, and crackers had to remove something from the program to be able to copy it. The Commandos protective software was ready for that though, and if it found that any audio tracks had been removed from the CD, the game refused to run.

This type of protection doesn't make much sense today though, since the price of 80-minute media is almost on par with 74-minute CD-Rs, and all better burning programs and burners can work with 80-minute media. This protection scheme would only make sense if the CD were larger than 80 minutes, but if it were, some CD-ROM drives would have trouble reading it.

Damaged TOC (Table of Contents)

If you try to copy a CD protected with a damaged table of contents, the burning program will display an error message and will refuse to copy the CD. Protection software uses this principle by adding an extra data block to the CD (besides the main one), often placing it between audio tracks. Because ISO format doesn't support two data blocks on one CD, the burning program will fail. The Achilles heel of this protection is that all better burning programs let the user switch off the warning and make the copy. (This copy protection was used with the Commandos game CD.)

Huge Files

This type of protection is often used together with the damaged TOC technique. The original CD contains files that are larger than 600MB once they are copied to a hard drive. In fact, once the entire CD has been copied to a hard drive, it may be larger than 2GB, causing the burning program to refuse to burn.

This type of protection was important because it prevented the CD from first being copied to a hard drive so that a 74-minute CD could be made from an 80-minute one. Currently though, with the availability of 80-minute CD-Rs (as discussed previously) this type of protection has lost its importance.

Physical Errors

This type of protection actually introduces physical errors onto the CD, such as a damaged track. (This technique hasn't been used very often, though it was used in the wonderful Settlers 3 protection.) Very few CD drives can read such errors. (I tried it with my TEAC drive, and I succeeded only after a long time. It was necessary to read it only at 1x speed and to be very patient, since reading the one CD took about six hours.)

Even though you can find a program on the Internet that makes the reading easier, this technique is still a good one. It may be difficult to produce the original CDs though, since the CD has to be mechanically damaged in just the right way, every time.

One or More Huge Files

This very good means of protection makes it difficult to create a ripped version from a program's CD. In this case, all files are combined into one or more very large files on the CD. If the files use encoding or compression, it is very difficult for the cracker to understand the file's structure, and to transform it back into small files in order to remove the files that he considers unnecessary.

When the protection is good, the cracker will have to combine the small files back again into a big file and replace, for example, the audio files that he wanted to remove with one-second pauses to shorten the file. Next, he will have to re-index the file header with the information about the lengths and locations of files in the large complex file. This isn't easy and it takes a lot of time, and besides which, it is easy to make a mistake and to create a useless copy of the game or program.

When combined with a program that checks to see whether changes have been made, this protection becomes even more difficult to remove.

Demo with Selected Program Functions Limited

In this situation, the protected program lacks several important functions; for example, Save is commonly disabled (see Figure 4.4). However, some programmers don't take enough care and they simply block the functions in the program code without removing them, in which case all the cracker needs to do is to unblock the function to make the program fully functional. When using this protection, important parts of the program should be removed rather than simply blocked.

There are wonderful programs for protecting demo versions called ASProtect and SVKP, which we'll discuss in Chapter 6. ASProtect and SVKP create and save a demo that becomes fully functional only once the correct registration number is entered. (Demos are one of the safest means of protection, and they are good for expensive software as well as shareware.)

Crackers cannot remove the protection from a program that doesn't contain important parts of the code to make it function. Their only way around protection that involves removing code from a program would be to write the missing code themselves, and this is highly unlikely.

In the next chapter we'll take a look at various programs that use compression and encoding techniques to protect software.

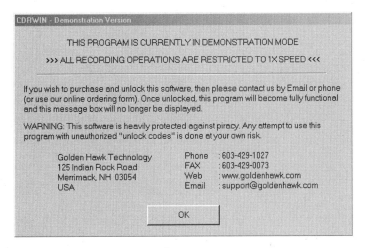

CDRWIN - Demonstration Version

THIS PROGRAM IS CURRENTLY IN DEMONSTRATION MODE

>>> ALL RECORDING OPERATIONS ARE RESTRICTED TO 1X SPEED <<<

If you wish to purchase and unlock this software, then please contact us by Email or phone (or use our online ordering form). Once unlocked, this program will become fully functional and this message box will no longer be displayed.

WARNING: This software is heavily protected against piracy. Any attempt to use this program with unauthorized "unlock codes" is done at your own risk.

Golden Hawk Technology   Phone : 603-429-1027
125 Indian Rock Road   FAX   : 603-429-0073
Merrimack, NH 03054   Web   : www.goldenhawk.com
USA   Email : support@goldenhawk.com

OK

Figure 4.4: Demo version of CDRWin, which allows you to write at only 1x speed. Notice the warning that the software is heavily protected against attempts to remove the protection. In fact, pirate versions do not write correctly.

5

PROGRAM COMPRESSION AND ENCODING: FREEWARE AND SHAREWARE

Compressing or encoding programs is an excellent way to add additional product protection. One advantage of compressing a program is that the program must be uncompressed before it can be changed. Also, better compression programs complicate program debugging, and, of course, you cannot disassemble a compressed file. (While it may still be possible to create a loader that will change the program code directly in memory once the program has been decompressed, no well-protected program should allow anything like this.)

Compressing all of a program's files makes it difficult to change things like text, but compressed programs will run a bit more slowly than uncompressed ones (though the performance hit with a good compression program will be insignificant.) Rather than compress all of a program, you can compress executables only—this will not slow the program down at all, though start-up will be slightly slower (because compressed programs are decompressed in memory during start-up).

When deciding whether to use compression, find out whether there is a decompressor for the particular compressor you want to use. If so, don't use it. For example, while PKLITE is the best compressor for EXE files in DOS, there are many decompressors. Your best bet, of course, is to create a new compressor. Still, most programmers will use the preprogrammed ones, so we'll take a look at a variety of compression and encoding programs for executables, as well as some other types of commercial protection.

aPLib

aPLib (home19.inet.tele.dk/jibz/apack/index.html) is a commercial compression library for programmers who want to compress data in their programs, created by the great programmer Joergen Ibsen. aPLib is used by many compression programs for executable files because it is one of the best products in the field.

ASPack

ASPack (www.aspack.com) is a compression program for EXE, DLL, and OCX files. It is easy to use, even for less-experienced users. On the other hand, more-experienced programmers may not like it because the program menu doesn't offer many options, as shown in Figure 5.1.

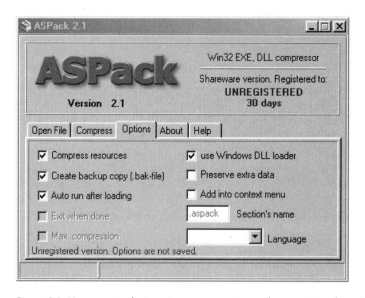

Figure 5.1: You cannot select maximum compression in the unregistered version of ASPack

ASPack's decompression routines contain several jumps that are designed to confuse a cracker but which really present problems only for the inexperienced ones. For example, ASPack's decoding routine contains only a few anti-debugging tricks. If a file is loaded into SoftICE's Symbol Loader, the program will not stop at the beginning. However, once you find the beginning of the program, insert INT 3h or an equivalent there, and set the breakpoint to this INT, then run the program, it will stop right at the beginning. Or, you can load the program into ProcDump and change the characteristics for the .text section. Here you will probably find C0000040; change that to E0000020 and the program should always stop at the beginning in the SoftICE loader. (I'll describe this more fully in Chapter 7.)

To remove ASPack, all you need is a special decompressor, though you can also create a loader that will change the program code directly in memory. (ASPack has no protection against anything like that.) I have even seen a program on the Internet that makes it possible to create these patches for ASPack.

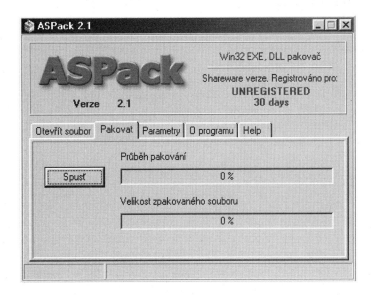

Figure 5.2: ASPack lets you choose from several languages

ASPack's Option menu contains the following items:

Compress Resources   Compresses resources along with the program.

Create Backup Copy (.bak-file)   Creates a copy of the compressed file.

Auto Run After Loading   Compresses the program automatically as soon as it is loaded.

Exit When Done   Closes ASPack once a program has been compressed.

Max Compression   Compresses the program as much as possible.

Use Windows DLL Loader   Uses the Windows DLL loader (this is important if you have an old Borland C++ linker).

Preserve Extra Data   Preserves extra data located after the end of a file. (This mostly concerns files with overlay data.)

Add Into Context Menu   Adds an ASPack item into the Explorer menu. If you right-click on a file, you can immediately compress it with ASPack.

Section's Name   Specifies a section name for the decompressor data in the compressed file (this is a kind of author's mark).

Language   Sets ASPack's language.

ASPack is a very good compression program, but it needs to be toughened up with more anti-debugging tricks. On the other hand, because its decompression routine doesn't contain any incompatible operations, it shouldn't cause problems with most programs, and it does offer very good compression.

In recent versions, the ASPack programmers have focused on dumping the program from memory in an effort to protect the import table as much as possible. They seem to have forgotten, though, that without good anti-debugging tricks and anti-disassembling macros, it is very easy to trace and view the ASPack code, so it will not take long before a new decompressor appears.

Test file compression: 486,400 bytes (using an unregistered version of ASPack with maximum compression option turned off)

Decompressors: ProcDump and UnASPack

Ding Boys PE-Crypt

Ding Boys PE-Crypt (shown in Figure 5.3) is another commonly used executable file encoder. It's particularly interesting because it implements anti-debugging tricks designed to make it impossible to run an encoded program when a debugger is present in memory. The creator's radical solution to this problem is also interesting because the program will freeze without warning if a debugger is in memory. Still, the program's encoding isn't too difficult, and it's no surprise that there is a decoding program freely available on the Internet.

The decoding routine in Ding Boy's PE-Crypt is clearly intended to make manual decoding annoying and time consuming. For one thing, it uses loops that only ever decode the following loop. Also, every loop decodes only 29 bytes, and each contains anti-debugging code, which means that the cracker has to remove this code from each individual loop. Manual decoding would therefore take several hours. (Of course, if you use a decoder, it will take only a few seconds.)

Once you run the program, you will see a menu from which you can select several encoding functions, as discussed in the list below. At the top you'll see a field where you can type a path to the program that you want to

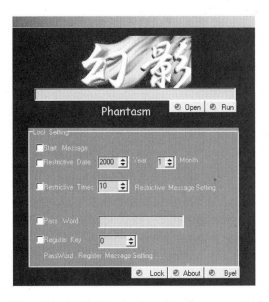

Figure 5.3: Luckily Ding Boy's PE-Crypt has a menu in English

encode, or you can click Open and browse to the program. Use Run to start the program.

Start Message   Sets a message that will appear when the program starts.

Restrictive Date   Sets a date on which the program will expire. (It is surprising that you can set only months.)

Restrictive Times   Sets how many times the program can be run.

Restrictive Message Setting   Specifies a message to appear after one of the time limits expires.

Pass Word   Sets a password that will always be required to run the program.

Register Key   Sets a registration number for the program. (Ding Boy's PE-Crypt supplies you with a program that will calculate such a number for you.)

Password. Register Message Setting   Sets the text of a message that will appear after an incorrect password or registration number has been entered.

Ding Boy's PE-Crypt is definitely one of the better encoding programs and, because it is not too widely used, it may be more effective against crackers. Manual decoding of PE-Crypt-encoded files is both difficult and very time consuming, though who knows whether decoders will really have a problem removing Ding Boy's PE-Crypt.

Ding Boy's PE-Crypt's universal functionality is diminished by the fact that it cannot be used under Windows NT, Windows 2000, or Windows XP. Also, while the program itself is in English, its documentation is in a language unknown to me, which may be a problem for many users.

> **Test file compression**: 1,729,553 bytes
> **Decoder**: Undbpe

NeoLite

NeoLite (www.neoworx.com) compresses executables including EXE, DLL, and OCX files. While the compression level is very high, the authors forgot to protect against unwanted decompression. In fact, the program itself can decompress files compressed by NeoLite, and the only way to safeguard against this is to select maximum compression.

I didn't manage to find any protection against debugging in the decompression routine. The only protection I did find was a set of changes in the PE header for the .text section: The program will immediately start running in the Symbol Loader for SoftICE. (I have already shown how easy it is to remove this protection in the ASPack discussion earlier in the chapter; manual decompression then takes only a short while.)

The program itself contains many functions for compression tuning and should therefore be considered a good professional compression program when protection against decompression isn't that important.

To begin using the program, choose the program you want to compress. After clicking Next, you can set several options on the next screen:

Information   Clicking this button will display information about the structure of the file that you chose to compress.

Create .BAK Backup File   Makes a backup copy of the compressed file.

Overwrite Existing Output Files   Overwrites a file with the same name if one is found.

Update Time & Date Stamp   Sets the current date and time in the compressed file. By default, the date and time are the same as those in the file that is being compressed.

Use Quick Compression Method   Enables a quick compression method that is less effective but which speeds up the decompression and subsequent starting of the program.

Force Executable Compression   Compresses a program even if NeoLite can't manage to shorten a program's length. The default behavior is for NeoLite not to perform any compression in this situation.

Compress   Compresses the program, but it will be possible to decompress the program with NeoLite.

MaxCmp   Compresses the program with maximum compression, and it will not be possible to decompress the program with NeoLite.

Change Advanced Settings   Settings for advanced users.

Advanced Compression Options

The screen shown in Figure 5.4 offers a series of advanced options as follows:

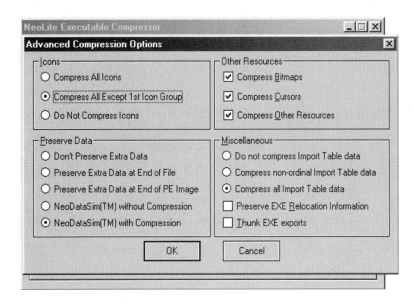

Figure 5.4: NeoLite

Icons

This section sets the options for handling icons.

Compress All Icons   Compresses all icons. It is recommended only for DLL files.

Compress All Except 1st Icon Group   This is the default setting because Windows Explorer uses the first icon group for displaying files. (If these icons were compressed, the files would not be displayed correctly.)

Do Not Compress Icons   No icons will be compressed.

Preserve Data

Determines whether extra data that may be located in the so-called overlay will be compressed.

Don't Preserve Extra Data　All extra data is ignored and removed from the final compressed file.

Preserve Extra Data at End of File　All extra data is located after the end of the file is preserved.

Preserve Extra Data at End of PE Image　All data is located after the PE image is preserved.

NeoDataSim without Compression　Extra data will not be compressed. This is a model developed by the authors of NeoLite for preserving extra data.

NeoDataSim with Compression　Extra data will be compressed. This is the default setting, and is a model developed by the authors of NeoLite for preserving extra data.

Other Resources

This section includes settings for compressing resources in files.

Compress Bitmaps　Compresses all images. This is a default setting.

Compress Cursors　Compresses all cursors. This is a default setting.

Compress Other Resources　Compresses all other resources. This is a default setting.

Miscellaneous

These are some other settings for the program.

Do not compress Import Table data　Does not compress the Import Table data.

Compress non-ordinal Import Table data　Enables the program to locate imported functions that use only numbers as names, which is not common. If a program prints out the message "Unable to locate exported function #<*ordinal*> in <*DLL name*>" after compression, switch this function on before compressing it.

Compress all Import Table data　Ensures that all data in the Import Table is compressed. This is done by default.

Preserve EXE Relocation Information　Preserves all relocation information in the file.

Thunk EXE exports　Adds a code into the decompressing routine code that deals with EXE files that set export function values, before running the main function itself. (This doesn't affect DLL files.)

　　NeoLite is one of the best professional compression software packages. However, as far as compression itself is concerned, it isn't that good at protecting against decoding and debugging. I would recommend NeoLite to professional programmers who care about the size of a file but who are not particularly concerned about security, and I hope that future versions will contain some protection.

Test file compression: 646,577 bytes

Decompressor: ProcDump

NFO

NFO is a very simple encoder for PE files that doesn't allow you to set parameters before file encoding. Files are only encoded and optimized, which shortens their length slightly, but they are not compressed. (Unfortunately, the programmers didn't take Windows NT, Windows 2000, and Windows XP into consideration, and an encoded program will not run under these operating systems.)

The decoding routine is well programmed and, at first sight, appears hard to debug because it contains many anti-debugging and anti-disassembling tricks. Still, you can easily find a decoder for this encoder on the Internet.

Test file compression: 1,583,104 bytes

Decompressor: unNFO

PECompact

PECompact from Collake Software (www.collakesoftware.com) is compression software for executable files. It was created by the excellent programmer Jeremy Collake and works with EXE, DLL, and OCX files.

The entire program is written in assembler and uses two compression libraries for compression: aPLiB is the first of them, and it is one of the best compression algorithms. The other library, JCALG1, was programmed by Jeremy Collake. Unlike aPLiB, it is open source, and you can use it for free.

I was surprised to discover that if you use maximum compression, JCALG1 compresses even better than aPLiB (though compression does take quite a long time). Loading compressed files will take about the same time with both libraries.

The software's design is really very practical. You set the compression level by means of a simple volume control, and then choose the type of program you want to compress. The advanced configuration item (shown in Figure 5.5) contains a detailed menu where you can set many switches, including settings for compression optimization, whether the decompressor in the file should be optimized for size or speed, which resources will be compressed, and other settings. (You can find detailed descriptions of the settings in the documentation.)

Another wonderful PECompact feature is its ability to use plug-ins. It supports plug-ins for encoding, decoding, post, and GPA and contains short examples that are easy to modify. For example, the post plug-in adds a message at the beginning of the program, which may be useful for an author's shareware.

Figure 5.5: PECompact's menu is a slightly larger one than those of other compression programs

I was slightly disappointed, however, in how easy it was to remove PECompact. The developer claims in the documentation that the program will complicate debugging, but I don't think is very true because I didn't find any anti-debugging tricks (which means it isn't difficult to debug). Otherwise, this is one of the best compression programs. If you need a high compression ratio and you don't care that the compressor may be easily removed, PECompact is a great choice.

Test file compression with JCALG: 526,336 bytes
Test file compression with aPLIB: 537,088 bytes
Decompressors: ProcDump and tNO-Peunc

PELOCKnt

PELOCKnt (shown in Figure 5.6) is one of the older but still among the best encoding programs for executable files. The Marquis de Soirée demonstrated considerable programming skills here. Debugging a program protected with PELOCKnt isn't easy at all, because it contains many anti-debugging tricks and the whole code is full of anti-disassembling macros. You can set several program switches, including:

-A1   Sets protection against breakpoints on API calls used by the program. This protects only against normal breakpoints, and debug breakpoints will not be discovered.

-V1   Sets 32-bit antivirus protection, which prevents program modification and protects against breakpoints. (Again, though, it discovers only classic breakpoints.)

```
Dos Navigator  Version 1.50  Copyright (C) 1991-96 RIT Research Labs   23:33:40

C:\7\PECOMP~1>pelocknt.exe

PELOCKnt v2.04  ■ EXE/DLL Protector 4 Win NT4/5/95/98 ■  (c) :MARQUIS:@UCF
Regname= unregistered                                email= martino@gmx.net

■ Usage   : PELOCKnt.exe File2Protect.exe -Options
■ Options: -A0      API protection against winice BPX      OFF (default=ON)
           -B0      Create BACKUP file .org                OFF (default=ON)
           -V0      32-bit CRC VIRUS check                 OFF (default=ON)
           -N       reNAME/hide objects to PELOCKnt        OFF (default=ON)
           -C       Crypt .CODE section ONLY              ON (default=OFF)
           -K       KILL generic Win9x tracer             ON (default=OFF)
           -W1      NAGSCREEN if winice found (NT/W95/W98) ON (default=OFF)
           -W2      EXIT program if winice found          ON (default=OFF)
           -W3      HANGUP windows if winice found        ON (default=OFF)
           -Xy      eXclude PE.object No.y from protection    (e.g. X3)
           -?       Display only fileinfos, don't crypt it
           -T"text" Displays a USER-defined TEXT inside a MessageBox
```

Figure 5.6: Don't waste your time looking for a classic 32-bit–application graphic display in PELOCKnt

-K   Provides protection against a ProcDump-type decoder.

-Wx   Lets you set an action in case SoftICE is found. You can select from
          three options: show a window, end the program, or crash the program.

PELOCKnt doesn't perform any compression, and the resulting code is
thus even slightly larger than the original. This is a pity, because even if the
compression algorithm wasn't the best, it would drastically shorten the length
of the program. On the other hand, PELOCKnt's file starts very quickly.

It has been some time since the last version of PELOCKnt appeared, and
a decoder has, naturally, appeared in the meantime. Unfortunately, it seems
that PELOCKnt is currently a dead project. This is unfortunate, since it truly is
a good program.

Test file encoding: 1,703,936 bytes
Decoder: PEUNLOCK-NT

PE-Crypt

PE-Crypt is a great example of what can happen when two of the best crackers
get down to writing protective software.

I encountered something like this for the first time in DOS when virus
creators tried to protect their works in this way against debugging and against
heuristic analysis. These systems are based on a simple principle but are very
difficult to program. Only a skilled assembler programmer will succeed, and
such a person must know the PE file structure perfectly. There aren't many
people who know both of these fields really well.

The whole file is either encoded or compressed. At the beginning, there is a routine that decodes (decompresses) the file. This opening routine is very interesting, since any fool who knows something about PE-Crypt will try to trace it. What is so interesting about it? The answer is very simple: The routine doesn't make any sense at all. I have managed to decode several programs encoded by PE-Crypt, but this work requires tremendous patience.

Figure 5.7 shows a list of PE-Crypt's options.

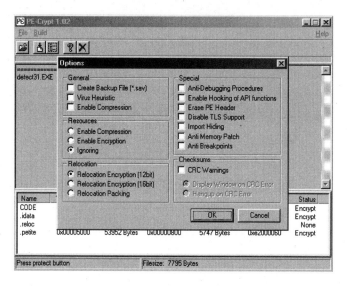

Figure 5.7: With PE-Crypt you have to think twice about which items to select in the menu before encoding an application

Here's a short example of PE-Crypt.

Address	Instruction Code	Instruction	Explanation
15F:42900F	85C0	test eax,eax	
15F:429011	7302	jae 429015	;jumps to address 429015
15F:429013	F70550E808000000EAFF	test dword ptr [8E850], FFEA0000	
15F:42901D	58	pop eax	
15F:42901E	E818	jmp 429038	;we will follow the program's ;correct branch
15F:429020	EB01	jmp 429023	
15F:429015	50	push eax	
15F:429016	E808000000	call 429023	;immediately jumps farther
15F:42901B	EAFF58EB18EB01	jmp 01EB:18EB58FF	;this code is wrong
15F:429022	0FEB02	por mm0, [edx]	
15F:429025	CD20	int 20 VXDCaII CDEA,03EB	

```
15F:429023      EB02            jmp   429027              ;jumps immediately
15F:429025      CD20            int   20 VXDCaII CDEA,03EB ;this code is wrong
15F:42902B      205840          and   [eax+40].bl
15F:42902E      EB01            jmp   429031

15F:429027      EB03            jmp   42902C              ;immediately jumps farther
15F:429029      EACD205840EB01  jmp   01EB:405820CD       ;this code is wrong
15F:429030      8B40EB          mov   eax,[eax-15]
15F:429033      0236            add   dh,[esi]

15F:42902C      58              pop   eax
15F:42902D      40              inc   eax
15F:42902E      EB01            jmp   429031              ;jumps farther
15F:429030      8B40EB          mov   eax,[eax-15]        ;this code is wrong
15F:429033      0236            add   dh,[esi]
15F:429035      8350C356        adc   dword ptr [eax-3D],56

15F:429031      40              inc   eax
15F:429032      EB02            jmp   429036              ;jumps farther
15F:429034      368350C356      adc   dword ptr ss:[eax-3D), ;this code is wrong
                56
15F:429039      57              push  edi
15F:42903A      55              push  ebp

15F:429036      50              push  eax                 ;saves an address of the jump
                                                          ;for ret
15F:429037      C3              ret                       ;jump to an address in the eax
                                                          ;register
15F:429038      56              push  esi                 ;the program will get here
                                                          ;later

15F:42901D      58              pop   eax
15F:42901E      EB18            jmp   429038              ;jumps farther
15F:429020      EB0l            jmp   429023
15F:429022      0FEB02          por   mm0,[edx]

15F:429038      56              push  esi
15F:429039      57              push  edi
15F:42903A      55              push  ebp
15F:42903B      50              push  eax
15F:42903C      E808000000      call  429049              ;jumps farther; this code is
                                                          ;wrong
15F:429041      EC              in    al,dx
15F:429042      FF58EB          call  far [eax-15]
15F:429045      18EB            sbb   b1,ch
15F:429047      010F            add   [edi],ecx
```

```
15F:429049      EB02                    jmp  42904D              ;immediately jumps farther
15F:429048      CD20                    int  20 VXDCaII CDEC,03EB ;this code is also wrong
15F:429051      205840                  and  [eax+40],bl
```

As you can see in the preceding example, PE-Crypt doesn't produce an easy survey at all.

I tried to apply PE-Crypt to a 4KB program. After encoding, the program was 35KB, meaning that the decoding routine takes about 30KB. Tracing such a routine would take an unbearably long time, which is bad news for those who would like to try it.

If PE-Crypt is traced or stopped by an API call breakpoint, it causes an error and the program will not run correctly. (PE-Crypt is protected by various anti-debugging tricks.)

It is possible to place anti-SoftICE routines into the program code, and rather difficult to discover them when a new and smart code is used. If a programmer takes care of other problems as well, he can rest assured that even the best crackers will spend endless hours or days on his work. Even if a cracker manages to get past all the protective software and find a place to make changes, he hasn't won yet.

When a file is encoded or compressed with PE-Crypt, you can't make a direct change to the program code. Your only choices when working with the file are to:

- Manually remove PE-Crypt from the file.
- Create a loader (a memory patcher).

Manual Removal

Manually removing PE-Crypt from a file is difficult, and it's very easy for a cracker to make a mistake. I don't want to claim that it is impossible, because there are people who have managed to do it. If you want to try it, I recommend using a less well-known debugger called TRW instead of SoftICE.

Another, much better, possibility is to use a PE-Crypt remover (such as Bye PE-Crypt). Once PE-Crypt has been removed, making changes in the protected application's code will not be a problem.

Creating a Loader

In order to create a loader you need to write a program that will run the compressed file, decompress it in memory, and then make changes directly in the memory.

You will have trouble if API hooking or anti-memory-patch functions were switched on before encoding. In these cases, PE-Crypt will try to prevent the loader from making code modifications. This function isn't very popular, though, because it isn't compatible with Windows NT, Windows

2000, or Windows XP. However, if a programmer is sure that his product will not be used under Windows NT, Windows 2000, or Windows XP, he may use these functions.

PE-Crypt Options

PE-Crypt offers a lot of options in its Options menu:

Create Backup File (*.sav)   This creates a backup of the original file.

Virus Heuristic   This inserts a heuristic routine into the file for antivirus and anti-change protection.

Resource Compression/Encryption/Ignoring:

> **Compression**   This uses LZW compression to compress the resource part, and it leaves icons and other information concerning the version of the program alone.

> **Encryption**   This encodes the resource part while leaving icons and other information concerning the version of the program alone.

> **Ignoring**   This function makes PE-Crypt ignore the resource part. This function is necessary when encoding fails or when the icons aren't correct.

Relocation Encryption 12-Bit/16-Bit/Relocation Packing:

> **Relocation Encryption 12-Bit or 16-Bit**   This will encode relocations (Fix-up Table) of the PE file and will add the Relocation-Loader.

> **Relocation Packing**   This compresses relocations (Fix-up Table) of the PE file by means of DELTA compression and the LZW routine.

Anti-Debugging Procedures   This adds anti-debugging tricks for SoftICE that are compatible with Windows 9x and Windows NT.

Enable Hooking of API Function   This enables a protective device against program-code changes in the memory. After you switch this function on, you will see a window with API calls in which you can select the API calls used by your program.

   PE-Crypt allows CRC warnings. With this function enabled, a CRC test of the code part of the program is performed with every API call that was selected. You shouldn't set API-hooking on frequently called APIs, or on API functions that are located in time-critical sections of the program. Problems under Windows NT, Windows 2000, and Windows XP could occur with these settings.

Erase PE Header   This will delete the program's PE header after the program has been started. This function won't work with Windows NT, Windows 2000, or Windows XP, or after compilation with some compilers.

Disable TLS Support   This switches off the internal TLS support of PE-Crypt. You only need to switch this function on when the program doesn't run after encoding.

Import Hiding   This adds protection against generic decoders, such as Proc-Dump or GTR95. You have to test it, though, since some programs don't want to run with this function enabled.

Anti-Memory Patch   This is similar to the Enable Hooking of API function. It also protects against changes in the program code. In contrast to the enable-hooking function, this one is focused on threads. It may not work with Windows NT, Windows 2000, or Windows XP.

Anti-Breakpoints   This function switches on protection against breakpoints with API calls in SoftICE (bpx API, bpm API). It may not work in Windows NT.

CRC Warnings:

> **Display Window on CRC Error**   If PE-Crypt encounters a CRC error (such as when the program code has been changed) it will display an error message.

> **Hang-up on CRC Error**   The process will freeze in case of a CRC error.

PE-Crypt Summary

PE-Crypt was probably the best product in program protection until its decoder Bye PE-Crypt appeared. While PE-Crypt was successfully used with Settlers 3, for example, there's not much point in using it today because it can be removed so easily.

NOTE   *There is one other version of PE-Crypt that is used by some cracker groups. This is a slightly different version, and you cannot remove it with Bye PE-Crypt. Unfortunately, it is only for internal use of the group and therefore is not accessible to the general public.*

I don't want to damn PE-Crypt here. You can still use it, and the less experienced crackers will have a tough job removing it. Unfortunately, there don't seem to be any hints of a new version in development.

Test file compression: 864,256 bytes
Test file encoding: 1,052,672 bytes
Decompressor: Bye PE-Crypt

PE-SHiELD

At this writing, PE-SHiELD (shown in Figure 5.8) is probably the best encoder for executable files, even though the current version cannot encode DLL files (parts of it are incompatible with them). On the other hand, because PE-SHiELD won't decode DLLs, it's safe to use to encode EXE files.

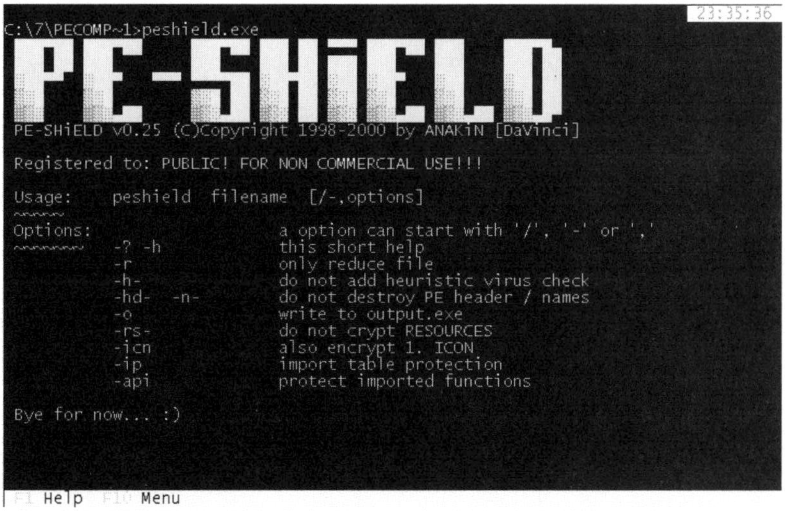

Figure 5.8: PE-SHiELD, presently the best encoding program

ANAKiN, PE-SHiELD's creator, is clearly at the top of his field and he created many of the anti-debugging routines that are now commonly used. (You can reach him at anakin@rockz.org.) In fact, it took almost a full year for a decoder to appear. The program is so good because its decoding is polymorphous, meaning that it changes with each new encoding, just like a virus. This polymorphous characteristic makes it impossible to find where the encoding ends or where any other orientation points.

The only way to correctly decode files encoded with PE-SHiELD is to analyze the code with heuristics to determine each particular instruction's function (this is precisely how the PE-SHiELD decoder works). While people have attempted to decode PE-SHiELD using ProcDump, they have failed because PE-SHiELD contains many protections against tracing in general, and ProcDump in particular.

PE-SHiELD contains many anti-debugging tricks that make debugging nearly impossible. For one thing, it checks all API calls on the breakpoints located in the Import table. It deletes debug breakpoints while running, and thus renders debugging programs useless.

I am not sure whether ANAKiN was the first to use heuristic API calls, but PE-SHiELD masters this method very well indeed. The program heuristically analyzes its opening before the API call, since its opening changes with various Windows versions. As such, it can start the API code elsewhere, omit the beginning of the API service, and jump to someplace like MessageBoxA+8, thus bypassing possible debug breakpoints for API calls.

Another great PE-SHiELD feature is its ability to optimize a file with the -r switch. Files optimized in this way, while not encoded, will be optimized in the best possible way. In my view, PE-SHiELD is absolutely one of the best optimization tools.

At this writing, ANAKiN is working on a new version of PE-SHiELD that should offer completely rewritten code, not a mere update or error correction (there are almost no errors to correct anyway). Considering ANAKiN's abilities, I can say with some certainty that the new version will be a hard program to break.

PE-SHiELD is shareware that may be used for private purposes for free. (The unregistered version is fully functional.) The encoded file shows that it was encoded with an unregistered version, along with other information.

Test file encoding: 1,622,016 bytes

Decoder: UnPEShield

Petite

Petite is also commonly used to compress executables, most often together with SecuROM. Before compression begins, you can set the classic ratio of speed to quality for the compression, though there aren't many additional options (see Figure 5.9).

If you choose maximum compression, the process may take up to several hours to complete for longer files, and the results aren't that great. ASPack and similar programs are faster and offer a better compression ratio, even when they are not set for maximum compression.

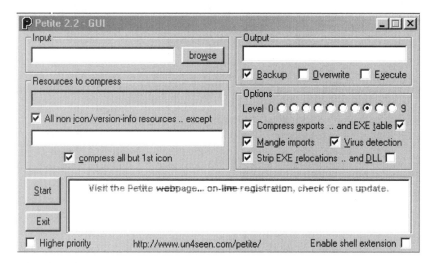

Figure 5.9: Petite is supplied with a graphical interface that makes working with it easier

Petite's decompression routine isn't very well protected against debugging, and it can be manually decompressed. While at this writing there was not yet a decompressor for the current version, 2.2, this version isn't very different from version 2.1, so it probably won't be long before a decompressor appears.

Test file compression: 538,490 bytes

Decompressor: ProcDump

Shrinker

Shrinker, shown in Figure 5.10, from Blink Inc. (www.blinkinc.com), is a rather expensive commercial compression tool. The latest version is over two years old, which suggests that it isn't in continuous development. This is a pity, because Shrinker offers pretty good compression and it is still usable. It also contains some good anti-debugging tricks.

The program interface is similar to ASPack's and is very easy to use. You can set the speed-to-compression ratio with a sliding bar, and most of its other settings should be familiar to you.

Test file compression: 723,456 bytes

Decompressor: ProcDump

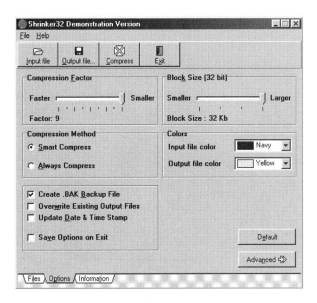

Figure 5.10: Demo version of Shrinker

UPX

UPX (upx.sourceforge.net) is a wonderful, free (GPL'd) compressor for executables that ranks among the best. There are versions for DOS, Linux, and Windows, but we'll focus only on the Windows version here because it's the most commonly used.

UPX's lack of a GUI may be a disadvantage these days, but one talented individual has created a GUI for it. Personally, I don't miss the GUI, though there is also an official UPX GUI in the works.

Because UPX was beta tested for almost two years, it's likely that any major faults have been removed and that your programs will work correctly after compression. My tests rank UPX as the second best compression program, after ASPack. While its compression routine takes a bit longer to run, the results are very good. Still, it is very hard to say which PE Compressor is the best. For some files, UPX is better than ASPack, but for others it is the reverse.

Unfortunately, UPX is much too easy to remove because it doesn't seem to contain any anti-debugging tricks or other protection. Programs compressed by UPX can even be decompressed with UPX, simply by setting the -d switch as shown in Figure 5.11 (though the current version may not always decompress programs compressed with older versions, probably due to changes in the compression algorithm).

The creators of UPX have done an excellent job, and they may even be able to defeat ASPack with future versions. They should consider developing a higher level of protection, however, to make the program even more useful.

Test file compression: 496,128 bytes

Decompressor: ProcDump

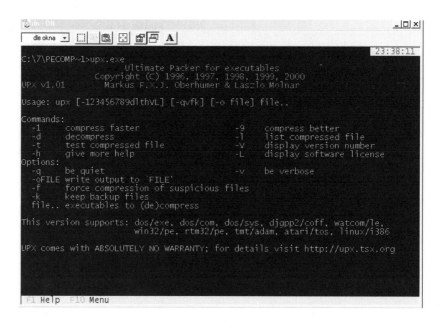

Figure 5.11: UPX can decompress files using the -d switch

WWPack32

The latest version of WWPack32 (www.webmedia.pl/wwpack32) is disappointing. Its compression isn't very good (certainly nowhere near as good as ASPack's), though the program looks good. The environment is fine and compression is really easy, but you cannot set many options, including the compression-to-speed ratio.

In the main window, you'll see a directory like those in Windows Explorer (see Figure 5.12). Select the files you want to compress, and click the compression icon. WWPack32 does the rest.

I don't recommend WWPack32 for software protection because its compression isn't that great and it's not hard to remove. Also, it has no anti-debugging tricks, and the anti-disassembling macros are very poor—they can only prevent disassembling in WinDasm. While at this writing there was no decompressor for WWPack32, it will certainly come soon.

Test file compression: 823,808 bytes

Decompressor: Currently none

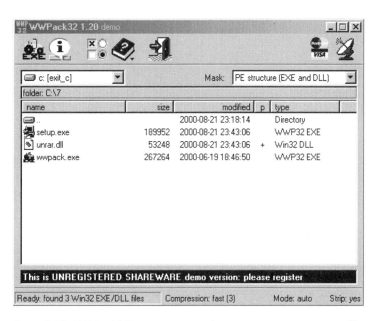

Figure 5.12: WWPack32's environment makes it easier to compress more files at a time

6

COMMERCIAL SOFTWARE
PROTECTION PROGRAMS

In addition to the freeware and shareware programs discussed so far, there are a number of commercial programs for software protection. These, too, vary in quality.

When planning this book, I intended to write about all the commercial software protection that I could find. I quickly learned, though, that there were far too many commercial packages to cover in a reasonable space, so I whittled my initial list down to about forty packages (perhaps one-third of what's available). I then selected what seemed to be not only the best-known, but also, in my view, the best packages, and studied each in detail. I focused both on the design of each package as well as the code itself.

Most of the current commercial software works like Armadillo, SVKP, Vbox, and ASProtect. However, only a few commercial software packages manage their protection well, and most of these programs aren't even protected against changes in the code, which I find to be very unprofessional.

There is quite a range of software protection available, and most of it has its weaknesses. As a software developer, you should understand the weaknesses in the programs you choose, and develop a good strategy for employing software protection. There are good solutions out there, and when used intelligently, one is sure to work for you, but don't expect any one solution to last forever.

ASProtect

ASProtect (shown in Figure 6.1), from ASPack Software (www.aspack.com), isn't just another commercial anti-cracking program; it is a truly revolutionary advance in software protection. It may be the prepackaged solution to software protection for those who don't want to spend long hours studying and programming custom protection for their own software.

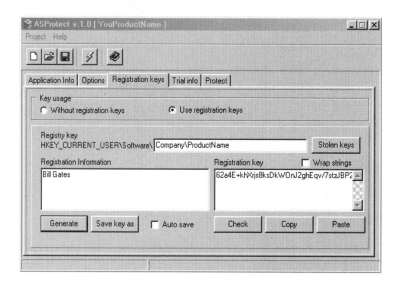

Figure 6.1: It isn't difficult to generate registration keys in ASProtect

ASProtect's creator Alexey Solodovnikov learned a lot from his work on ASPack and applied that experience to ASProtect. He claims that because all anti-cracking defenses can be defeated, the only important thing is under what circumstances they can be broken.

While it was created especially for shareware developers, ASProtect can be used for professional software as well. While it's not as versatile as FLEXlm (discussed later in this chapter), and it works only under Windows, I daresay that it is currently the most difficult commercial software protection to break. Its only weakness is that it doesn't have the best anti-debugging tricks.

Compared to other commercial software protection, ASProtect is simple and well-programmed, reflecting the simple but wonderful idea behind it. Like similar programs, the original program is compressed and then uncompressed by ASProtect before it is run.

ASProtect's compression is based on the ASPack algorithm, which is among the best. While it adds about 60KB of code to the original program, this additional code doesn't matter at all, since the resulting compressed program is much smaller then the original one.

ASProtect's decompression routine checks to see whether there have been attempts to change the file, and it tries to prevent changes in memory. Naturally, without decompression, the original program can't be disassembled, and it isn't easy to decompress ASProtect because it tries to prevent memory dumps by programs like ProcDump. Once the import section has been dumped from memory, the PE file will not be correct. Still, there is a way to decompress ASProtect (not by just dumping), but ASProtect is still not defeated even after successful decompression.

Like FLEXlm, ASProtect tries to prevent the use of certain functions in the protected program when it is unregistered, and it does so beautifully compared with other software. For example, if a programmer wants to disable Preview in the unregistered version, he need only encode this function with ASProtect (as shown in Figure 6.2). After registration, the disabled part is decoded using a constant from the registration key, and it is not possible to decode it without this registration key. ASProtect's exceptionally strong encoding prevents even direct (brute-force) attacks.

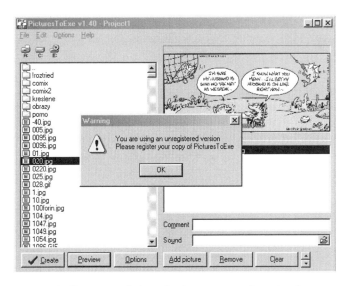

Figure 6.2: The preview function for this program only works after registration

There are three ways to secure an application with ASProtect. The first way uses classic compression and is not recommended because it's relatively easy to decode.

The second possibility is much more interesting, though still not the best. With this method, the original protection is first authenticated after the ASProtect API is called with a constant for decoding the encoded part of the program. You might use this method if, for example, the program you want to protect already has its own registration control and you don't want to change it. This method would be a poor choice if the original protection is weak, since it would not prevent the cracker from getting the correct constant.

The third and best possibility doesn't add any protection to your program (although additional protections are possible). Basically, when using this third method, you specify in the Registration Keys tab in ASProtect that you want your project to contain a registration key (as shown in Figure 6.3 on page 80). The program then creates a basic constant that will serve as a base for other keys, and that will also be used to encode the protected part of the program. You can generate the keys according to user names, and you can also save them. Finally, you determine where the registration key will be saved in the registry following registration.

NOTE *ASProtect's key files have KEY endings but are essentially REG files that are imported into registers once they have been double-clicked. This is an advantage, because ASProtect's registration keys are rather long, and it would be tedious for users to enter them by hand.*

The next step is to verify the registration. If you have only a registration key, the program will print the name of the registered user. You can also specify keys that have been illegally made public if you don't want them to function in future versions of the program. Subsequent versions of ASProtect will probably be able to generate keys for only one computer, which will prevent the illegal distribution of registration keys.

Finally, in the program code you specify the parts of the program that you want to encode—this is a simple procedure that can be performed by almost any programmer. Currently ASProtect contains code examples for Delphi, Visual C++, and Visual Basic. For instance, here's a short example in Visual C++:

```
include <windows.h>
#include "include\asprotect.h"
char *message;
void RegisterAction()
{
REG_CRYPT_BEGIN
message = "Registered version !";
REG_CRYPT_END
}
int WINAPI WinMain (HINSTANCE hInstance, HINSTANCE hPrevInstance,
```

```
PSTR szCmdLine, int iCmdShow)
{
message = "Unregistered version !";
RegisterAction();
MessageBox (0,message,"",0);
return 0;
}
```

You must add REG_CRYPT_BEGIN to the beginning of the encoded program and REG_CRYPT_END to the end.

At the beginning of the encoded part of the program, you must add the following data:

```
OEBh, 04h, OEBh, 05h, 89h, 89h, OE9h, 0, 0, 0, 0
```

And the following data is added at the end:

```
OEBh, 04h, OEBh, 05h, 99h, 99h
```

This data enables ASProtect to find the areas that you want to encode.

Next, you need only call the procedure and the rest will be done for you. If a program isn't registered, the encoded part will be skipped, or else an error will occur. If the program is registered, this part will be decoded at the start of the program, and it will be used later when it is called.

You can get the user's name with the apiGetRegInfo() API function.

Should you need to create many registration keys at once, ASProtect makes it easy by supplying the library keygen.dll. You can generate registration keys with its two functions. The GenerateKeyAsRegFile() function creates a registration file based on user information. Alternatively, the GenerateKeyAsString() function returns the memory pointer to where the registration key was created.

ASProtect allows you to set the number of times that a program can be run or the number of days it will be useable. Unlike similar commercial programs, all protection is placed in the PE file, and not in added DLL or OCX files.

As of this writing, it is impossible for a cracker to correctly remove ASProtect's protection. To do so, he would need to use the correct registration key to decode the program and then dump it from memory. Of course, should the program's creators consider this attack, they may prevent it too by adding additional protections.

Test file original: 1,691,648 bytes
Test file encoding: 693,760 bytes
Decoder: AspackDie

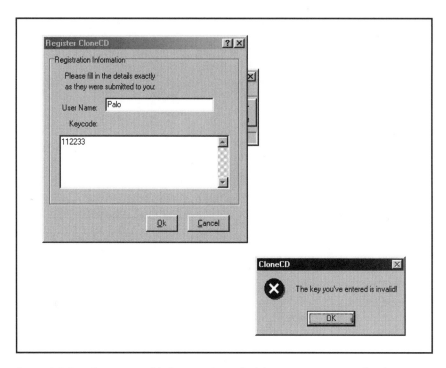

Figure 6.3: It is almost impossible for a cracker to find the correct registration key for a program protected by ASProtect

FLEXlm

FLEXlm, from Globetrotter Software (www.globetrotter.com) is one of the most frequently used protection programs for pricier commercial software. While originally used mostly with Unix software, in the last few years it has been used with other systems as well, especially Windows. FLEXlm is used by the largest software producers, including Adobe Systems, Sun Microsystems, Texas Instruments, Sybase, and SGI.

FLEXlm supports most operating systems and many network protocols, and it offers many ways to protect a product. I will briefly describe the most important ones. The Enable/Disable product features option is the most frequently used.

Demo (Time-Limited License)   Demo or time-limited programs may disable certain features found in the full product. The time limit may be determined by a date when the license expires, by a number of days, or by a number of program starts.

Enable/Disable Product Features   This option lets you disable some program features and use various types of licenses. For example, in the "lite" version of a program, some functions might be disabled and then enabled once a user registers for the "pro" version.

Floating Over a Network   This option lets you determine the maximum number of users who may use a particular program over a network at one time.

Named-User   This setting specifies that the program may be used only on computers that have their network names specified in a list of users.

Node-Locked   This option locks the product to one particular computer.

Node-Locked Counted   This option locks the program to one computer and only for a limited number of starts.

Time-Limited   This option sets a date after which the license for the product will expire and the program will no longer be usable.

Domain Only   This option restricts use of the product to computers in a specific Internet domain.

Protected products call FLEXlm's protection using API functions, and this protection then checks the license in a file, usually license.dat (see Figure 6.4). Before the program uses a protected function, it checks to see whether a particular user has a right to use the function.

FLEXlm's protection isn't unbreakable though. At this writing, there is a generator that capitalizes on failures in FLEXlm to produce correct license files. Naturally, the existence of this generator diminishes FLEXlm's effectiveness.

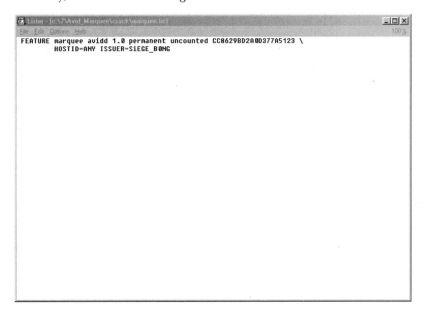

Figure 6.4: At first glance, the registration file for an application protected by FLEXlm doesn't seem complicated

On the other hand, though, when used correctly and combined with other protections, FLEXlm may still offer a very good solution. For example, if another program is used to test the license again in some other way once a protected function has been used, that program will often reveal an illegally created license file.

It is sometimes difficult to find all of FLEXlm's protected functions, and it is absolutely essential to avoid placing their names directly in the EXE file in readable form. Because crackers often set a breakpoint on the lc_checkout call when searching for FLEXlm function calls, it's better to check the protected functions only when they are used, rather than to check them all as soon as the program has started. Be sure, too, to check the breakpoints set to this call, and to use other protections in the program.

While FLEXlm is breakable, it is easy to use. Its wide range of options and support for a variety of operating systems make it an attractive software protection option.

InstallShield

The InstallShield software (shown in Figure 6.5) is designed for creating installation packages. Probably anyone who works in Windows has already seen it, and it is most likely the best application in the field for doing so. Many programs have attempted to compete with InstallShield, but none have beaten it (though a few come close).

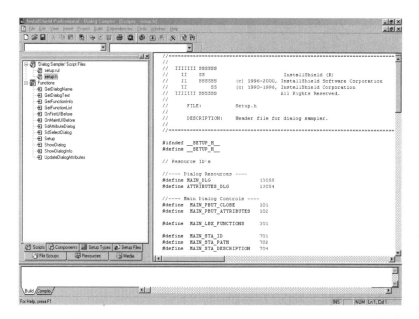

Figure 6.5: The InstallShield environment is a pleasant surprise

Because a faulty installation package can cause huge problems for product distribution, you should use the best installation product you can find, even if it is a bit more expensive. InstallShield has been extensively tested and has been used for several years without problems, which itself is a good test for errors.

InstallShield can perform simple as well as highly complicated installations. It can even call the API calls of external libraries, which is good for protection. And, it can check for various registration conditions during installation (see Figure 6.6). The hardware key is often tested during installation, and the installation is halted if the correct hardware key is missing. The difficulty of removing this protection depends only on the quality of the DLL library.

InstallShield uses its own simple scripting language, which is probably most like C, and once the installation package has been created, the files are compressed into special files. When installing, all of the files necessary for installation are decompressed into the temp directory and then run only from there. This has the advantage that even when the protection can be removed, it is still not easy to change the files within the installation package. (At this writing, a decompressor for version 5 of InstallShield could update its compressed files, but there was still nothing like it for version 6.)

The most difficult part of cracking InstallShield-protected files lies in breaking the protection programmed in the InstallShield script language. Debugging the language is difficult because it is very similar to Visual Basic in the p-code. The attacker will encounter a problem when trying to change the

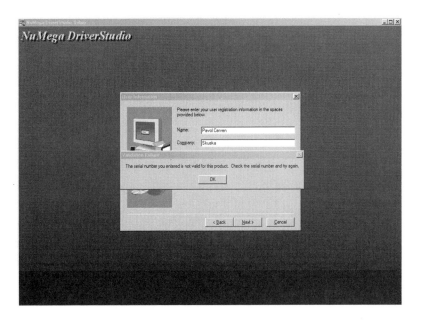

Figure 6.6: Registration check during application installation

file containing the script—the file is protected by a CRC check, and it is very difficult to perform the change correctly because the file's structure is rather confusing and complicated. Still, the protection can be broken.

Install Shield is clearly the best program for creating installation packages. It has been used not only with games but also with the most expensive applications.

ShareLock

ShareLock from Nesbitt Software (www.nesbitt.com) is commercial protection that uses DLL API calls. While it has been discontinued by Nesbitt, it is still used today, so let's have a look at it.

ShareLock's protection is more complex than a program like Vbox (discussed later in the chapter), requiring you to insert an API call into the code to test the protected application. You can test either for the expiration of a time limit or for the correctness of the entered registration number. The entire protection is secured by one DLL library called ShareLk20.dll, which must be located either in the directory with the protected application or in the Windows system directory.

ShareLock's weakest point lies in the protection of the DLL library itself, which is very easy to modify because it has no CRC checks. On the other hand, the registration number calculation is very good, and it is hard to find; to find it, an attacker would have to debug ShareLk20.dll and find a location for the change in the program code, at which point the program would behave as if registered.

Unfortunately, if the protection can be broken this easily, there is no way to protect the application against attack. (Perhaps the protected application could perform the checksum of the DLL library to detect an attack.) Still, the worst news is that once the ShareLk20.dll protection is broken, it is possible to use (illegally) all applications that use this commercial protection, which may well be why this product has been discontinued.

The Armadillo Software Protection System

The Armadillo Software Protection System (see Figure 6.7) is commercial protection from Silicon Realms Toolworks (www.siliconrealms.com/armadillo.htm). Programs are encoded and compressed by means of a randomly generated encoding key.

Armadillo contains one particularly interesting function that allows developers to enter illegal registration numbers found by crackers into a database so that such numbers will be non-functional in subsequent versions. Armadillo also contains anti-debugging tricks that protect against SoftICE.

It's easy to manage Armadillo, and we'll look at a few of its more interesting features in the following list. Armadillo has a very good help system too; to learn more about a particular option, simply select it to read its description or access the help system.

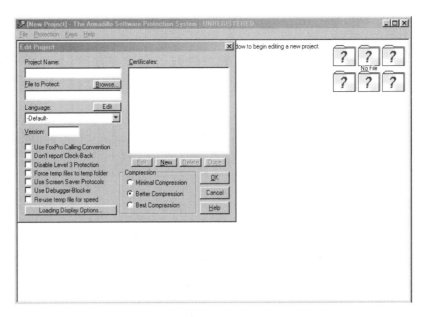

Figure 6.7: Creating a project in the Armadillo Software Protection System

Hardware Locking Options (Pro) With hardware locking, the registration number changes for each computer, according to the various parameters that you set here.

Don't Report Clock-Back Protection checking will be disabled if the time wasn't turned back on the user's system. This protection should be disabled only if your program has problems with it.

Certificates Box Defines Keys for Product Protection When certificates are used, the program can be registered only with these certificates. You can set various options for these certificates in sub-menus.

Create FixClock Key If a user breaks the time protection and changes the date, the program protected by Armadillo will cease to function. When the user runs the program in this format: program_name fixclock, he will be asked to enter the so-called "fixclock" key. If he enters the correct key, the program will start working normally.

Armadillo is a very good program, but it's too easy to remove from a protected product. For example, all the cracker needs to do is wait until the program loads into memory and decodes itself, at which point he can dump the program from memory to disc and make some small changes for the program to be fully functional. Armadillo itself makes the cracker's job easier because it creates a process in memory with the same name as the protected program, except for the suffix, TMPO. This process is fully decoded after loading into memory, and all the cracker needs to do is dump it to the hard drive.

Armadillo may be a good choice for shareware programmers who have less experience with protection programming. This application looks really professional, and I hope that its creators will find a way to improve it in newer versions. Currently, though, I cannot recommend Armadillo because it is so easy to remove, even though less experienced crackers will probably fail to do so—unless, of course, they use a decoder found on the Internet.

Test file compression: 1,007,806 bytes

Decompressor: Un-Armadillo and Armadillo Killer

Vbox

Vbox from Aladdin Knowledge Systems (www.ealaddin.com) is one of the oldest and most frequently used commercial protection programs for Windows (see Figure 6.8). While it is used mostly for shareware, demo versions of expensive programs are sometimes protected with it as well.

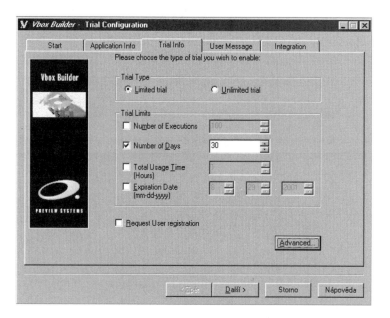

Figure 6.8: Almost anybody can learn how to work with Vbox Builder

The Vbox protection is based on time limits. A window appears every time a Vbox-protected program is launched, and from this window you can run the program itself until the time limit expires.

The first versions of Vbox were called TimeLock and were very popular. For protection, TimeLock 2 uses API calls from the tl32v20.dll library, called from the protected program. The protected application tests the return values and decides whether it will continue to run or not. It looks like this in the program:

```
call CallTimeLock
```

After this returns, the EAX register should contain a return value that will vary depending on whether the test was successful or not.

TimeLock 3.03 Through 3.10

Improvements in these versions of TimeLock include the encoding of certain parts of the program and a preview that sets the entry point (beginning) of the program. This preview contains a lot of the Vbox code that makes debugging difficult.

An API call at the beginning of the program has a rather unusual name:

```
call tl303inj.PleaseTraceIntoMe_MrCracker
```

The encoded part of the application is decoded in this function, and the return value is the entry point of the protected program (or in case of an error, the address for the ExitProcess API call). The return value is in the EAX register again, and the last instruction is to call eax, which jumps on this real entry point of the program (or on the ExitProcess API call in case of an error).

TimeLock 3.13 Through 3.15

These versions brought several innovations:

- Encoding of all program code
- Encoding of section .idata
- Calculation of the CRC of the protection's DLL library in memory

Program decoding with these versions isn't as easy as with previous ones. For one thing, encoding information is saved in an encoded .idata part. Also, the CRC control of the tl315inj.dll is in memory, which secures the protection against breakpoints (of course, not debug breakpoints), as well as against changes in the code. (You can find Weijun Li's initials in the code; he is probably the lead programmer.)

Vbox 4.0 Through 4.03

In this version, Vbox first appeared as we know it today. This version, sometimes called TimeLock 4, contains many improvements. The protected EXE is compressed, and the encoded .idata section is in a separate file. The protection itself is located in three DLL libraries:

Vboxp4xx.dll	Decompresses and loads DLL files
Vboxt4xx.dll	Contains the basic routine for protection of the PreviewParadise_WJ
Vboxb4xx.dll	Loads vboxt4xx.dll and calls PreviewParadise

The last two DLL libraries are compressed but not encoded, and information about the imported calls are saved.

Two parts in the file, called Preview and WeijunLi, contain a good bit of code and encoded data. The first part contains normal code, while the second is compressed. Once a protected program is launched, the first call is to vboxpxx.PreviewExecGate_By_WeijunLi, which decompresses the original program in the Preview.

Once everything has been decoded, a small piece of the code contains a call to a function exported from vboxbxx.dll. This function is also first decompressed with vboxpxx.PreviewExecGate_By_WeijunLi before being launched, and it calls vboxtxx.PreviewParadise_WJ. This function also performs the CRC on the protected file, as well as on the vboxt4xx.dll and vboxb4xx.dll files. If CRC is incorrect, the program will work with a wrong decoding key, and after incorrect decoding, the CRC will also be incorrect for the decoded data. The program will then display an error message.

Vbox 4.10

This version contains the following novelties:

- CRCs for all important files are authorizing signals
- CRCs for DLL file copies are calculated in memory
- The program tries to detect a debugger in memory

If someone tries to disassemble the vboxp410.dll code in WinDasm, an error will occur in the program. IDA (Interactive Disassembler) will work fine, but it will create incorrect code.

Vbox 4.3

This latest version of Vbox offers good protection, though it is vulnerable to dumping from memory (just like Armadillo). No matter how extensive the code, you don't have to try to understand it all to crack it. All you have to do is find the beginning of the encoding program and dump it from memory. (Should the authors solve this problem in future versions, Vbox will definitely be one of the best of the commercial protection packages.) Vbox's Vbox Builder application makes it very easy to create a protected application (see Figure 6.9).

When you launch the program, you set a path to the Vbox privilege file, which each user obtains from the software publisher. To obtain this privilege file, click the Get Privilege File button. Your browser will display the pub-

Figure 6.9: It is very easy to create an initial dialog box for your program with Vbox

lisher's page, and you will have to fill out a questionnaire. Within a few minutes, you should receive an email containing a short file with the .prv extension. Click Next and enter a file name for the Vbox license information file, and then enter a password to prevent unauthorized people from working with your license file. Next, select the language in which you want to work, and enter the author's name, product, version, year, and product identification number.

In following menus, you will enter the most important information, including limitations on the maximum number of launches or days, or a date on which the application's trial period will expire. In the Advanced Security Options menu, you'll set the application's protection. If you select Software Binding, users will be unable to copy the application to another computer because of secret files on the hard drive. If you choose Hardware Binding, information about the computer's hardware will be used to identify the licensed machine.

Test file compression: 835,320 bytes
Decompressor: Vbox Unwrapper

The Slovak Protector (SVKP)

It is especially tough to write about your own product without bias and with maximum objectivity, as you might imagine, and the Slovak Protector is my product. Still, I promise to stick to the facts and to be as objective as possible.

The *Slovak Protector* (SVKP) is the youngest of the commercial protection products described here. When developing the SVKP, I adopted the best of the latest trends and, as a result, the SVKP might look like ASProtect. However, that similarity extends only to their appearance and some functions. The SVKP's inner structure is completely different from ASProtect, and it is the only one of the protections I've discussed that is programmed in assembler. The fact that it is built with assembler guarantees high speed and allows for some special programming techniques that are unavailable to many other advanced programming languages.

As with ASProtect, the SVKP is able to encode parts of a protected application, which will then be able to be decoded only with the right registration key, as shown in Figure 6.11. It uses RSA keys of 2048-bytes' length, which makes it impossible to generate false registration keys. To do so, a cracker would have to have found the private key, but obtaining the private key of such a long length by calculation is simply not possible with current computer systems.

Figure 6.11: It's really easy to work with keys in SVKP

There are protected, compiled programs in the destination executables (EXE, DLL, OCX, or SCR). The protected application is not compressed, but it is encoded by the *Rijndael algorithm* (also known as *AES*). This algorithm protects against brute-force attacks, and the lack of compression guarantees that the program will run quickly.

These types of application protection are similar to those used in ASProtect:

- Coding of the compiled application that, while though not very secure, is adequate in some cases. The advantages of this protection are ease of use and high speed, and that the application can use its own registration control.

- The protected application uses the SVKP registration keys. It utilizes *API functions* (described later in this chapter) to determine whether the right registration key is used.

- Blocks (functions) in the protected application are decoded only with the right registration file. To use these blocks, simply mark places or parts of the application that you want to prevent people from using without the right registration key, before compiling the application to be protected. This is a very easy way to create a protected demo version of a program. For example, if you mark SAVE to be disabled before compilation, the user (without the right registration key) will be notified that the SAVE function is disabled in the demo version. Once the program is registered with the correct registration key, the marked functions will be accessible immediately.

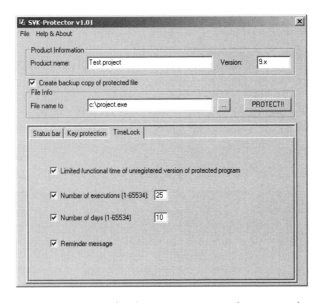

Figure 6.12: Set up of trial version parameters takes no more than a minute

We presently have a very serious problem facing us when it comes to commercial protection: the publishing of registration keys on the Internet. If a cracker buys a program (usually using a stolen credit card) and obtains the right registration key, he has two possibilities. First, he can attempt to remove the protection, which is not easy if the program is protected by the SVKP. Second (and a much more attractive possiblity to him), he can publish the stolen registration key on the Internet. In this case, anyone who uses this actual key can turn their demo version into a fully functional program.

The SVKP, ASProtect, and Armadillo all offer the protected application special key types generated for a specific computer to users intending to register. One advantage of these keys is that they cannot be moved between computers; thus, their publication on the Internet does not threat the application's protection.

Of course, there are some disadvantages, as well. For one, registration requires the user to send data about his computer to a server before the key is generated, but not every user likes to do that. Too, none of the listed protections work online, so a registration could be made directly using its API functions. (Further development will likely head toward enabling and paying for registration directly through a protection program, without needing to go to registration website or the producer's site.)

The biggest problem, however, arises with a change of hardware. If the user changes his hardware, the key stops working, and a brand new one needs to be generated. It is for this reason that most developers allow keys to be transferred between computers.

The SVKP includes some other progressive technologies too, the most important of which are API calls that enable a protected application to communicate with its protection, namely the function SVKP_GetRegistrationInformation. Unlike other protections, the SVKP also contains API functions with active protection, including SVKP_LockKeybord, SVKP_KillDebugger, names which reveal their purpose.

In addition to classical coded blocks, which are decoded only with the right registration key, the SVKP includes two other block types. The first type is decoded right before start-up and, after execution, the program code that contains the block is immediately deleted. I recommend that you use this first block type in initial code parts.

The second block type is also decoded right before start-up, but it is coded again immediately after execution. Use this block type for critical code parts.

Athough all of the above technologies protect against dumping, and the SVKP and other commercial protection contain active protection against dumping from memory, it is not enough. This technology offers a very effective protection against dumping a program from memory and then disassembling it.

Let's take another look at some of the technology built into the SVKP and consider the way it addresses the problems of tracers and debuggers, as well as the way it attempts to incorporate metamorphism to increase protection.

Tracers

A *tracer* is a program that crackers use to try to analyze the protected application on start-up or while it is running. The best-known tracer is IceDump, which is a plug-in to Soft-ICE.

The tracer analyzes instructions directly in machine code, which means that it is a really simple program. But when a tracer is well-designed it can be used in a variety of ways, depending only on the cracker's imagination. Crackers mostly use tracers to repair Import tables, which are frequently used by commercial protections to prevent a program from simply being dumped from the memory. Tracers are also used to decode protected applications by analyzing the code and waiting until the application is decoded. Once the tracer finds that the application has been decoded, it dumps it from memory. The SVKP is one of only a few commercial protections that fights tracers.

Debuggers

Debuggers are yet another problem, as we have discussed throughout this book. The SVKP uses some brand new tricks to detect debuggers, and it is the only protection able to detect and remove all types of breakpoints used by debuggers.

Metamorphism

Metamorphism is a technology with a very promising future, though it is rarely used. The youngest (and most complicated) of all listed technologies, metamorphism tries to solve the problem of protected code repeatability, which stems from the fact that current protections are more or less alike. Once a cracker figures out how to break a type of protection scheme, it is easy for him to break it again and again and in less and less time. Metamorphism tries to prevent this by changing the protection each time it is used, thus making it harder for the cracker to break the protection. None of the protections currently offered use full metamorphism, though the SVKP comes close, since it is much easier to use metamorphism in assembler than in advanced programming languages.

I leave it to you to decide whether the SVKP's protection is any better (or worse) than any other, and I hope that you have not found my opinion to be too biased.

7

ANTI-DEBUGGING, ANTI-DISASSEMBLING, AND OTHER TRICKS FOR PROTECTING AGAINST SOFTICE AND TRW

Few programmers realize just how important it is to prevent their code from debugging or disassembly. It's essential to do so, because if a program can be debugged, it is easy for a cracker to understand how the protection works. Fortunately, even the simplest anti-debugging tricks can complicate debugging, and we can use anti-disassembling macros to make it harder to understand the debugged code. When well-executed, both tricks will make it much more difficult for a cracker to remove even the simplest protection.

We've had a look at the compression and encoding programs that many programmers rely on to do the dirty work of software protection. Using these programs alone, though, is really not a good solution, because it will only be a matter of time before a new decoder becomes available, and before the better crackers remove the encoding programs themselves, thus leaving the application without protection against debugging.

Anti-debugging and anti-disassembling tricks aren't hard to use, but it is very important to test your protected application carefully.

NOTE *As of this writing, there are only a few anti-debugging tricks for Windows NT, Windows 2000, and Windows XP because their internal structure differs from that of Windows 9x. You may find it necessary to have your program test to see which operating system is running and then decide which trick to use. Anti-disassembling tricks, on the other hand, are not operating-system-dependent and will work without such problems. It is therefore advisable to use them as much as possible.*

All of the example programs discussed in the following pages are written in assembler, and it is a good idea to avoid programming them in a higher-level programming language. While not every programmer knows assembler, most higher-level languages let you insert assembly code. If your language of choice does not, it will be much more difficult for you to work with the code you'll find here. In that case, your best bet will be to insert the anti-debugging tricks into a separate DLL library, and then to call those functions from the protected application. (Of course, this is not ideal, because a cracker will be able to remove such protection quickly and easily.)

NOTE *You only need to use anti-disassembling macros to protect critical points in the program that should remain hidden from an attacker. You do not need to use these macros throughout the program.*

Your program should perform a simple test for the presence of a debugger in memory as soon as it starts. If a debugger is found, the program should refuse to run and possibly display a warning that the debugger should be removed (see Figure 7.1). While a cracker will probably be able to get around the first test easily, you should consider having the program, in a later test, check a second time for the presence of a debugger. Then, if it finds that a debugger is still active, the program could "freeze," or do something else to make it difficult or impossible for the cracker to continue. I do not, however,

Figure 7.1: ASProtect has just found an active debugger

recommend displaying a warning under any circumstances, because such a warning makes it clear that this is an attack.

The examples that follow are tuned for Turbo Assembler v5.0 from Borland. The code isn't completely optimized and should therefore be understandable by less-than-expert assembler programmers. (I hope that the pros will excuse me.) While it wouldn't be hard to optimize the examples, doing so would result in less-readable code.

My advice to those of you who don't know how to work in assembler is to learn it. Even though many people claim that it is a dead language, there are still fields where it is necessary, and programming good software protection is one of them, especially when tuning your application (which can only be done well in assembler). When tuning your code, you will discover the holes that make it easy for crackers to conquer and remove software protection.

Let's begin.

Detecting SoftICE by Calling INT 68h

Here's a way to detect the presence of SoftICE in memory by calling INT 68h. The AH register must contain the value 43h before calling INT 68h. If SoftICE is active in memory, the return value 0F386h will be in the AX register.

This is a well-known method of detecting SoftICE that is safe and commonly used, but only in Windows 9x. You can see it in action, for example, in SafeDisc:

```
.386
.MODEL FLAT,STDCALL
locals
jumps
UNICODE=0
include w32.inc
Extrn SetUnhandledExceptionFilter : PROC
.data
message1     db "Detection by calling INT 68h",0
message3     db "SoftICE found",0
message2     db "SoftICE not found",0
delayESP     dd 0                          ;the ESP register saves here
previous     dd 0                          ;the ESP register will save the address of the
                                           ;previous SEH service here


.code
Start:

;--------------------------------------------------------------------------------
;Sets SEH in case of an error
;--------------------------------------------------------------------------------
```

```
        mov  [delayESP],esp
        push offset error
        call SetUnhandledExceptionFilter
        mov  [previous], eax
```
;--
;The new address for Structured Exception Handling (SEH) is set here to ensure that in case of an
;error, the program will continue from an error label and will end correctly. This is important
;if, for example, the program calls an interrupt that will be performed correctly only if SoftICE
;is active, but which will cause an error and crash the program if SoftICE is not active. Finally,
;the previous SEH service address is saved.
;--
```
        mov  ah,43h                    ;service number
        int  68h                       ;calls the INT 68h interruption
        push eax                       ;saves the return value
```
;--
;Sets previous SEH service
;--
```
        push dword ptr [previous]
        call SetUnhandledExceptionFilter
```
;--
;Sets the original SEH service address
;--
```
        pop  eax                       ;restores the return value
        cmp  ax, 0f386h                ;tests to see whether the return value is
                                       ;a "magic number"
```
;--
;If SoftICE is active in memory, the return value will be F386h in the AX register.
;--
```
        jz   jump                      ;if yes, the program jumps because SoftICE is
                                       ;active in memory

continue:
        call MessageBoxA,0, offset message2,\
        offset message1,0

                                       ;if the return value was other than F386h,
                                       ;SoftICE was not found, and an error message
                                       ;will be displayed.
        call ExitProcess, -1

                                       ;ends the program

jump:
        call MessageBoxA,0, offset message3,\
        offset message1,0

                                       ;prints a message that SoftICE was found. Any
                                       ;code may follow from this point.
```

```
call ExitProcess, -1
                                        ;ends the program

error:
                                        ;starts a new SEH service in case of an error.

        mov  esp, [delayESP]
        push offset continue
        ret

                                        ;if an error occurs in the program, SEH
                                        ;ensures that the program will continue from the
                                        ;error label.



ends
end Start
                                        ;end of program
```

Detecting SoftICE by Calling INT 3h

This is one of the most well known anti-debugging tricks, and it uses a back door in SoftICE itself. It works in all versions of Windows, and it is based on calling INT 3h with registers containing the following values: EAX=04h and EBP=4243484Bh. This is actually the "BCHK" string. If SoftICE is active in memory, the EAX register will contain a value other than 4.

This trick has often been used in the code of various compression and encoding programs, and it is well known because of its wide use. When used well, it may cause trouble even for the more experienced crackers.

2

```
.386
.MODEL FLAT,STDCALL
locals
jumps
UNICODE=0
include w32.inc
Extrn SetUnhandledExceptionFilter : PROC
.data
message1    db "Detection by calling INT 3h",0
message3    db "SoftICE found",0
message2    db "SoftICE not found",0
delayESP    dd 0                        ;the ESP register is saved here.
previous    dd 0                        ;the ESP register will save the address of the
                                        ;previous SEH service here.

.code
Start:
```

```
;------------------------------------------------------------------------------
;Sets SEH in case of an error
;------------------------------------------------------------------------------
            mov  [delayESP], esp
            push offset error
            call SetUnhandledExceptionFilter
            mov  [previous], eax
;------------------------------------------------------------------------------
;The new address for Structured Exception Handling (SEH) is set here to ensure that in case of an
;error, the program will continue from an error label and will end correctly. This is important
;if, for example, the program calls an interrupt that will be performed correctly only if SoftICE
;is active, but which will cause an error and crash the program if SoftICE is not active.
;Finally, the previous SEH service address is saved.
;------------------------------------------------------------------------------
            mov  eax,4                       ;"magic" values to be found
            mov  ebp,"BCHK"                  ;whether SoftICE is active
            int  3h                          ;calls the INT 3h interruption
            push eax                         ;saves the return value
;------------------------------------------------------------------------------
;Sets previous SEH service
;------------------------------------------------------------------------------
            push dword ptr [previous]
            call SetUnhandledExceptionFilter
;------------------------------------------------------------------------------
;Sets the original SEH service address
;------------------------------------------------------------------------------
            pop  eax                         ;restores the return value
            cmp  eax,4                       ;tests to see whether eax was changed
            jnz  jump                        ;if it was changed, SoftICE is active
                                             ;in memory
continue:
            call MessageBoxA,0, offset message2,\
            offset message1,0
;------------------------------------------------------------------------------
;If the return value is 4 SoftICE wasn't found and the program prints out an error message.
;------------------------------------------------------------------------------
            call ExitProcess, -1
;ends program
jump:
            call MessageBoxA,0, offset message3,\
            offset message1,0
;------------------------------------------------------------------------------
;Displays a message that SoftICE was found; any code may follow this point.
;------------------------------------------------------------------------------
```

```
call ExitProcess, -1

;ends program

error:
                                                ;starts a new SEH service in case of an error.
        mov  esp, [delayESP]
        push offset continue
        ret
;------------------------------------------------------------------------------------------
;If an error occurs in the program, SEH will ensure that the program will continue from the
;error label.
;------------------------------------------------------------------------------------------

ends
end Start                                       ;end of program
```

Detecting SoftICE by Searching Memory

This detection searches the memory in the V86 mode for the WINICE.BR string. Because this method is infrequently used, it's worth considering, though it can only be used in Windows 9x.

This routine can be easily hidden because it doesn't use calls (neither API nor INT). This will make it impossible to detect, and, if you use it well, it may discover a debugging attempt—for an attacker to make the program continue, he will have to change its code or the register's contents.

To discover the debugging attempt, all you need to do is check after this trick to see if the registers really contain the values that they should contain, and you'll need to perform a CRC test to see if the program code has been changed in memory. If SoftICE isn't active in memory, your checking routine will run without problems.

This method's one disadvantage is that it works well only with older versions of SoftICE, and an error will occur if one of SoftICE's newer versions is active in memory.

3

```
.386
.MODEL FLAT,STDCALL
locals
jumps
UNICODE=0
include w32.inc
Extrn SetUnhandledExceptionFilter : PROC
.data
message1    db "Detection by memory search",0
```

```
message2     db "SoftICE not found",0
message3     db "SoftICE found",0
delayESP     dd 0                                    ;the ESP register saves here
previous     dd 0                                    ;the ESP register will save the address of the
                                                     ;previous SEH service here.


.code
Start:
;-------------------------------------------------------------------------------
;Sets SEH in case of an error
;-------------------------------------------------------------------------------
            mov    [delayESP],esp
            push   offset error
            call   SetUnhandledExceptionFilter
            mov    [previous], eax
            mov    al, "W"                            ;searches for the WINICE.BR string in
                                                     ;V86 memory
            mov    edi, 10000h                        ;begins the search here
            mov    ecx, 400000h - 10000h             ;specifies the number of bytes to search
more:
            repnz SCASB                               ;searches for a "W" string in memory
            jecxz notfound                            ;if the string is not found, the memory search
                                                     ;ends because SoftICE isn't active in memory.
            cmp    dword ptr [edi], "INIC"            ;when a "W" string is found, this tests to see
                                                     ;whether the "INIC" string follows.
            jz     found1                             ;ends when "INIC" is found
            jmp    more                               ;otherwise it searches all memory
found1:
            add    edi, 4                             ;move by 4 characters (bytes)
            cmp    dword ptr [edi], "RB.E"            ;when "WINIC" is found it checks to see if the
                                                     ;"E.RB" string follows
            jnz    more                               ;if it does not, the memory search ends
            push   word ptr 1                         ;go here if SoftICE is active in memory and
                                                     ;save 1 into the stack to show that SoftICE
                                                     ;was found.


            jmp    short found
notfound:
            push   word ptr 0                         ;Go here if SoftICE is not found in memory.
found:
;-------------------------------------------------------------------------------
;Sets previous SEH service
;-------------------------------------------------------------------------------
            push   dword ptr [previous]
            call   SetUnhandleExceptionFilter
```

```
;-------------------------------------------------------------------------------
          pop  ax                        ;restores the return value
          test ax,ax                     ;tests to see if the return value is 1
          jnz  jump                      ;if it is, the program jumps because SoftICE is
                                         ;active.


continue:
          call MessageBoxA,0, offset message2,\
          offset message1,0
          call ExitProcess, -1


jump:
          call MessageBoxA,0, offset message3,\
          offset message1,0
          call ExitProcess, -1


error:                                   ;starts a new SEH service in case of an error
          mov  esp, [delayESP]
          push offset continue
          ret
ends
end Start
```

Detecting SoftICE by Opening Its Drivers and Calling the API Function CreateFileA (SICE, NTICE)

This is the most frequently used detection for SoftICE. It will also find other active VxD (Virtual Device Driver) and Sys drivers.

The principle of this detection is simple: You try to open a file with the same name as the active VxD or Sys file. If the driver is active in memory, and you specify the type of file opening as OPEN_EXISTING (i.e., open the existing file), it will be possible to open it. Once you have called CreateFileA, the EAX register will contain a return value other than –1 (0FFFFFFFFh) if it has been opened successfully.

4

```
.386
.MODEL FLAT,STDCALL
locals
jumps
UNICODE=0
include w32.inc
Extrn SetUnhandledExceptionFilter : PROC


.data
```

```
message1    db "Detection by means of CreateFileA",0
message3    db "SoftICE found",0
message2    db "SoftICE not found",0
delayESP    dd 0                                    ;the ESP register is saved here
previous    dd 0                                    ;the ESP register will save the address of the
                                                    ;previous SEH service here
SOFT9x      db "\\.\SICE",0                         ;the name of the SoftICE driver for Windows 9x
SOFTNT      db "\\.\NTICE",0                        ;the name of the SoftICE driver for Windows NT
                                                    ;and 2000


.code
Start:
;-----------------------------------------------------------------------------------------
;Sets SEH in case of an error
;-----------------------------------------------------------------------------------------
            mov  [delayESP],esp
            push offset error
            call SetUnhandledExceptionFilter
            mov  [previous], eax
;-----------------------------------------------------------------------------------------
            call CreateFileA, OFFSET SOFT9x,\
            FILE_FLAG_WRITE_THROUGH, FILE_SHARE_READ,\
            NULL,OPEN_EXISTING, FILE_ATTRIBUTE_NORMAL,\
            NULL
                                        ;tries to open a file
                                        ;\\.\SICE
            cmp eax, -1                 ;tests for success
            jz  noSOFT9x                ;if not, the program jumps to the test for
                                        ;SoftICE NT and 2000
            push word ptr 1             ;saves the value 1 into the stack to
            jmp short found             ;show that SoftICE is active in memory
noSOFT9x:
            call CreateFileA, OFFSET SOFTNT,\
            FILE_FLAG_WRITE_THROUGH, FILE_SHARE_READ,\
            NULL, OPEN_EXISTING, FILE_ATTRIBUTE_NORMAL,\
            NULL
                                        ;tries to open a file
                                        ;\\.\NTICE
            cmp eax, -1                 ;tests for success
            push dword ptr 1            ;saves value 1 into the stack to show that
                                        ;SoftICE is active in memory
            jnz short found             ;if SoftICE for Windows NT and 2000 is active,
                                        ;the program ends
            pop eax                     ;when SoftICE isn't active.
```

```
                                                 ;calls the value 1 from the stack
            push dword ptr 0                      ;and saves 0 here to show that SoftICE isn't
                                                 ;active
found:
;------------------------------------------------------------------------------------------
;Sets previous SEH service
;------------------------------------------------------------------------------------------
            push dword ptr [previous]
            call SetUnhandledExceptionFilter
;------------------------------------------------------------------------------------------
            pop  eax                             ;restores the return value
            test eax,eax                         ;tests the return value
            jnz  jump                            ;if eax is 1, the program jumps because SoftICE
                                                 ;is active in memory

continue:
            call MessageBoxA,0, offset message2,\
            offset message1,0
            call ExitProcess, -1

jump:
            call MessageBoxA,0, offset message3,\
            offset message1,0
            call ExitProcess, -1

error:                                           ;starts a new SEH service in case of an error
            mov  esp, [delayESP]
            push offset continue
            ret
ends
end Start
```

This means of SoftICE detection is used frequently (probably because it is easy to apply with higher-level programming languages), and is very well known. Since you will need to call the API CreateFileA, you should test to see whether a breakpoint was set on this call. It is best to use this detection as the first test for active SoftICE and to then warn the user to remove it.

```
#include <stdio.h>
#define WIN32_LEAN_AND_MEAN
#include <windows.h>
BOOL IsSoftIce95Loaded( )
{
        HANDLE hFile;
```

```c
          // "\\.\SICE" for Windows 9x
          hFile = CreateFile( "\\\\.\\SICE",
                         GENERIC_READ | GENERIC_WRITE,
                         FILE_SHARE_READ | FILE_SHARE_WRITE.
                         NULL,
                         OPEN_EXISTING,
                         FILE_ATTRIBUTE_NORMAL,
                         NULL);
          if( hFile != INVALID_HANDLE_VALUE )
          {
               CloseHandle(hFile);
               return TRUE;
          }
          return FALSE;
}
BOOL IsSoftIceNTLoaded()
{
          HANDLE hFile;
          // "\\.\NTICE" for Windows NT
          hFile = CreateFile( "\\\\.\\NTICE",
                         GENERIC_READ | GENERIC_WRITE,
                         FILE_SHARE_READ | FILE_SHARE_WRITE,
                         NULL,
                         OPEN_EXISTING,
                         FILE_ATTRIBUTE_NORMAL,
                         NULL);
          if( hFile != INVALID_HANDLE_VALUE )
          {
               CloseHandle(hFile);
               return TRUE;
          }
          return FALSE;
}
int main(void)
{
          if( IsSoftIce95Loaded() )
               printf("SoftICE for Windows 9x is active in memory.\n");
          else if( IsSoftIceNTLoaded() )
               printf("SoftICE for Windows NT or 2000 is active in memory.\n");
          else
               printf("SoftICE wasn't found.\n");
          return 0;
}
```

Detecting SoftICE by Measuring the Distance Between INT 1h and INT 3h Services

This detection routine is one of the best ways to detect SoftICE when it is active in memory, and the most difficult to discover. It's based on the fact that when SoftICE is active, the distance between the INT 1h and INT 3h services will always be 1Eh.

This method is great to use when you don't have to call any interrupts, API, or VxD calls, and discovery is difficult but not impossible. Unfortunately it can be used only in Windows 9x.

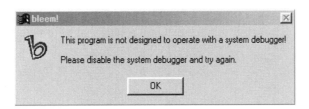

Figure 7.2: Bleem! contains powerful protection that also tries to discover a debugger

```
.386p
.MODEL FLAT,STDCALL
locals
jumps
UNICODE=0
include w32.inc
Extrn SetUnhandledExceptionFilter : PROC
.data
message1    db "Detection of service distance INT 1h and INT 3h",0
message3    db "SoftICE found",0
message2    db "SoftICE not found",0
delayESP    dd 0                        ;the ESP register saves here
previous    dd 0                        ;the ESP register will save the address of the
                                        ;previous SEH service here
pIDT        db 6 dup (0)                ;IDT is saved here

.code


Start:
;------------------------------------------------------------------------------------------
;Sets SEH in case of an error
;------------------------------------------------------------------------------------------
            mov  [delayESP], esp
            push offset error
```

```
            call SetUnhandledExceptionFilter
            mov  [previous], eax
            sidt fword ptr pIDT                ;saves IDT
            mov  eax,dword ptr [pIDT + 2]      ;puts a pointer to the interrupt table into eax
            add  eax,8                         ;inserts the INT 1h vector address into eax
            mov  ebx, [eax]                    ;inserts the INT 1h service address into ebx
            add  eax,16                        ;inserts the INT 3h vector address into eax
            mov  eax, [eax]                    ;inserts the INT 3h service address into eax
            and  eax, 0ffffh                   ;selector will not be used
            and  ebx, 0ffffh                   ;even with INT 1h
            sub  eax,ebx                       ;calculates the distance between interrupt
                                               ;services
            push eax                           ;saves the result
;------------------------------------------------------------------------------------
;Sets previous SEH service
;------------------------------------------------------------------------------------
            push dword ptr [previous]
            call SetUnhandledExceptionFilter
            pop  eax                           ;restores the result
            cmp  eax, 01eh                     ;when 01Eh is the value in eax, SoftICE is
                                               ;active in memory
            jz   jump                          ;and the program jumps

continue:
            call MessageBoxA,0, offset message2,
            offsetmessage1,0

            call ExitProcess, -1

jump:
            call MessageBoxA,0, offset message3,
            offsetmessage1,0
            call ExitProcess, -1
error:                                         ;starts a new SEH service in case of an error
            mov  esp, [delayESP]
            push offset continue
            ret


ends
end Start
```

Detecting SoftICE by Opening Its Drivers and Calling the API Function CreateFileA (SIWVID)

This means of detection is like the detection we used in the "Detecting Soft-ICE by Opening Its Drivers and Calling the CreateFileA API function (SICE, NTICE)" section, and it is based on the fact that SoftICE uses its own graphic driver, VxD siwvid, in Windows 9x. When SoftICE is active in memory, this graphic driver will run, and you can detect it, just as we did the SICE or NTICE drivers, by using an API call at CreateFileA.

This particular method is slightly less used than the one in that earlier section, and as such may be more useful. This trick is valid only in Windows 9x.

6

```
.386
.MODEL FLAT,STDCALL
locals
jumps
UNICODE=0
include w32.inc
Extrn SetUnhandledExceptionFilter : PROC
.data
message1    db "Detection2 by means of CreateFileA",0
message3    db "SoftICE found",0
message2    db "SoftICE not found",0
delayESP    dd 0                        ;the ESP register saves here
previous    dd 0                        ;the ESP register will save the address of the
                                        ;previous SEH service here
SOFTVIDEO   Db "\\.\SIWVID",0           ;the name of the SoftICE graphic driver

.code
Start:
;------------------------------------------------------------------------------------
;Sets SEH in case of an error
;------------------------------------------------------------------------------------
        mov [delayESP], esp
        push offset error
        call SetUnhandledExceptionFilter
        mov [previous], eax
;------------------------------------------------------------------------------------
        call CreateFileA, OFFSET SOFTVIDEO,\
        FILE_FLAG_WRITE_THROUGH, FILE_SHARE_READ,\
        NULL, OPEN_EXISTING, FILE_ATTRIBUTE_NORMAL,\
        NULL
                                        ;tries to open a file \\.\SIWVID
        push eax                        ;saves the return value
```

```
;-------------------------------------------------------------------
;Sets previous SEH service
;-------------------------------------------------------------------
          push dword ptr [previous]
          call SetUnhandledExceptionFilter
          pop  eax                          ;restores the return value
          cmp  eax, -1                      ;tests for success
          jnz  jump                         ;if found, the program ends because SoftICE is
                                            ;active in memory

continue:
          call MessageBoxA,0, offset message2,\
          offset message1,0
          call ExitProcess, -1

jump:
          call MessageBoxA,0, offset message3,\
          offset message1,0
          call ExitProcess, -1

error:                                      ;starts a new SEH service in case of an error
          mov  esp, [delayESP]
          push offset continue
          ret


ends
end Start
```

Detecting SoftICE by Calling the NmSymIsSoftICELoaded DLL Function from the nmtrans.dll Library

The SoftICE DLL library nmtrans.dll contains the NmSymIsSoftICELoaded function, which we can use to see whether SoftICE is active in memory. This trick can be used in all Windows versions, and it is not used very often.

To use this trick, first load the nmtrans.dll library into memory by API-calling LoadLibraryA. Next, find its address by API-calling GetProcAddress, and then calls it. If the return value is other than 0 then SoftICE is active in memory.

The nmtrans.dll library uses an API call to CreateFileA for SoftICE detection, as shown in the section above titled "Detecting SoftICE by Opening Its Drivers and Calling the CreateFileA API Function (SICE, NTICE)." It is important to test breakpoints at API calls to the LoadLibraryA, GetProcAddress, CreateFileA, and possibly even to NmSymIsSoftICELoaded.

Because paths for Windows 9x and Windows NT are firmly set, this isn't an ideal tool, because SoftICE could be installed anywhere. In the "Using the

Windows Registry to Find the Directory Where SoftICE Is Installed" section later in this chapter, I will show you how to use the Windows registers to determine where SoftICE has been installed.

7

```asm
.386
.MODEL FLAT,STDCALL
locals
jumps
UNICODE=0
include w32.inc
Extrn SetUnhandledExceptionFilter : PROC
Extrn GetProcAddress            : PROC
Extrn LoadLibraryA              : PROC
.data
message1    db "Detection using nmtrans.dll",0
message3    db "SoftICE found",0
message2    db "SoftICE not found",0
delayESP    dd 0                                    ;the ESP register saves here
previous    dd 0                                    ;the ESP register will save the address of
                                                    ;the previous SEH service here
SOFT95sym   db "C:\program\sice\SoftICE\nmtrans.dll",0   ;adjust this path according to the SoftICE
                                                    ;installation
SOFTNTsym   db "C:\program\NTICE\nmtrans.dll",0     ;this may be performed by reading from
                                                    ;registers
SOFTsym     db "NmSymIsSoftICELoaded",0             ;the name of the function in nmtrans.dll

.code

Start:
;------------------------------------------------------------------------------------------------
;Sets SEH in case of an error
;------------------------------------------------------------------------------------------------
        mov   [delayESP],esp
        push  offset error
        call  SetUnhandledExceptionFilter
        mov   [previous], eax
;------------------------------------------------------------------------------------------------
        call  LoadLibraryA, offset SOFT95sym        ;loads DLL (nmtrans.dll) for SoftICE
                                                    ;Windows 9x

        test  eax,eax
        jz    no95                                  ;jump on error
        call  GetProcAddress, eax, offset SOFTsym   ;finds the address of the
        test  eax,eax                               ;NmSymIsSoftICELoaded function
        jz    no95                                  ;jump on error
        call  eax                                   ;calls the function NmSymIsSoftICELoaded
                                                    ;whose address is in EAX
```

```
                test eax,eax                                    ;jump if eax is not 0, because SoftICE is
                                                                ;active in memory

                jnz  exit
no95:
                call LoadLibraryA, offset SOFTNTsym             ;loads DLL (nmtrans.dll) for SoftICE
                                                                ;Windows NT and 2000

                test eax,eax
                jz   exit                                       ;jump on error
                call GetProcAddress, eax, offset SOFTsym        ;detects the address of the
                                                                ;NmSymIsSoftICELoaded function

                test eax,eax
                jz   exit                                       ;jump on error
                call eax                                        ;calls NmSymIsSoftICELoaded function whose
                                                                ;address is in EAX
exit:
                push eax                                        ;saves the return value
                                                                ;Sets previous SEH service

                push dword ptr [previous]
                call SetUnhandledExceptionFilter
                pop  eax                                        ;restores the return value
                test eax,eax                                    ;if EAX isn't 0, SoftICE is active
                                                                ;in memory

                jnz  jump                                       ;and the program ends

continue:
                call MessageBoxA,0, offset message2,\
                offset message 1, 0
                call ExitProcess, -1

jump:
                call MessageBoxA,0, offset message3,\
                offset message 1, 0
                call ExitProcess, -1

error:                                                          ;starts a new SEH service in case of
                                                                ;an error

                mov  esp, [delayESP]
                push offset continue
                ret


ends
end Start
```

Detecting SoftICE by Identifying Its INT 68h Service

This rarely used means of detection tests the first bytes of the INT 68h service to see whether it is a SoftICE service. This detection routine is hard to discover, but the test may only be launched from a DOS program running under Windows, because the INT 68h service is for DOS only.

Because it cannot be used directly in a 32-bit Windows program, this routine is almost useless. Its other disadvantage is that the beginning of the service is different for various SoftICE versions. The compared values shown in this code are from SoftICE v4.05 for Windows 9x.

8

```
.MODEL TINY
.386P

.DATA
message    db "SoftICE detection by means of its INT 68h service identification", 0dh, 0ah, 24h
found      db "SoftICE active", 24h
notfound   db "SoftICE not found", 24h

.CODE
.STARTUP
        lea  dx, message
        mov  ah,9                       ;function number --> show string
        int  21h                        ;the INT 21h call shows the label
        xor  ax,ax                      ;nulls ax
        mov  es,eax                     ;sets 0 into es
        mov  bx, word ptr es: [68h*4]   ;puts the offset part of the INT 68h service
                                        ;address into bx
        mov  es, word ptr es: [68h*4+2] ;puts the segment part of the INT 68h service
                                        ;address into es
        mov  eax, 0f43fc80h             ;puts the first bytes of the SoftICE INT 68h
                                        ;service into eax
        cmp  eax,dword ptr es: [ebx]    ;tests to see if SoftICE is active in memory
        jz   short jump                 ;jumps if SoftICE is active in memory
        lea  dx, notfound
        jmp  short farther
jump:
        lea  dx, found
farther:
        mov  ah,9                       ;function number --> show string
;chain
        int  21h                        ;INT 21h call
        mov  ax,4c00h                   ;Function number causes the program to end
        int  21h                        ;INT 21h call
END
```

Detecting SoftICE by Detecting a Change in the INT 41h Service

This detection is based on the fact that your program will change the INT 41h vector to your new service. If SoftICE is active in memory, this will not be possible; if SoftICE is not in memory, your new service will be performed.

As with the previous example, this technique only runs in a DOS box under Windows 9x. It cannot be used in 32-bit Windows applications.

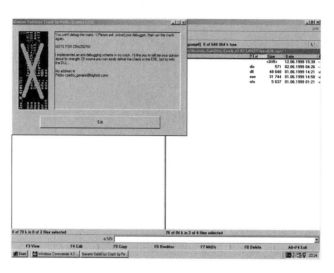

Even some programs created by crackers contain protection against debugging

9

```
.MODEL TINY
.386P


.DATA
message     db "SoftICE detection by means of its INT 41h", 0dh, 0ah,24h service identification
found       db "SoftICE active",24h
notfound    db "SoftICE not found",24h


.CODE
.STARTUP
        lea  dx, message
        mov  ah,9                    ;function number --> Show string
        int  21h                     ;INT 21h call shows label
        xor  ax,ax                   ;nulls ax
        mov  es,ax                   ;puts 0 into es (sets interrupt vector segment)
        mov  bx, cs                  ;puts the program segment into bx
        lea  dx, new_int41           ;puts the offset part of the new int 41h
                                     ;service into dx
```

```
        xchg dx, es:[41h*4]              ;sets an offset part of the new int 41h service
                                         ;address and puts the offset part of the old
                                         ;service address into dx

        xchg bx, es:[41h*4+2]            ;sets the segment part of the new int 41h
                                         ;service address and puts the segment part of
                                         ;the old service address into bx

        in   al, 40h                     ;reads a value into al
        xor  cx,cx                       ;nulls cx
        int  41h                         ;calls INT 41h. If SoftICE isn't active in
                                         ;memory, the program will perform the new
                                         ;service

        xchg dx, es:[41h*4]              ;sets the offset part of the original INT 41h
                                         ;service address

        xchg bx, es:[41h*4+2]            ;sets the segment part of the original int 41h
                                         ;service address

        cmp  cl,al                       ;compares cl and al and if the result is
                                         ;negative SoftICE is active in memory
        jnz  short jump                  ;jumps if SoftICE is active in memory
        lea  dx, notfound
        jmp  short farther
jump:
        lea  dx, found
farther:
        mov  ah,9                        ;function number --> Show string
        int  21h                         ;INT 21h call
        mov  ax,4c00h                    ;function number --> Ends program
        int  21h                         ;INT 21h call this is your new INT 41h service
new_int41 PROC
        mov  cl,al                       ;moves the value from al into cl to show that
                                         ;SoftICE isn't active in memory

        iret                             ;returns from the service
new_int41 ENDP

END
```

Detecting SoftICE by Opening Its Driver and
Calling the API Function CreateFileA (SIWDEBUG)

This trick is also based on searching for a SoftICE driver in memory. The API function CreateFileA is used because it can find out whether the driver is active in memory, and it is also necessary to use the API function GetLastError once it has been called. CreateFileA will return the value −1 in the EAX register, which means that it didn't succeed in opening the file. Once you call

GetLastError, you will be able to find out whether SoftICE is active in memory. If it is, the EAX will be 02; if it is not, this value will be 32h.

This is a less widely known anti-debugging trick than the detection method described in the "Detecting SoftICE by Opening Its Drivers and Calling the CreateFileA API Function (SICE, NTICE)" section. It works only in Windows 9x.

10

```
.386
.MODEL FLAT,STDCALL
locals
jumps
UNICODE=0
include w32.inc
Extrn SetUnhandledExceptionFilter : PROC


.DATA
message1    db "Detection by means of CreateFileA and SIWDEBUG driver",0
message3    db "SoftICE found",0
message2    db "SoftICE not found",0
delayESP    dd 0                            ;the ESP register saves here
previous    dd 0                            ;the ESP register will save the address of the
                                            ;previous SEH service here
SIWDEBUG    db "\\.\SIWDEBUG",0             ;the name of the SoftICE driver

.CODE
Start:
;----------------------------------------------------------------------------------
;Sets SEH in case of an error
;----------------------------------------------------------------------------------
            mov  [delayESP],esp
            push offset error
            call SetUnhandledExceptionFilter
            mov  [previous], eax
;----------------------------------------------------------------------------------
            call CreateFileA, OFFSET SIWDEBUG, FALSE,\
            FALSE, NULL, FALSE, OPEN_EXISTING, NULL
                                            ;tries to open the \\.\SIWDEBUG file
call GetLastError                           ;returns an error number (if SoftICE is
                                            ;active EAX=32h; if it is not, EAX=02)
            push eax                        ;saves the return value
;----------------------------------------------------------------------------------
;Sets previous SEH service
;----------------------------------------------------------------------------------
            push dword ptr [previous]
            call SetUnhandledExceptionFilter
;----------------------------------------------------------------------------------
```

```
        pop  eax                              ;restores the return value
        cmp  eax, 32h                         ;tests to see if SoftICE is active in memory
        jz   jump                             ;jumps if it is active

continue:
        call MessageBoxA,0, offset message2,\
        offset message1,0
        call ExitProcess, -1

jump:
        call MessageBoxA,0, offset message3,\
        offset message1,0
        call ExitProcess, -1
error:                                        ;starts a new SEH service in case of an error
        mov  esp, [delayESP]
        push offset continue
        Ret


ends
end Start
```

Detecting SoftICE by Calling Int 2Fh and Its Function GET DEVICE API ENTRY POINT for VxD SICE

This infrequently used trick calls the INT 2Fh interrupt and its function, GET DEVICE API ENTRY POINT. The service must be called with ES and DI equal to 0. It's not hard to use this trick in a DOS box under Windows.

BX contains the value 0202h, which is a VxD ID for SoftICE. If VxD is active, a non-zero value will return in es and di, which is the address for the DEVICE API ENTRY POINT. This means that SoftICE is active in memory.

11

```
.MODEL TINY
.386P


.DATA
message   db 'SoftICE detection through calling Int 2fh and its function GET DEVICE API ENTRY
          POINT for VXD SICE', 0dh, 0ah,24h
found     db 'SoftICE active',24h
notfound  db 'SoftICE not found',24h

.CODE
.STARTUP
```

```
        lea  dx, message
        mov  ah,9                          ;function number --> show string
        int  21h                           ;INT 21h call shows label
        xor  di,di                         ;nulls di
        mov  es,di                         ;nulls es
        mov  ax, 1684h                     ;the number of GET DEVICE API ENTRY POINT
                                           ;function
        mov  bx, 202h                      ;VxD ID for SICE VxD
        int  2fh                           ;calls GET DEVICE API ENTRY POINT
        mov  ax, es                        ;puts the value from es into axf
        add  ax, di                        ;adds di to ax
        test ax,ax                         ;tests whether ax=0
        jnz  short jump                    ;if not, it jumps since SoftICE is active in ;
                                           ;memory

        lea  dx, notfound
        jmp  short farther

jump:

        lea  dx, found

farther:

        mov  ah,9                          ;function number --> show string
        int  21h                           ;INT 21h call shows label
        mov  ax,4c00h                      ;function number --> ends the program
        int  21h                           ;INT 21h call
END
```

As you can see, it's very easy to use this trick in a DOS program. There is a problem, though, with using it in a 32-bit Windows application, because the simple INT 2Fh can't be used without the program ending with an error. After considering this problem for some time, I figured out a way to solve it, as follows.

The program first finds the address of the INT 5h service, sets your new service instead of it, and then calls the new INT 5h service. In this way, the program is switched into ring0, the high privilege state. Once in ring0, you can call a VxD and then set a new INT 68h service. At this point, the INT 5h service will end, and the program will switch back into ring3, the low privilege state.

The program will call INT 68h with the AH register set to 43h, which is the same means of detection as that used in the preceding DOS example. The AH register doesn't have to be set, because this is just a trick to fool an attacker into thinking that you are trying to detect the debugger in this way, though you are not.

You call your new service for this interrupt by calling INT 68h, using the same INT 2Fh call as in a DOS program running under Windows. If SoftICE is found, it sets a mark and returns to the main program.

At this point, the INT 5h running in the ring0 service is called again, and the original INT 68h service is set there. Later, the program switches back into ring3 and sets the original INT 5h service. Finally, it tests to see whether the mark indicating that SoftICE had been found was set.

This is a somewhat complicated solution, but it's the best I've been able to come up with. There may well be a better one.

11 (32-bit)

```
.386p
.MODEL FLAT,STDCALL
locals
jumps
UNICODE=0
include w32.inc


Extrn SetUnhandledExceptionFilter : PROC
Interrupt        equ 5                          ;interrupt 3 will make debugging more difficult


.DATA
message1        db "Detection by means of the Int 2Fh_GET DEVICE API ENTRY POINT for VxD SICE",0
message2        db "Debugger not found",0
message3        db "Debugger found",0
delayESP        dd 0                            ;the ESP register will be saved here
previous        dd 0                            ;the ESP register will save the address of the
                                                ;previous SEH service here
mark            db 0                            ;a value of 1 will be set here if SoftICE is
                                                ;active in memory


.CODE
Start:


;------------------------------------------------------------------------------------------------
;Sets SEH in case of an error
;------------------------------------------------------------------------------------------------
                mov   [delay, ESP]
                push offset error
                call SetUnhandledExceptionFilter
                mov   [previous], eax
;------------------------------------------------------------------------------------------------
                push edx
                sidt [esp-2]                     ;reads IDT into the stack
                pop   edx
                add   edx,(Interrupt*8)+4        ;reads a vector of the required interrupt
                                                 ;(INT 5h)
                mov   ebx,[edx]
                mov   bx,word ptr [edx-4]         ;reads an address of the old service of the
                                                 ;required interrupt (INT 5h)
```

```
                lea   edi,InterruptHandler
                mov   [edx-4],di
                ror   edi,16                    ;sets a new service for the interrupt (INT 5h)
                mov   [edx+2],di
                push  ds                        ;saves registers for
                push  es                        ;security
                int   Interrupt                 ;jump into Ring0 (the newly defined service
                                                ;INT 5h)
                pop   es                        ;restores registers
                pop   ds
                push  ds                        ;saves registers for
                push  es                        ;security
                mov   ah,43h
                int   68h                       ;calls INT 68h and function 43h (which will call
                                                ;your new service INT 68h)
                stc                             ;sets a mark that your service INT 68h may be
                                                ;cancelled
                int   Interrupt                 ;jumps into Ring0 (your new service INT 5h)
                pop   es                        ;restores registers
                pop   ds
                mov   [edx-4],bx                ;sets the original service
                ror   ebx,16                    ;of the INT 5h interrupt
                mov   [edx+2],bx
;-------------------------------------------------------------------------------------------
;Sets the previous SEH service
;-------------------------------------------------------------------------------------------
                push  dword ptr [previous]
                call  SetUnhandledExceptionFilter
;-------------------------------------------------------------------------------------------
                cmp   byte ptr mark,1           ;tests to see whether a mark has been set that
                                                ;SoftICE is active in memory
                jz    jump                      ;if yes the program will end

continue:
                call MessageBoxA,0, offset message2,
                offsetmessage1,0
                call ExitProcess, -1

jump:
                call MessageBox, 0, offset message3,
                offsetmessage1,0
                call ExitProcess, -1
error:                                          ;sets a new SEH service in case of an error
                mov  esp, [delayESP]
                push offset continue
                ret
```

```
;-------------------------------------------------------------------------------
;A new INT 5h service (runs in Ring0)
;-------------------------------------------------------------------------------
InterruptHandler:
                pushad                          ;saves registers
                jc   uninstall                  ;tests your mark and if it is set it will jump
                                                ;to uninstall your INT 68h service
                mov  eax, 68h                   ;interrupt number where it will set your new
                                                ;service
                mov  esi, offset HookInt68      ;address of your new service
                db   0cdh,20h                   ;calls the VxD call
                dd   000010041H                 ;Hook_V86_Int_Chain
;       VMMCall Hook_V86_Int_Chain
                mov  eax, 68h                   ;interrupt number where it will set your new
                                                ;service
                mov  esi, OFFSET HookInt68      ;address of your new service
                db   0cdh,20h                   ;calls the VxD call
                dd   000010080H                 ;Hook_PM_Fault
;       VMMCall Hook_PM_Fault
                popad                           ;restores registers
                iretd                           ;jump back to Ring3
uninstall:                                      ;the program will jump here if it is to
                                                ;uninstall your INT 68h service
                mov  eax, 68h                   ;interrupt number where your new service has
                                                ;been set
                mov  esi, OFFSET HookInt68      ;the address of your new service
                db   0cdh,20h                   ;calls the VxD call
                dd   000010118H                 ;UnHook_V86_Int_Chain
;       VMMCall  UnHook_V86_Int_Chain
                mov  eax, 68h                   ;the interrupt number where your new service
                                                ;has been set
                mov  esi, OFFSET HookInt68      ;the address of your new service
                db   0cdh,20h                   ;calls the VxD call
                dd   00001011AH                 ;UnHook_PM_Fault
;       VMMCall UnHook_PM_Fault
                popad                           ;restores registers
                iretd                           ;jump back to ring3
;-------------------------------------------------------------------------------
;The new service INT 68h
;-------------------------------------------------------------------------------
HookInt68:
                pushfd                          ;
                pushad                          ;saves registers
                xor  di, di                     ;
                mov  es, di                     ;nulls es:di
```

```
            mov  bx, 202h                    ;VxD ID for SICE VxD
            mov  ax, 1684h                   ;GET DEVICE API ENTRY POINT function number
            int  2Fh                         ;calls the GET DEVICE API ENTRY POINT
            ;mov  ax, es                      ;moves a value from es into ax
            ;add  ax, di
;-------------------------------------------------------------------------------
;The preceding two lines must always be left out because the ES is always set to a value other than
;0 when calling the INT 2Fh. This is the main difference between the DOS version and the 32-bit
;Windows version of this detection.
;-------------------------------------------------------------------------------
            mov  ax,di                       ;saves only the DI register
            test ax,ax                       ;tests if ax=0
            jz   short none                  ;if yes, it will jump because SoftICE isn't
                                             ;active in memory
            mov  byte ptr mark, 1            ;sets a mark that SoftICE is active

none:
            popad                            ;
            popfd                            ;restores registers
            ret                              ;jumps back from the service


ends
end Start
```

One advantage of this method of detection is that some detectors of anti-debugging tricks have problems with it. For example, if FrogsICE were running, Windows would "freeze." (This method only works in Windows 9x, though.)

Detecting SoftICE by Calling INT 2Fh and Its Function GET DEVICE API ENTRY POINT for VxD SIWVID

This detection is based on the same principle as the previous one, except that instead of searching for the VxD of the SICE driver, it searches for the VxD SIWVID whose VxD ID is 7A5Fh.

Here's how it looks as a DOS program running under Windows.

12

```
.MODEL TINY
.386P


.DATA
message       db 'Detecting SoftICE by calling Int 2fh and its function GET DEVICE API ENTRY
              POINT for VXD SIWVID', 0dh, 0ah,24h
found         db 'SoftICE active',24h
notfound      db 'SoftICE not found',24h
```

```
.CODE
.STARTUP
                lea  dx, message
                mov  ah,9               ;a number of the function -> display the string
                int  21h                ;the INT 21h call displays the label
                xor  di,di              ;nulls di
                mov  es,di              ;nulls es
                mov  ax, 1684h          ;GET DEVICE API ENTRY POINT function number
                mov  bx, 7A5Fh          ;VxD ID for SIWVID VxD
                int  2fh                ;calls the GET DEVICE API ENTRY POINT
                mov  ax, es             ;puts the value from es into ax
                add  ax, di             ;adds di to ax
                test ax,ax              ;tests if ax=0
                jnz  short jump         ;if not, it will jump since SoftICE is active
                                        ;in memory

                lea  dx, notfound
                jmp  short farther
jump:
                lea  dx, found

farther:
                mov  ah,9               ;a number of the function -> display the string
                int  21h                ;INT 21h call
                mov  ax,4c00h           ;a number of the function -> ends the program
                int  21h                ;INT 21h call
END
```

No great changes had to be made to make this method run as a 32-bit Windows application.

---

12 (32-bit)

```
.386p
.MODEL FLAT,STDCALL
locals
jumps
UNICODE=0
include w32.inc


Extrn SetUnhandledExceptionFilter : PROC
Interrupt        equ 5                  ;interrupt number 3 makes debugging more
                                        ;difficult


.DATA

message1         db "Detection by Int 2Fh_GET DEVICE API ENTRY POINT for VXD SIWVID",0
message2         db "Debugger not found",0
message3         db "Debugger found",0
```

```
delayESP            dd 0                        ;the ESP register saves here
previous            dd 0                        ;the ESP register will save the address of the
                                                ;previous SEH service here
mark                db 0                        ;a value of 1 will be set here if SoftICE is
                                                ;active in memory


            .CODE
            Start:


;------------------------------------------------------------------------------------
;Sets SEH in case of an error
;------------------------------------------------------------------------------------
            mov  [delay, ESP]
            push offset error
            call SetUnhandledExceptionFilter
            mov  [previous], eax
;------------------------------------------------------------------------------------
            push edx
            sidt [esp-2]                        ;reads IDT into the stack
            pop  edx
            add  edx,(Interrupt*8)+4            ;reads the vector of the required interrupt
                                                ;(INT 5h)
            mov  ebx,[edx]
            mov  bx,word ptr [edx-4]
                                                ;reads the address of the old service of the
                                                ;required interrupt (INT 5h)
            lea  edi, InterruptHandler
            mov  [edx-4],di
            ror  edi,16                         ;sets the new service of the interrupt (INT 5h)
            mov  [edx+2],di
            push ds                             ;saves registers
            push es                             ;for security
            int  Interrupt                      ;jump into the Ring0 (newly defined INT 5h
                                                ;service)
            pop  es                             ;restores registers
            pop  ds
            push ds                             ;saves registers
            push es                             ;for security
            mov  ah,43h
            int  68h                            ;calls INT 68h and the 43h function (your new
                                                ;INT 68h service will be called)
            stc
            int  Interrupt                      ;jump into Ring0 (your INT 5h service)
            pop  es                             ;restores registers
            pop  ds
```

```
mov  [edx-4],bx    ;sets the original service
             ror  ebx,16                        ;of the INT 5h interrupt
             mov  [edx+2],bx
;----------------------------------------------------------------------------------------------
;Sets the previous SEH service
;----------------------------------------------------------------------------------------------
             push dword ptr [previous]
             call SetUnhandledExceptionFilter
;----------------------------------------------------------------------------------------------
             cmp  byte ptr mark, 1              ;tests to see if a mark was set indicating that
                                                ;SoftICE is active in memory
             jz   jump

continue:
             call MessageBoxA,0, offset message2,\
             offset message1,0
             call ExitProcess, -1

jump:
             call MessageBoxA,0, offset message3\
             offset message1,0
             call ExitProcess, -1

error:                                          ;sets a new SEH service in case of an error
             mov  esp, [delayESP]
             push offset continue
             ret
;----------------------------------------------------------------------------------------------
;The new INT 5h service (runs in Ring0)
;----------------------------------------------------------------------------------------------
InterruptHandler:
             pushad                             ;saves registers
             jc   uninstall                     ;tests our mark when it is set; jumps uninstall
                                                ;our service INT 68 h
             mov  eax, 68h                      ;the interrupt number where your new service has
                                                ;been set.
             mov  esi, offset HookInt68         ;the address of your new service
             db   0cdh,20h                      ;calls VxD
             dd   000010041H                    ;Hook_V86_Int_Chain
;            VMMCall Hook_V86_Int_Chain
             mov  eax, 68h                      ;the interrupt number where your new service has
                                                ;been set.
             mov  esi, OFFSET HookInt68
             db   0cdh,20h                      ;calls VxD
             dd   000010080H                    ;Hook_PM_Fault
```

```
;          VMMCall Hook_PM_Fault
              popad                            ;restores registers
              iretd                            ;jump back to ring3; jumps here when it has to
                                               ;uninstall our service INT 68 h
uninstall:
              mov   eax, 68h
              mov   esi, OFFSET HookInt68      ;the interrupt number where your new service has
                                               ;been set.
              db    0cdh,20h                   ;calls VxD
              dd    000010118H                 ;UnHook_V86_Int_Chain
;          VMMCall UnHook_V86_Int_Chain
              mov   eax, 68h                   ;the interrupt number where your new service has
                                               ;been set.
              mov   esi, OFFSET HookInt68      ;the address of your new service
              db    0cdh,20h                   ;calls VxD
              dd    00001011AH                 ;UnHook_PM_Fault
;          VMMCall UnHook_PM_Fault
              popad                            ;restores registers
              iretd                            ;jumps back into ring3
;-------------------------------------------------------------------------------
;The new INT 68h service
;-------------------------------------------------------------------------------
HookInt68:
              pushfd                           ;
              pushad                           ;saves registers
              xor   di, di                     ;
              mov   es, di                     ;nulls es:di
              mov   bx, 7A5Fh                  ;VxD ID for SIWVID VxD
              mov   ax, 1684h                  ;number of the GET DEVICE API ENTRY POINT
                                               ;function
              int   2Fh                        ;calls the GET DEVICE API ENTRY POINT
;             mov   ax, es                     ;puts the value from es into ax
;             add   ax, di                     ;adds di to ax
;-------------------------------------------------------------------------------
;The preceding two lines must always be left out because the ES is always set to a value different
;from 0 when calling the INT 2Fh. This is the major difference between this and the DOS version of
;this detection.
;-------------------------------------------------------------------------------
              mov   ax, di                     ;saves only the DI register
              test  ax, ax                     ;tests to see if ax=0
              jz    short none                 ;if yes it ends because SoftICE isn't active
                                               ;in memory
              mov   byte ptr mark, 1           ;sets a mark that SoftICE is active in memory
```

```
none:
            popad                           ;
            popfd                           ;restores registers
            ret                             ;jump back from the service

ends
end Start
```

As with the previous example, this detection works only in Windows 9x.

Using the CMPXCHG8B Instruction with the LOCK Prefix

This slightly different trick uses the LOCK CMPXCHG8B instruction to make SoftICE detect an error and stop. The correct usage is LOCK CMPXCHG8B [EAX].

The instruction CMPXCHG8B is used for 64-bit values. It compares a value in the EDX:EAX registers with the 64-bit value saved in the address determined by the pointer in the EAX register. If the values are the same, it saves the value from the ECX:EBX registers here, and sets the ZF flag in the flag register. If they do not match, it reads the 64-bit value from the address saved in the EAX register into the EDX:EAX registers, and nulls the ZF flag.

The register that determines the location of the 64-bit value may also be used incorrectly. It is a special instruction that will stop as an error if SoftICE is active, because it doesn't handle this instruction correctly (some Pentium processors had this problem too).

There are several possibilities for the instruction LOCK CMPXCHG8B:

Prefix					Instruction		
FO	OF	C7	C8	-	LOCK	CMPXCHG8B	EAX
FO	OF	C7	C9	-	LOCK	CMPXCHG8B	ECX
FO	OF	C7	CA	-	LOCK	CMPXCHG8B	EDX
FO	OF	C7	CB	-	LOCK	CMPXCHG8B	EBX
FO	OF	C7	CC	-	LOCK	CMPXCHG8B	ESP
FO	OF	C7	CD	-	LOCK	CMPXCHG8B	EBP
FO	OF	C7	CE	-	LOCK	CMPXCHG8B	ESI
FO	OF	C7	CF	-	LOCK	CMPXCHG8B	EDI

If a program running without SoftICE encounters this incorrect instruction, it will continue to run by virtue of its SEH service. However, if that same program is run together with SoftICE, it will stop at the incorrect function.

Most attackers will be content with only removing the instruction, and they will let the program run on. You can take advantage of this fact because the code that follows LOCK CMPXCHG8B EAX will only run if the above-mentioned instruction was removed or jumped over, which would mean that someone had tried to work with the program code.

```
.386p
.MODEL FLAT,STDCALL
locals
jumps
UNICODE=0
include w32.inc

Extrn SetUnhandledExceptionFilter : PROC
.data
message1    db "CMPXCHG8B instruction usage with the LOCK prefix",0
message3    db "Program doesn't run properly, it has been changed while running!",0
message2    db "SEH service was called (OK)",0
delayESP    dd 0                                    ;the ESP register saves here
previous    dd 0                                    ;the ESP register will save the address of the
                                                    ;previous SEH service here

.code
Start:

;-------------------------------------------------------------------------------
;Sets SEH if there is an error
;-------------------------------------------------------------------------------
            mov   [delayESP],esp
            push  offset error
            call  SetUnhandledExceptionFilter
            mov   [previous], eax
;-------------------------------------------------------------------------------
;LOCK CMPXCHG8B EAX
            db    0F0h, 0F0h, 0C7h, 0C8h            ;jumps to your SEH service, a label error.
                                                    ;Normally the program should never get this far.
            jmp   jump
;-------------------------------------------------------------------------------
;Sets the previous SEH service
;-------------------------------------------------------------------------------
            push  dword ptr [previous]
            call  SetUnhandledExceptionFilter
;-------------------------------------------------------------------------------

continue:
            call  MessageBoxA,0, offset message2,\
            offset message1,0
            call  ExitProcess, -1
```

```
jump:
            call MessageBoxA,0, offset message3,\
            offset message1,0
            call ExitProcess, -1

error:                                          ;sets a new SEH service in case of an error
            mov  esp, [delayESP]                ;the program will jump here in case of an error
                                                ;in the LOCK CMPXCHG8B EAX instruction

            push offset continue
            ret


ends
end Start
```

This trick can be used in all Windows versions. Nevertheless, I don't recommend using it often because it might cause problems with some processors.

Detecting SoftICE with the VxDCall

A VxD is really nothing more than a DLL running at the processor's highest privilege level (ring0). Since VxD runs at ring0, there's essentially nothing they can't do. In Windows 9x, it is possible to call VxDCall, but only from ring0 (not from ring3). (Though as I'll demonstrate later, this isn't completely true.)

In this example, we'll use the VxD calls from ring0 without having to program a VxD driver. We'll call the VMMCall Get_DDB, which will find the Device Description Block. You must define the driver name or its VxD ID before the call.

Your goal is to find the two drivers, SICE and SIWVID. The VxD ID of the first one is 202h and the second one is 7A5Fh. If a VxD driver hasn't been installed, the ECX register value will be 0, meaning that SoftICE isn't active in memory. If ECX contains any other value, the VxD is active, which tells us that SoftICE is active in memory.

14

```
.386p
.MODEL FLAT,STDCALL
locals
jumps
UNICODE=0
include w32.inc

Extrn SetUnhandledExceptionFilter : PROC
Interrupt   equ 5                              ;interrupt numbers 1 or 3 will make debugging
                                               ;more difficult
```

```
.DATA
message1     db "Detection by means of VxDCALL - VMMCall Get_DDB",0
message2     db "Debugger not found",0
message3     db "Debugger found",0
delayESP     dd 0                              ;the ESP register saves here
previous     dd 0                              ;the ESP register will save the address of the
                                               ;previous SEH service here

Device_ID    dd 202h                           ;the VxD ID for SICE
Device_ID2   dd 7a5Fh                          ;the VxD ID for SIWVID
Device_Name  dd 0                              ;the VxD name will not be needed


.CODE
Start:


;-------------------------------------------------------------------------------
;Sets SEH if there is an error
;-------------------------------------------------------------------------------
            mov  [delayESP],esp
            push offset error
            call SetUnhandledExceptionFilter
            mov  [previous], eax
;-------------------------------------------------------------------------------
            push edx
            sidt [esp-2]                        ;reads IDT into the stack
            pop  edx
            add  edx,(Interrupt*8)+4            ;reads the vector of the required interrupt
                                               ;(INT 5h)

            mov  ebx,[edx]
            mov  bx,word ptr [edx-4]            ;reads the address of the required interrupt's
                                               ;old service

            lea  edi,InterruptHandler
            mov  [edx-4],di
            ror  edi,16                         ;sets a new interrupt service
            mov  [edx+2],di
            push ds                             ;saves registers for security
            push es
            int  Interrupt                      ;jumps into ring0 (newly defined service INT 5h)
            pop  es                             ;restores registers
            pop  ds
            mov  [edx-4],bx                     ;sets the original service of the interrupt
                                               ;(INT 5h)
            ror  ebx,16
            mov  [edx+2],bx
            push eax                            ;saves the return value
```

```
;-----------------------------------------------------------------------------------------
;Sets the previous SEH service
;-----------------------------------------------------------------------------------------
          push dword ptr [previous]
          call SetUnhandledExceptionFilter
;-----------------------------------------------------------------------------------------
          pop  eax                          ;restores the return value
          cmp  eax,1                        ;tests to see if the return value is 1. If so,
                                            ;SoftICE is active in memory
          jz   jump                         ;and the program jumps

continue:
          call MessageBoxA,0, offset message2,\
          offset message1,0
          call ExitProcess, -1

jump:
          call MessageBoxA,0, offset message3,\
          offset message1,0
          call ExitProcess, -1
error:                                      ;sets a new SEH service in case of an error
          mov  esp, [delayESP]
          push offset continue
          ret
;-----------------------------------------------------------------------------------------
;Your new INT 5h service (runs in Ring0)
;-----------------------------------------------------------------------------------------

InterruptHandler:
          mov  eax, Device_ID               ;202h is for SICE VxD ID
          mov  edi, Device_Name             ;This will be set only if Device_ID is unknown,
                                            ;otherwise it will be 0 (as is the case here)
          ;VMMCall Get_DDB                   ;calls the service
          db   0cdh, 20h                    ;this is actually INT 20h
          dd   000010146H                   ;0001h is a type of call=VMM 0146h Get_DDB
                                            ;function is called
          test ecx, ecx                     ;ecx=DDB or 0 if VxD is not installed
          jnz  Debugger_detect              ;if SoftICE wasn't found by the first method,
                                            ;the program will try the next one

          mov  eax, Device_ID2
                                            ;7a5Fh for SIWVID VxD ID
          mov  edi, Device_Name             ;this will be set only if Device_ID is unknown,
                                            ;otherwise it is 0 (as is the case here)

          ;VMMCall Get_DDB                   ;service call
```

```
db    0cdh, 20h                              ;this is actually INT 20h
          dd    000010146H                   ;0001h is a type of call=VMM 0146h Get_DDB
                                             ;function is called
          test ecx,ecx                       ;ecx=DDB or 0 if VxD is not installed
          jnz  Debugger_detect
          xor  eax,eax                        ;nulls EAX to show that SoftICE isn't active
                                             ;in memory
          iretd                              ;jump back to ring3
Debugger_detect:
          xor  eax,eax
          inc  al                            ;sets value 1 into EAX to show that SoftICE is
                                             ;active in memory
          iretd                              ;jump back to ring3

ends
end Start
```

This is a good method of detection, and one that's hard to detect. Its only disadvantage, as with all detection programs that use ring0, is that it works only in Windows 9x.

Finding an Active Debugger Through the DR7 Debug Register

You can also use the debug registers with x86 processors to determine whether a debugger is active. Debug register 7 (DR7) is the most important one for you in this trick. If there is no debugger in memory, DR7 will be default to 400h. If there is a debugger, it will have a different value.

The detection routine searches in the following way:

```
mov  eax,dr7                                ;reads a value from DR7
cmp  eax, 400h                              ;tests to see if it is 400h value
jnz  Debugger_detect                        ;if not, a debugger is active in memory
```

While it is possible to detect a debugger with only three instructions, Windows just cannot make it that simple. The problem is that you can work with the debug registers only in ring0. This changes the situation substantially, because the trick is then usable only with the VxD or Sys drivers, or by using it to switch into ring0 for Windows 9x.

```
.386p
.MODEL FLAT,STDCALL
locals
jumps
UNICODE=0
include w32. inc
```

```
Extrn SetUnhandledExceptionFilter : PROC
Interrupt    equ 5                                  ;the interrupt numbers 1 or 3 will make
                                                    ;debugging more difficult

.DATA
message1    db "Detection by means of the DR7 debug register",0
message2    db "Debugger not found",0
message3    db "Debugger found",0
delayESP    dd 0                                    ;the ESP register saves here
previous    dd 0                                    ;the ESP register saves the address of the
                                                    ;previous SEH service here

.CODE
Start:


;-------------------------------------------------------------------------------
;Sets SEH if there is an error
;-------------------------------------------------------------------------------
            mov  [delayESP],esp
            push offset error
            call SetUnhandledExceptionFilter
            mov  [previous], eax
;-------------------------------------------------------------------------------
            push edx
            sidt [esp-2]                             ;reads IDT into the stack
            pop  edx
            add  edx,(Interrupt*8)+4                 ;reads a vector of the required interrupt
            mov  ebx,[edx]
            mov  bx,word ptr [edx-4]                 ;reads the address of the required interrupt
            lea  edi,InterruptHandler
            mov  [edx-4],di
            ror  edi,16                              ;sets a new interrupt service
            mov  [edx+2],di
            push ds                                  ;saves register for security
            push es
            int  Interrupt                           ;jumps into ring0 (the newly defined service
                                                     ;INT 5h)
            pop  es                                  ;restores registers
            pop  ds
            mov  [edx-4],bx                          ;sets the original interrupt service (INT 5h)
            ror  ebx,16
            mov  [edx+2],bx
            push eax                                 ;saves the return value
;-------------------------------------------------------------------------------
;Sets the previous SEH service
;-------------------------------------------------------------------------------
```

```
                push dword ptr [previous]
                call SetUnhandledExceptionFilter
;--------------------------------------------------------------------------------
                pop  eax                          ;restores the return value
                cmp  eax, 400h                    ;tests to see if the return value is 400h, the
                                                  ;correct value of the DR7 register. If it is, a
                                                  ;debugger isn't active.
                jnz  jump                         ;if the return value is other than 400h, a
                                                  ;debugger is active in memory.

continue:
                call MessageBoxA,0, offset message2,\
                offset message1,0
                call ExitProcess, -1

jump:
                call MessageBoxA,0, offset message3,\
                offset message1,0
                call ExitProcess, -1
error:                                            ;sets a new SEH service in case of an error
                mov  esp, [delayESP]
                push offset continue
                ret
;--------------------------------------------------------------------------------
;Your new service INT 5h (runs in Ring0)
;--------------------------------------------------------------------------------

InterruptHandler:
                mov  eax,dr7                      ;reads a value from DR7
                iretd                             ;jump back to ring3

ends
end Start
```

This is a rarely used trick that you can see, for example, in an older version of SafeDisc. It is one of the best detection methods because it is very hard to discover, particularly because it doesn't use any API calls or interrupts.

However, you can discover this trick if you set the GD flag in the DR7 register to switch on a breakpoint (int 01h) and then read the value of the DR6 flag BD register to see if the next instruction is read/write DRx. The need to switch into ring0 might give this method away, though. It works only in Windows 9x.

Detecting SoftICE by Calling VxDCall Through Kernel32!ORD_0001

This method of detection, which is very similar to the example in the "Detecting SoftICE by Detecting a Change in the INT 41h Service" section, calls the VWIN32_Int41Dispatch function 4fh. If SoftICE is active in the memory, the AX register will contain the value 0F386h. This trick can only be used in Windows 9x.

While VxDCall cannot be called directly from ring3, we're fortunate that the developers of Windows 9x "forgot" to remove a way to do it in the system. KERNEL32.DLL contains many exported functions called API calls, and these API calls are listed normally in the file's export table, so it's simple to import them into a program. Some functions are hidden from the programmer's eyes, and they are exported in another way (ordinal). Although it isn't possible to import them normally into a program and then call them, there is another way to call them.

This is a good detection method but it is somewhat tricky because it is necessary to find the export address of the Kernel32!ORD_0001. My friend EliCZ has found a way to use the hidden exports of the KERNEL32.DLL library without finding its address in the program code. The problem is that its direct importing into the machine code during program compilation isn't functional in the TASM compiler, for which the examples have been optimized.

Chapter 10 about the PE file's structure should help you better understand this example.

16

```
.386
.MODEL FLAT,STDCALL
locals
jumps
UNICODE=0
include w32.inc

include pe.inc
Extrn SetUnhandledExceptionFilter : PROC
.DATA
message1    db "Detection by means of the VxDCALL called through Kernel32!ORD_0001",0
message3    db "SoftICE found",0
message2    db "SoftICE not found",0
delayESP    dd 0                        ;the ESP register saves here
previous    dd 0                        ;the ESP register will save the address of the
                                        ;previous SEH service here
            dd 0                        ;the address of the beginning (base) of the
                                        ;KERNEL32 in memory
KernelAddress
a_VxDCall   dd 0                        ;the address for calling VxDCall
                                        ;(Kernel32!ORD_0001)
```

```
.CODE
Start:

        mov  ecx,[esp]                          ;puts the address from which it was called into
                                                ;the ecx. (This is always somewhere in
                                                ;KERNEL32.DLL.)
        push ecx                                ;saves the address
;------------------------------------------------------------------------------------------------
;Sets SEH if there is an error
;------------------------------------------------------------------------------------------------
        mov  [delayESP],esp
        push offset error
        call SetUnhandledExceptionFilter
        mov  [previous], eax
;------------------------------------------------------------------------------------------------
        pop  ecx                                ;restores the address
GetKrnlBaseLoop:                                ;starts searching for the beginning address
                                                ;(base) of the KERNEL32.DLL in memory
        xor  edx,edx                            ;nulls the edx register
        dec  ecx                                ;searches backward
        mov  dx,[ecx+03ch]                      ;tries to read parts of the file header from the
                                                ;MZ start of the PE header
        test dx,0f800h                          ;tests to see if the correct value was found
        jnz  GetKrnlBaseLoop                    ;if not, the program jumps to search farther
        cmp  ecx,[ecx+edx+34h]                  ;compares the actual address with the address
                                                ;where this PE file (KERNEL32.DLL) was supposed
                                                ;to be loaded (its image base)


;------------------------------------------------------------------------------------------------
;Basically, this tests to see if it's found the beginning of KERNEL32.DLL
;------------------------------------------------------------------------------------------------
        jnz  GetKrnlBaseLoop                    ;if divided, the program jumps to search farther
        mov  [KernelAdress],ecx                 ;it found the beginning address (base) of the
                                                ;KERNEL32.DLL and saves it
        mov  ebx,ecx                            ;puts the beginning (base) address of the
                                                ;KERNEL32.DLL into EBX
        or   ebx,ebx
        jz   continue                           ;if the beginning of the KERNEL32.DLL wasn't
                                                ;found, there has been an error and it will jump
                                                ;(if EBX=0)
        mov  eax,dword ptr [ebx+3ch]            ;reads the file header from the MZ part of the
                                                ;PE header
        add  eax,ebx                            ;sets the EAX register at the beginning of the
                                                ;PE header
```

```
                mov   edi,dword ptr [eax+NT_OptionalHeader. \
                                  OH_DirectoryEntries. \
                                        DE_Export. \
                              DD_VirtualAddress]
;----------------------------------------------------------------------------------
;This is actually mov  edi, dword ptr [eax+78h]
;----------------------------------------------------------------------------------
                                          ;reads the relative virtual address (RVA) from
                                          ;the Export table
                add   edi,ebx             ;sets on Export table in the KERNEL32.DLL
;----------------------------------------------------------------------------------
;The program searches for the Kernel32!ORD_0001 call address entrance values: ebx = base address of
;the KERNEL32.DLL, and edi = address of the export table in the KERNEL32.DLL file
;----------------------------------------------------------------------------------
                mov   esi,dword ptr [edi+ED_AddressOfFunctions]
;----------------------------------------------------------------------------------
;This is actually mov  esi, dword ptr [edi+1Ch]
;----------------------------------------------------------------------------------
                                          ;reads the RVA address for the list of exported
                                          ;functions
                add   esi,ebx             ;sets on the list of the exported functions
                xor   edx,edx             ;nulls the edx register (there will be a
                                          ;counter here).


address_loop:
                cmp   edx,dword ptr [edi+ED_NumberOfFunctions]
;----------------------------------------------------------------------------------
;This is actually mov esi, dword ptr [edi+14h]
;----------------------------------------------------------------------------------
                                          ;tests edx (counter) against the number of
                                          ;exported functions to determine if all numbers
                                          ;have been tested
                jae   continue            ;if yes the program jumps because VxDCall
                                          ;(Kernel32!ORD_0001) wasn't found; this is
                                          ;an error
                mov   ecx,00000008h-01h   ;puts 7 into the cx register and, as a result,
                                          ;repeats 8 times

function_loop:
                inc   edx                 ;increases the edx register (counter) by 1
                lodsd                     ;reads the address of the exported function
                cmp   eax,dword ptr[esi]  ;tests to see if this is the beginning of the
                                          ;PE header of the KERNEL32.DLL
                jne   address_loop        ;if not, the program jumps to search farther
```

```
            loop function_loop             ;if yes, it tests 7 more times
            add   eax,ebx                  ;the RVA address for the VxDCall
                                           ;(Kernel32!ORD_0001) is in the eax register. By
                                           ;adding the value from ebx, the beginning (base)
                                           ;address of the KERNEL32.DLL in memory, it sets
                                           ;on the real VxDCall address

            mov   dword ptr [a_VxDCall], eax   ;saves the address for the VxDCall
                                               ;(Kernel32!ORD_0001)


;-------------------------------------------------------------------------------
; SoftICE detection starts here
;-------------------------------------------------------------------------------
            push 0000004fh                 ;4fh function, the same as in the "Detecting
                                           ;SoftICE by Detecting a Change in the INT 41h
                                           ;Service" example.
            push 002a002ah                 ;the upper word determines which type of VxD
                                           ;call is called (VWIN32); the lower word
                                           ;determines which function is called
                                           ;(VWIN32_Int41Dispatch)
            call [a_VxDCall]               ;calls VxDCall (KERNEL32!ORD_0001)
            push eax                       ;saves the return value
;-------------------------------------------------------------------------------
;Sets the previous SEH service
;-------------------------------------------------------------------------------
            push dword ptr [previous]
            call SetUnhandledExceptionFilter
;-------------------------------------------------------------------------------
            pop  eax                       ;restores the return value
            cmp  ax, 0f386h                ;if SoftICE is active in memory, the return
                                           ;value will be 0f386h
            jz   jump                      ;and the program ends

continue:
            call MessageBoxA,0, offset message2,0\
            offset message1,0
            call ExitProcess, -1

jump:
            call MessageBoxA,0, offset message3,0\
            offset message1,0
            call ExitProcess, -1
```

```
error:                                          ;sets a new SEH service in case of an error
            mov  esp, [delayESP]
            push offset continue
            ret


ends
end Start
```

Using the Windows Registry to Find the Directory Where SoftICE Is Installed

In the section entitled "Detecting SoftICE by Calling the NmSymIsSoftICE-Loaded DLL Function from the nmtrans.dll Library," on page 109 we had to specify the SoftICE installation directory, and here's how to find it. Like most Windows programs, SoftICE saves various bits of information into the registers, such as the version number, registration number, user name, and installation directory. This information can be found in two locations:

```
HKEY_LOCAL_MACHINE\Software\Microsoft\Windows\CurrentVersion\Uninstall\SoftICE
```

and

```
HKEY_LOCAL_MACHINE\Software\NuMega\SoftICE
```

We'll use the second location in the following program. As you'll see, I have used two functions from the ADVAPI32.DLL library to work more easily with the Windows registers. This trick works in all Windows versions.

17

```
.386
.MODEL FLAT,STDCALL
locals
jumps
UNICODE=0
includelib advapi32.lib
include w32.inc
Extrn SetUnhandledExceptionFilter      : PROC
Extrn RegOpenKeyExA                    : PROC    ;a function exported from the ADVAPI32.DLL
Extrn RegQueryValueExA                 : PROC    ;a function exported from the ADVAPI32.DLL

.DATA
message1    db "Searching for SoftICE installation directory by means of registers",0
message3    db "SoftICE found",0
message2    db "SoftICE not found",0
message4    db "SoftICE installed in the following directory: ",0
```

```
message5      db "Installed SoftICE version: ",0
delayESP      dd 0                              ;the ESP register saves here
previous      dd 0                              ;the ESP register will save the address of the
                                                ;previous SEH service here

result        dd 0
size          dd 5                              ;the size of the data buffer for the SoftICE
                                                ;version
size2         dd 80h                            ;the size of the data buffer for the SoftICE
                                                ;installation directory

subkey        db "Software\NuMega\SoftICE\",0
current_ver   db "Current Version",0
install_dir   db "InstallDir",0
data_buffer   db 200 dup (0)                    ;the SoftICE version number will be saved here
value_buffer  db  20 dup (0)
data_buffer2  db 200 dup (0)                    ;the location where SoftICE is installed will be
                                                ;saved here

.CODE
Start:


;-------------------------------------------------------------------------------
;Sets SEH if there is an error
;-------------------------------------------------------------------------------
              mov  [delayESP], esp
              push offset error
              call SetUnhandledExceptionFilter
              mov  [previous], eax
;-------------------------------------------------------------------------------
              push offset result               ;the result will be saved here
              push 20016h                      ;access type
              push 0                           ;non-essential (must be 0)
              push offset subkey               ;string with the subkey name
              push 80000002h                   ;HKEY_LOCAL_MACHINE = 80000002 where a subkey
                                               ;will be opened

              call RegOpenKeyExA                ;opens the required access in registers and
                                                ;saves the result for further handling

              test eax,eax
              jnz  not_found                    ;jump if error
              push offset size                  ;size of the data buffer
              push offset data_buffer           ;address of the data buffer
              push offset value_buffer          ;address of the value buffer
              push 0                            ;non-essential (must be 0)
              push offset current_ver           ;name of the value for comparison (Current
                                                ;Version)
              push result                       ;where the result was saved
```

```
          call RegQueryValueExA                   ;reads the installed version of SoftICE into
                                                  ;the data_buffer

          test eax,eax
          jnz  not found                          ;if an error occurred, the program jumps
          push offset size2                       ;size of the data buffer
          push offset data_buffer2                ;address of the data buffer
          push offset value_buffer                ;address of the value buffer
          push 0                                  ;non-essential (must be 0)
          push offset install_dir                 ;name of the value for comparison
          push result                             ;where the result was saved
          call RegQueryValueExA                   ;reads the SoftICE installation directory into
                                                  ;the data_buffer

          test eax,eax
          jnz  not found                          ;if an error occurred, the program jumps
          inc  al                                 ;increases the al register by 1 (if there was
                                                  ;no error eax=0) to show that everything is OK

          jmp short ok

not found:
          xor eax,eax                             ;nulls the eax register to show that there was
                                                  ;an error
ok:
          push eax                                ;saves the result
;------------------------------------------------------------------------------------------
;Sets the previous SEH service
;------------------------------------------------------------------------------------------
          push dword ptr [previous]
          call SetUnhandledExceptionFilter
;------------------------------------------------------------------------------------------
          pop  eax                                ;restores the result
          test eax,eax
          jnz  jump                               ;jumps if everything was OK

continue:
          call MessageBoxA,0, offset message2,\
          offset message1,0                       ;prints out an error message
          call ExitProcess, -1

jump:
          call MessageBoxA,0, offset message3,\
          offset message1,0                       ;prints out a message that SoftICE was found
          call MessageBoxA,0, offset data_buffer,\
          offset message5,0                       ;prints out the SoftICE version number
          call MessageBoxA,0, offset data_buffer2,\
          offset message4,0                       ;prints out location where SoftICE is installed
          call ExitProcess, -1
```

```
error:                                  ;sets a new SEH service in case of an error
        mov  esp, [delayESP]
        push offset continue
        ret


ends
end Start
```

TRW Detection Using the Distance Between the Int 1h and the Int 3h Services

This detection is based on the same principle as the method described in the "Detecting SoftICE by Measuring the Distance Between INT 1h and INT 3h Services" section, except that it will try to detect TRW instead of SoftICE. The distance between the Int 1h and Int 3h services is 2FCh. Because this is the same trick used to detect SoftICE, we can test for the presence of both debuggers in memory. It detects only older types of TRW, not the new TRW2000.

This wonderful detection method doesn't require you to call any interrupts, API functions, or VxD calls. It works only in Windows 9x, but the same is true for TRW.

18

```
.386p
.MODEL FLAT,STDCALL
locals
jumps
UNICODE=0
include w32.inc


Extrn SetUnhandledExceptionFilter : PROC
.DATA
message1    db "TRW detection using the distance between Int 1h and Int 3h",0
message3    db "TRW found",0
message2    db "TRW not found",0
delayESP    dd 0                        ;the ESP register saves here
previous    dd 0                        ;the ESP register will save the address of the
                                        ;previous SEH service here
pIDT        db 6 dup (0)                ;IDT will be saved here

.CODE

Start:
;-------------------------------------------------------------------------------
;Sets SEH if there is an error
;-------------------------------------------------------------------------------
```

```
        mov  [delayESP], esp
        push offset error
        call SetUnhandledExceptionFilter
        mov  [previous], eax
;-----------------------------------------------------------------------------------
        sidt fword ptr pIDT               ;saves the IDT
        mov  eax,dword ptr [pIDT+2]       ;puts pointer to the interrupt table into eax
        add  eax, 8                       ;puts int 1h vector address into eax
        mov  ebx, [eax]                   ;puts int 1h service address into ebx
        add  eax, 16                      ;puts int 3h vector address into eax
        mov  eax, [eax]                   ;puts Int 3h service address into eax
        and  eax, 0ffffh                  ;selector will not be used
        and  ebx 0ffffh                   ;selector will not be used even with int 1h
        sub  eax,ebx                      ;calculates the distance between the interrupt
                                          ;services
        push eax                          ;saves the result
;-----------------------------------------------------------------------------------
;Sets the previous SEH service
;-----------------------------------------------------------------------------------
        push dword ptr [previous]
        call SetUnhandledExceptionFilter
;-----------------------------------------------------------------------------------
        pop  eax                          ;restores the result
        cmp  eax, 2fch                    ;if eax is 2FCh, TRW is active in memory
        jz   jump                         ;and the program jumps

continue:
        call MessageBoxA,0, offset message2,\
        offset message1,0
        call ExitProcess, -1

jump:
        call MessageBoxA,0, offset message3,\
        offset message1,0
        call ExitProcess, -1

error:                                    ;sets a new SEH service in case of an error
        mov  esp, [delayESP]
        push offset continue
        ret

ends
end Start
```

Detecting TRW by Opening Its Driver Through Calling the API of the CreateFileA (TRW)

This detection program is based on the same principle as the SoftICE detection. It too tries to open the driver file and, if it succeeds, the driver is active in memory.

19

```
.386p
.MODEL FLAT,STDCALL
locals
jumps
UNICODE=0
include w32.inc

Extrn SetUnhandledExceptionFilter : PROC
.data
message1    db "TRW detection by means of CreateFileA",0
message3    db "TRW found",0
message2    db "TRW not found",0
delayESP    dd 0                          ;the ESP register saves here
previous    dd 0                          ;the ESP register will save the address of the
                                          ;previous SEH service here
SOFT9x      db "\\.\TRW,"0                 ;name of the TRW driver

.code
Start:

;-----------------------------------------------------------------------------------------
;Sets SEH if there is an error
;-----------------------------------------------------------------------------------------
        mov  [delayESP],esp
        push offset error
        call SetUnhandledExceptionFilter
        mov  [previous], eax
;-----------------------------------------------------------------------------------------
        call CreateFileA, OFFSET SOFT9x,\
        FILE_FLAG_WRITE_THROUGH, FILE_SHARE_READ,\
        NULL, OPEN_EXISTING, FILE_ATTRIBUTE_NORMAL,\
        NULL                              ;tries to open \\.\TRW file
        push eax                          ;saves the return value
;-----------------------------------------------------------------------------------------
;Sets the previous SEH service
;-----------------------------------------------------------------------------------------
        push dword ptr [previous]
        call SetUnhandledExceptionFilter
;-----------------------------------------------------------------------------------------
```

```
        pop  eax                          ;restores the return value
        cmp  eax, -1                      ;tests to see if it succeeded
        jnz  jump                         ;if yes, it jumps since TRW is active in memory

continue:
        call MessageBoxA,0, offset message2,\
        offset message1,0
        call ExitProcess, -1

jump:
        call MessageBoxA,0, offset message3,\
        offset message1,0
        call ExitProcess, -1

error:                                    ;sets a new SEH service in case of an error
        mov  esp, [delayESP]
        push offset continue
        ret

ends
end Start
```

This trick works only for older versions of TRW and is ineffective against TRW2000.

Launching the BCHK Command of the SoftICE Interface

In the "Detecting SoftICE by Calling INT 3h" section, I showed you how to determine whether SoftICE is active in memory using the BCHK interface. This interface also lets you launch various commands for SoftICE that can be used, for example, for setting, switching off, switching on, and deleting breakpoints.

The BCHK interface contains 32 functions for SoftICE in Windows 9x, and 36 functions in Windows NT and 2000. Because there is no documentation, it isn't easy to determine the command usage, so I'll show a few tricks here that my friend EliCZ discovered and demonstrate their practical use with an example. (My thanks to Eli.)

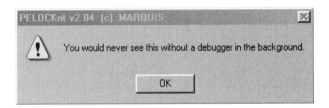

PELOCKnt can find SoftICE easily

In the following example, I'll show how to work with SoftICE breakpoints; a good trick that complicates program tracing. This example uses a different method to set the SEH service than I have been using so far, and one that is simpler, easier to understand, and doesn't need any API calls. (You'll find comments throughout the example because it is hard to understand at first glance.)

20

```
.386p
.MODEL FLAT,STDCALL
locals
jumps
UNICODE=0
include w32.inc
;---------------------------------------------------------------------------
;There is no need for any API calls
;---------------------------------------------------------------------------

.data
message1        db "Running commands of the BCHK interface of the SoftICE",0
message3        db "SoftICE commands functional",0
message2        db "SoftICE isn't active, an error occurred, the program was traced or breakpoints
                have been set",0
mark            db 0                            ;a sign that everything went OK

.code
Start:

                xor  eax,eax                    ;nulls the eax register
                call real_start                 ;jumps to the real start of the program

;---------------------------------------------------------------------------
;Sets a new SEH service if there is an error
;---------------------------------------------------------------------------
;The program will get here under two circumstances:
;1. If SoftICE isn't active in memory, an error will occur while calling the Int 3h, and the SEH
;service will be called (it will be called more times, always at the Int 3h).
;2. If SoftICE is active, an error will occur after a breakpoint was set on the NOP instruction,
;after which the SEH service will be called, and it will have you jump over the instruction. If
;the program has been traced, SoftICE will stop at the NOP instruction, and will refuse to
;continue tracing, and will not display any messages.
;---------------------------------------------------------------------------
                mov  ecx, [ecx+0B8h]            ;reads the context address
                sub  eax,eax                    ;nulls the eax register
                inc  dword ptr [ecx+0B8h]       ;increases the EIP register by 1 and moves 1
                                                ;byte farther in the program
```

```
;----------------------------------------------------------------------------
;In short, this means that it moves by one instruction, which is only one byte long. The Int 3h
;instruction is one byte long and, therefore, if SoftICE isn't active in memory, it will be jumped
;over. The NOP instruction is also one byte long, and once a breakpoint has been set on it, an
;error will occur, the SEH service will be called, and the program will jump over it.
;----------------------------------------------------------------------------
                inc  byte ptr mark
;----------------------------------------------------------------------------
;sets the mark on value 1 to show that everything went OK. If this is any value other than 1, your
;SEH service has been called repeatedly, which is bad since SoftICE isn't active in memory. If the
;mark is 0, your SEH service wasn't called at all, which means that the program has been traced.
;----------------------------------------------------------------------------
                ret                             ;returns back to the program from the SEH
                                                ;service
;----------------------------------------------------------------------------


real_start:
                push dword ptr fs:[eax]         ;saves the original SEH service
                mov  dword ptr fs:[eax], esp
;----------------------------------------------------------------------------
;Sets your new SEH service (which you have ended by means of CALL) to be able to save the following
;return address into the stack. This is your new SEH service.
;----------------------------------------------------------------------------
                mov  eax,4                      ;"magic" values for finding out if SoftICE is
                                                ;active
                mov  ebp,"BCHK"                 ;if SoftICE is active,
                int  3h                         ;calls interrupt 3. (If SoftICE isn't active, an
                                                ;error will occur and our new SEH service will
                                                ;be called.)
                cmp  eax,4                      ;tests to see if the eax has been changed
                jz   continue                   ;if not, SoftICE isn't active in memory and the
                                                ;program jumps
                mov  eax,0                       ;Get ID function (returns an ID for SoftICE)
                mov  ebp,"BCHK"                 ;calls the BCHK interface
                int  3h                         ;calls SoftICE
                cmp  eax, 0ff01h                ;tests to see if the return value is 0FF01h
                jnz  continue                   ;if not, SoftICE isn't active in memory
                sub  edi,edi                    ;use the edi register as a mark if it is
                                                ;necessary to deactivate breakpoints. You will
                                                ;set this to 0 to say that it isn't necessary.
                mov  eax,8                       ;Deactivates the lowest breakpoint function
                                                ;deactivates the nearest breakpoint
                int  3h                         ;calls SoftICE
                inc  eax                        ;returns -1 (0FFFFFFFFh) if an error occurs
                jz   not needed                 ;jumps if there was an error; it is not
                                                ;necessary to deactivate breakpoints
```

```
            dec  edi                              ;says that it is necessary to deactivate
                                                  ;breakpoints
            dec  eax                              ;returns the error value (-1) into the eax
            xchg eax,ebx                          ;exchanges values in the ;unneeded registers
            mov  ecx, cs                          ;selector (segment) of the breakpoint
            lea  edx, breakpoint                  ;address where you will set the breakpoint
            mov  bh, 0+0                          ;0 represents the breakpoint type (BT_EXECUTE);
                                                  ;+ 0 represents the length of the breakpoint
                                                  ;(BL_BYTE)
            mov  eax, 0ah                         ;sets the breakpoint function (which sets a
                                                  ;breakpoint)
            int  3h                               ;calls SoftICE
;-------------------------------------------------------------------------------------
;You set a breakpoint to the label "breakpoint" where the NOP instruction is located. If the
;program encounters the breakpoint, an error will occur, and your SEH service will be called.
;-------------------------------------------------------------------------------------
            mov  eax,9                            ;activate the breakpoint function to explicitly
                                                  ;activate breakpoints.
            int  3h                               ;calls SoftICE
            nop
breakpoint:
            nop                                   ;SoftICE will stick here during tracing, or an
                                                  ;error will occur here and the program will call
                                                  ;your new SEH service
            mov  eax, 0ch                         ;get breakpoint status function (saves the DR6
                                                  ;register into the eax register)
            int  3h                               ;calls SoftICE
            push eax                              ;saves the status (DR6)
            mov  eax, 0bh                         ;clears the breakpoint function (removes a
                                                  ;breakpoint)
            int  3h                               ;calls SoftICE
            inc  edi
            je   not needed2                      ;tests to see if it is necessary to deactivate
                                                  ;the breakpoint
            mov  eax,8                            ;deactivate the lowest breakpoint function,
                                                  ;which deactivates the lowest breakpoint
            int  3h                               ;calls SoftICE

not needed2:
            pop  ecx                              ;restores the status (DR6)
            xor  eax,eax
            pop  dword ptr fs:[eax]               ;sets the original SEH service
            pop  eax                              ;clears the stack
            xchg eax,ecx                          ;puts the status into the eax
```

```
;bsf eax,eax                                    ;because TASM has a problem translating this
                                                ;function, you will enter its byte form
            db 0fh, 0bch, 0c0h                  ;tests if the program was traced. If so, there
                                                ;will be a value other than 0 in the eax

            cmp  byte ptr mark, 1
            jnz  continue                       ;tests for an error
            cmp  al,bl                          ;tests to see if everything was OK
            jz   jump                           ;if so, the program jumps


continue:
            call MessageBoxA,0, offset message2,\
            offset message1,0
            call ExitProcess, -1


jump:
            call MessageBoxA,0, offset message3,\
            offset message1,0
            call ExitProcess, -1


ends
end Start
```

This is a good method of detecting SoftICE, and it can seriously complicate debugging. It works in all Windows versions.

Detecting TRW by Calling Int 3h

This trick uses the fact that when calling Int 3h while tracing a program, TRW handles the error and continues without calling the SEH service, which lets you discover it.

21a

```
.386p
.MODEL FLAT,STDCALL
locals
jumps
UNICODE=0
include w32.inc

Extrn SetUnhandledExceptionFilter : PROC
.data
message1    db "Detecting TRW by calling Int 3h",0
message3    db "TRW found",0
message2    db "TRW not found",0
delayESP    dd 0                                ;the ESP register saves here
previous    dd 0                                ;the ESP register will save the address of the
                                                ;previous SEH service here
```

```
        .code
        Start:

;------------------------------------------------------------------------
;Sets SEH in case of an error
;------------------------------------------------------------------------
                mov   [delayESP],esp
                push  offset error
                call  SetUnhandledExceptionFilter
                mov   [previous], eax
;------------------------------------------------------------------------
                int   3h                        ;calls int 3h. If the program has been traced in
                                                ;TRW it will continue past INT 3h without
                                                ;calling the SEH service, which is an error


;------------------------------------------------------------------------
;Sets the previous SEH service
;------------------------------------------------------------------------
                push  dword ptr [previous]
                call  SetUnhandledExceptionFilter
;------------------------------------------------------------------------
                jmp   jump                      ;the program will get here only if it has been
                                                ;traced in TRW

continue:
                call  MessageBoxA,0, offset message2,\
                offset message1,0
                call  ExitProcess, -1

jump:
                call  MessageBoxA,0, offset message3,\
                offset message1,0
                call  ExitProcess, -1
error:                                          ;sets a new SEH service in case of an error
                mov   esp, [delayESP]
                push  offset continue
                ret

        ends
        end Start
```

Surprisingly, this detection doesn't work with older versions of TRW, though it does work with TRW2000. Its only disadvantage is that the program must be traced for the trick to succeed. Fortunately, we can hide the detection program in a routine deeper in the program code, like this:

21b

```
.386p
.MODEL FLAT,STDCALL
locals
jumps
UNICODE=0
include w32.inc


Extrn SetUnhandledExceptionFilter : PROC
.data
message1    db "TRW detection by calling Int 3h",0
message3    db "TRW found",0
message2    db "TRW not found",0
delayESP    dd 0                        ;the ESP register saves here
previous    dd 0                        ;the ESP register saves the address of the
                                        ;previous SEH service here


.code
Start:


;-----------------------------------------------------------------------------------------
;Sets SEH in case of an error
;-----------------------------------------------------------------------------------------
            mov  [delayESP],esp
            push offset error
            call SetUnhandledExceptionFilter
            mov  [previous], eax
;-----------------------------------------------------------------------------------------
            call test                   ;jumps to the test; if the program continues on
                                        ;TRW is active
;-----------------------------------------------------------------------------------------
;Sets the previous SEH service
;-----------------------------------------------------------------------------------------
            push dword ptr [previous]
            call SetUnhandledExceptionFilter
;-----------------------------------------------------------------------------------------
            jmp jump                    ;the program gets here only if it has been
                                        ;traced in TRW

continue:
            call MessageBoxA,0, offset message2,\
            offset message1,0
            call ExitProcess, -1
```

```
jump:
        call MessageBoxA,0, offset message3,\
        offset message1,0
        call ExitProcess, -1


error:                                  ;sets a new SEH service in case of an error
        mov  esp, [delayESP]
        push offset continue
        ret


test:

        int  3h                         ;calls int 3h. If the program has been traced in
                                        ;TRW it will continue past INT 3h without
                                        ;calling the SEH service, which is an error
        ret                             ;the program will get here only if TRW is active


ends
end Start
```

This is a slightly less conspicuous method of detection. Unfortunately, the Int 3h call can be hidden only one level deeper in the program; any deeper than that and the SEH service will be called.

On the other hand, it is possible to use the method from the "Launching the BCHK Command of the SoftICE Interface" section, where the SEH service secures a move to the other instruction in case of an Int 3h call, thus preventing the program from failing. It is then possible to insert one Int 3h call into each program branch, which will make debugging in TRW very difficult.

Detecting SoftICE by Opening Its Driver with an API Call to the CreateFileA (SIWVIDSTART) Function

This SoftICE detection program is based on finding its driver, SIWVIDSTART. I don't think much explanation is needed here because this is only another version of a well-known trick.

This method of detection works only with SoftICE for Windows NT and 2000.

```
.386p
.MODEL FLAT,STDCALL
locals
jumps
UNICODE=0
include w32.inc
```

```
Extrn SetUnhandledExceptionFilter : PROC
.data
message1        db "Detection by means of CreateFileA (SIWVIDSTART)",0
message3        db "SoftICE found",0
message2        db "SoftICE not found",0
delayESP        dd 0                                  ;the ESP register saves here
previous        dd 0                                  ;the ESP register will save the address of the
                                                      ;previous SEH service here

SIWVIDSTART     db "\\.\SIWVIDSTART, 0"               ;name of the SoftICE driver


.code
Start:


;-------------------------------------------------------------------------------------------
;Sets SEH if there is an error
;-------------------------------------------------------------------------------------------
                mov  [delayESP], esp
                push offset error
                call SetUnhandledExceptionFilter
                mov  [previous], eax
;-------------------------------------------------------------------------------------------
                call CreateFileA, OFFSET SIWVIDSTART,\
                FILE_FLAG_WRITE_THROUGH, FILE_SHARE_READ,\
                NULL, OPEN_EXISTING, FILE_ATTRIBUTE_NORMAL,\
                NULL
                                                      ;tries to open the SIWVIDSTART file
                push eax                              ;saves the return value


;-------------------------------------------------------------------------------------------
;Sets the previous SEH service
;-------------------------------------------------------------------------------------------
                push dword ptr [previous]
                call SetUnhandledExceptionFilter
;-------------------------------------------------------------------------------------------
                pop  eax                              ;restores the return value
                cmp  eax, -1                          ;tests to see if it succeeded
                jnz  jump                             ;if yes the program will jump since SoftICE is
                                                      ;active in memory

continue:
                call MessageBoxA,0, offset message2,\
                offset message1,0
                call ExitProcess, -1
```

```
jump:
                call MessageBoxA,0, offset message3,\
                offset message1,0
                call ExitProcess, -1
error:                                          ;sets a new SEH service in case of an error
                mov  esp, [delayESP]
                push offset continue
                ret


ends
end Start
```

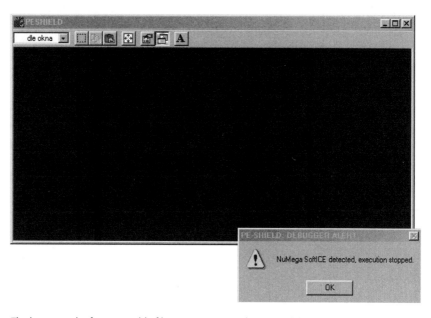

The best encoder for executable files cannot exist without anti-debugging tricks

Detecting SoftICE by Opening Its Driver with an API Call to the CreateFileW (NTICE, SIWVIDSTART) Function

The API function CreateFile is the most commonly used method of detecting SoftICE drivers. It has a twin, though, in Windows NT and 2000—CreateFileW. The only difference is that the function works with a Unicode string, which means that each character of the string is a zero value. This is an almost unknown method of detection.

I don't know why so many people blindly use the API function CreateFileA, the most well-known anti-debugging trick. If you aren't afraid to experiment a bit, you can find other ways.

23

```
.386p
.MODEL FLAT,STDCALL
locals
jumps
UNICODE=0
include w32.inc


Extrn SetUnhandledExceptionFilter : PROC
Extrn CreateFileW                 : PROC


.DATA
message1    db "Detection by means of CreateFileW (SIWVIDSTART)",0
message3    db "SoftICE found",0
message2    db "SoftICE not found",0
delayESP    dd 0                            ;the ESP register saves here
previous    dd 0                            ;the ESP register will save the address of the
                                            ;previous SEH service here
SIWVIDSTART db "\",0,"\",0,".",0,"\",0,"S",0,"I",0,
            "W",0,"V",0,"I",0,"D",0,"S",0,"T",0,"A",
            0,"R",0,"T",0,0,0
                                            ;name of the SoftICE driver


.CODE
Start:


;---------------------------------------------------------------------------------------------
;Sets SEH if there is an error
;---------------------------------------------------------------------------------------------
            mov [delayESP], esp
            push offset error
            call SetUnhandledExceptionFilter
            mov [previous], eax
;---------------------------------------------------------------------------------------------
            call CreateFileW, OFFSET SIWVIDSTART,\
            FILE_FLAG_WRITE_THROUGH, FILE_SHARE_READ,\
            NULL, OPEN_EXISTING, FILE_ATTRIBUTE_NORMAL,\
            NULL
                                            ;tries to open the SIWVIDSTART file
            push eax                        ;saves the return value
```

```
;-------------------------------------------------------------------
;Sets the previous SEH service
;-------------------------------------------------------------------
          push dword ptr [previous]
          call SetUnhandledExceptionFilter
;-------------------------------------------------------------------
          pop  eax                            ;restores the return value
          cmp  eax, -1                         ;tests to see if it succeeded
          jnz  jump                            ;if yes, the program jumps since SoftICE is
                                               ;active in memory

continue:
          call MessageBoxA,0, offset message2,\
          offset message1,0
          call ExitProcess, -1

jump:
          call MessageBoxA,0, offset message3,\
          offset message1,0
          call ExitProcess, -1

error:                                         ;sets a new SEH service in case of an error
          mov  esp, [delayESP]
          push offset continue
          ret


ends
end Start
```

I used the SIWVIDSTART driver in this example, but you could also use NTICE. This trick works only in Windows NT and 2000, and it's not possible to search for the SICE and other drivers in Windows 9x.

Detecting SoftICE by Opening Its Driver with an API Call to Function _lcreat (SICE, NTICE, SIWVID, SIWDEBUG, SIWVIDSTART)

This method of detecting the SoftICE driver uses the API function _lcreat, which is almost never used. It is included in Windows only to make it compatible with older 16-bit programs. As such, you can use it right away.

(24)

```
.386
.MODEL FLAT,STDCALL
locals
jumps
UNICODE=0
include w32.inc
```

```
Extrn SetUnhandledExceptionFilter : PROC
Extrn _lcreat                     : PROC

.DATA
message1    db "Detection through _lcreat",0
message3    db "SoftICE found",0
message2    db "SoftICE not found",0
delayESP    dd 0                              ;ESP register saves here
previous    dd 0                              ;the ESP register saves the address of the
                                              ;previous SEH service here

SOFTVIDEO   db "\\.\SIWVID",0                 ;the name of the SoftICE driver

.CODE
Start:

;------------------------------------------------------------------------------
;Sets SEH if there is an error
;------------------------------------------------------------------------------
            mov  [delayESP],esp
            push offset error
            call SetUnhandledExceptionFilter
            mov  [previous], eax
;------------------------------------------------------------------------------
            push 0                            ;opening attributes (0=normal)
            push offset SOFTVIDEO             ;address with the driver name
            call _lcreat                      ;tries to open the SIWVID file
            push eax                          ;saves the return value
;------------------------------------------------------------------------------
;Sets the previous SEH service
;------------------------------------------------------------------------------
            push dword ptr [previous]
            call SetUnhandledExceptionFilter
;------------------------------------------------------------------------------
            pop  eax                          ;restores the return value
            cmp  eax, -1                      ;tests to see if it succeeded
            jnz  jump                         ;if yes, it will jump since SoftICE is active
                                              ;in memory

continue:
            call MessageBoxA,0, offset message2,\
            offset message1,0
            call ExitProcess, -1
```

```
jump:
            call MessageBoxA,0, offset message3,\
            offset message1,0
            call ExitProcess, -1


error:                                          ;sets a new SEH service in case of an error
            mov  esp, [delayESP]
            push offset continue
            ret


ends
end Start
```

This is definitely a better trick than using the API function CreateFileA. It can also be used for detecting the driver in older versions of TRW (\\ .\TRW). This trick works in all Windows versions.

Detecting SoftICE by Opening Its Driver with an API Call to Function _lopen (SICE, NTICE, SIWVID, SIWDEBUG, SIWVIDSTART)

If you aren't already fed up with all the tricks for finding SoftICE drivers, I will show you one more. It uses the API function _lopen, which almost isn't used at all. It is in Windows only to make it compatible with older 16-bit programs.

This is the same detection method as in the preceding example, so the description is the same.

25

```
.386
.MODEL FLAT,STDCALL
locals
jumps
UNICODE=0
include w32.inc


Extrn SetUnhandledExceptionFilter : PROC
Extrn _lopen                      : PROC
.DATA
message1    db "Detection by means of _lopen",0
message3    db "SoftICE found",0
message2    db "SoftICE not found",0
delayESP    dd 0                                ;the ESP register saves here
previous    dd 0                                ;the ESP register saves the address of the
                                                ;previous SEH service here
SOFTVIDEO   db "\\.\SIWVID", 0                  ;the name of the SoftICE driver
```

```
.CODE
Start:

;-------------------------------------------------------------------------------
;Sets SEH if there is an error
;-------------------------------------------------------------------------------
          mov  [delayESP], esp
          push offset error
          call SetUnhandledExceptionFilter
          mov  [previous], eax
;-------------------------------------------------------------------------------
          push 0                          ;a type of opening 0 = OF_READ (opens a file
                                          ;for reading only)
          push offset SOFTVIDEO           ;the address with the driver name
          call _lopen                     ;tries to open the SIWVID file
          push eax                        ;saves the return value


;-------------------------------------------------------------------------------
;Sets the previous SEH service
;-------------------------------------------------------------------------------
          push dword ptr [previous]
          call SetUnhandledExceptionFilter
;-------------------------------------------------------------------------------
          pop  eax                        ;restores the return value
          cmp  eax, -1                    ;tests to see if it succeeded
          jnz  jump                       ;if yes it will jump since SoftICE is active
                                          ;in memory

continue:
          call MessageBoxA,0, offset message2,\
          offset message1,0
          call ExitProcess, -1

jump:
          call MessageBoxA,0, offset message3,\
          offset message1,0
          call ExitProcess, -1

error:                                    ;sets a new SEH service in case of an error
          mov  esp, [delayESP]
          push offset continue
          ret

ends
end Start
```

Anti-FrogsICE Trick

FrogsICE is an application that crackers use for hiding SoftICE from anti-debugging tricks (see Figure 7.3). Unfortunately, it is currently able to detect most tricks. Fortunately, because its creator chose to hide SoftICE with a VxD driver, you can find errors just like in any other program. Therefore, detecting FrogsICE isn't impossible.

When detecting FrogsICE, you cannot use the driver-detection methods that we looked at earlier to detect SoftICE. Also, because the application can change its name, you can't use either VxD ID or other well-known methods.

NOTE *One good thing about Windows 9x is that you can find many ways to do what you want in it. This is not possible in Windows NT, 2000, or XP because of their restrictions. FrogsICE is a Windows 9x application and, as such, you can take advantage of the operating system's possibilities.*

The following trick cannot detect FrogsICE, but it will cause an error in the program if FrogsICE is active. It is performed by the VxD call VMM_GetDDBList. The VxD call can be used only in ring0, so you must either first switch into it or use your own VxD driver. Because it's easier to switch into ring0, I'll use this method in the following example.

If FrogsICE isn't active, the program will end correctly. If it is active, an error will occur after the VMM_GetDDBList call. Unfortunately, you will also lose control over your program then, because it will end right after the error has occurred.

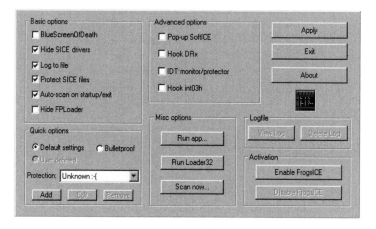

Figure 7.3: FrogsICE is one of the biggest enemies of anti-debugging tricks

```
.386
.MODEL FLAT,STDCALL
locals
jumps
UNICODE=0
include w32.inc

Extrn SetUnhandledExceptionFilter : PROC
Interrupt    equ 5                              ;an interrupt number; numbers 1 or 3 will make
                                                ;debugging more difficult

.DATA
message1      db "Anti-FrogsICE trick",0
message2      db "FrogsICE isn't active",0
delayESP      dd 0                              ;the ESP register saves here
previous      dd 0                              ;the ESP register will save the address of the
                                                ;previous SEH service here

.CODE
Start:


;-----------------------------------------------------------------------------------------
;Sets SEH if there is an error
;-----------------------------------------------------------------------------------------
          mov  [delayESP],esp
          push offset error
          call SetUnhandledExceptionFilter
          mov  [previous], eax
;-----------------------------------------------------------------------------------------
          push edx
          sidt [esp-2]                          ;reads the IDT into the stack
          pop  edx
          add  edx,(Interrupt *8)+4             ;reads the vector of the required interrupt
                                                ;(Int 5h)
          mov  ebx,[edx]
          mov  bx,word ptr [edx-4]              ;reads the address of the old service of the
                                                ;required interrupt (INT 5h)
          lea  edi,InterruptHandler
          mov  [edx-4],di
          ror  edi,16                           ;sets a new interrupt service (INT 5h)
          mov  [edx+2],di
          push ds                               ;saves registers for security
          push es
          int  Interrupt                        ;jump into Ring0 (a new service INT 5h that you
                                                ;have defined)
          pop  es                               ;restores registers
          pop  es
```

```
              mov    [edx-4],bx                              ;sets the original service of the INT 5h
                                                             ;interrupt

              ror    ebx,16
              mov    [edx+2],bx
;-----------------------------------------------------------------------------------------------------
;Sets the previous SEH service
;-----------------------------------------------------------------------------------------------------
              push dword ptr [previous]
              call SetUnhandledExceptionFilter
;-----------------------------------------------------------------------------------------------------


continue:
              call MessageBoxA,0, offset message2,\
              offset message1,0
              call ExitProcess, -1
error:                                                       ;sets a new SEH service in case of an error
              mov  esp, [delayESP]
              push offset continue
              ret
;-----------------------------------------------------------------------------------------------------
;Your new INT 5h service (runs in Ring0)
;-----------------------------------------------------------------------------------------------------
InterruptHandler:
              db 0cdh, 20h
              dd 00001013FH

;VMMCall       VMM_GetDDBList                                ;this call will cause FrogsICE to crash
              iretd                                          ;if the program gets here FrogsICE isn't active
                                                             ;in memory

ends
end Start
```

FrogsICE is a great threat to protection developers. If you cannot prevent debugging, then protecting the application from crackers' attacks will be more and more difficult. Fortunately, even FrogsICE isn't foolproof, and it is possible to protect against it. The protection program should first focus on the application that FrogsICE is trying to hide, and only then should it detect FrogsICE itself.

NOTE *There is one other application like FrogsICE that runs in Windows NT and 2000, a sort of port for these systems, called NTALL. Fortunately, it isn't able to hide SoftICE as well.*

Detecting SoftICE by Searching for the
Int 3h Instruction in the UnhandledExceptionFilter

If SoftICE is active in memory, the interrupt instruction Int 3h will be set at the API address of the UnhandledExceptionFilter function. The following sample program first searches for the address of this API function, and then it searches for the Int 3h at its beginning.

27

```
.386
.MODEL FLAT,STDCALL
locals
jumps
UNICODE=0
include w32.inc

Extrn SetUnhandledExceptionFilter : PROC
Extrn UnhandledExceptionFilter    : PROC
.DATA
message1    db "Detecting SoftICE by searching for the Int 3h instruction in
            UnhandledExceptionFilter",0
message3    db "SoftICE found",0
message2    db "SoftICE not found",0
delayESP    dd 0                                 ;the ESP register saves here
previous    dd 0                                 ;the ESP register will save the address of
                                                 ;the previous SEH service here.


.code
Start:


;-------------------------------------------------------------------------------
;Sets SEH if there is an error
;-------------------------------------------------------------------------------
            mov  [delayESP], esp
            push offset error
            call SetUnhandledExceptionFilter
            mov  [previous], eax
;-------------------------------------------------------------------------------
            mov  eax, offset UnhandledExceptionFilter ;puts the address for a jump into
                                                      ;the UnhandledExceptionFilter into eax
            mov  eax, [eax+2]                     ;reads the address of the API function of the
                                                 ;UnhandledExceptionFilter in the Import table
            mov  eax, [eax]                       ;reads the address of the
                                                 ;UnhandledExceptionFilter function from the
                                                 ;Import table
            push eax                             ;saves the API address of the
                                                 ;UnhandledExceptionFilter function
```

```
;--------------------------------------------------------------------------------
;Sets the previous SEH service
;--------------------------------------------------------------------------------
          push dword ptr [previous]
          call SetUnhandledExceptionFilter
          pop  eax                            ;restores the API address of the
                                              ;UnhandledExceptionFilter function
          cmp  byte ptr [eax], 0cch           ;tests to see if the Int 3h instruction is
                                              ;present
          jz   jump                           ;if so, the program will jump because SoftICE
                                              ;is active in memory

continue:
          call MessageBoxA,0, offset message2,\
          offset message1,0
          call ExitProcess, -1

jump:
          call MessageBoxA,0, offset message3,\
          offset message1,0
          call ExitProcess, -1

error:                                        ;sets a new SEH service in case of an error
          mov  esp, [delayESP]
          push offset continue
          ret

ends
end Start
```

This is a fairly good detection method that works in Windows NT, Windows 2000, and Windows XP.

Detecting SoftICE Through Int 1h

This trick for discovering SoftICE utilizes the Int 1h interrupt. A new SEH service is set before the SEH service is called. This service is called once the Int 1h instruction has been performed. The EIP register in the Context field is increased by one, causing a 1-byte move in the program, at which point the SEH service identifies the error.

If it is an exception breakpoint, the program will finish without any changes. Otherwise the EIP register in the Context field is increased by one again, resulting in a one more 1-byte move in the program.

Next, the service tests to see if the Exception Single Step error has occurred. If it has, then SoftICE is active in memory (or the error would have been the

Exception Access Violation), and the program sets a mark. The service then finishes and the program continues to run.

Finally, the program tests to see if the mark has been set, and if it has, SoftICE is active in memory.

28

```
.386
.MODEL FLAT,STDCALL
locals
jumps
UNICODE=0
include w32.inc

.data
message1    db "Detecting SoftICE through Int 1h",0
message2    db "SoftICE not found",0
message3    db "SoftICE found",0
Mark        db 0

.code
Start:

        xor eax,eax                     ;nulls the eax register before setting the
                                        ;new SEH service

        push offset xhandler            ;address for your new SEH service (xhandler)
        push dword ptr fs:[eax]         ;saves the address of the original SEH service
        mov  dword ptr fs:[eax], esp    ;sets your new SEH service
        mov  eax, cs
        test ax, 100bh                  ;tests to see if the operating system is
                                        ;Windows 9x
        jne  Win9x                      ;if so, the program jumps because this trick
                                        ;is only for Windows NT and Windows 2000
        int  1h                         ;this causes an error so the program calls
                                        ;your new SEH service (xhandler)
        nop
        nop
        pop  dword ptr fs:[0]           ;sets the original SEH service
        add  esp,4                      ;clears the stack
        cmp  mark, 1                    ;tests to see if the mark is set
        jz   jump                       ;if the mark is set, the program jumps because
                                        ;SoftICE is active in memory.
Win9x:
        call MessageBoxA,0, offset message2,\
        offset message1,0
        call ExitProcess, -1

                                        ;ends the program
```

```
jump:
        call MessageBoxA,0, offset message3,\
        offset message1,0
        call ExitProcess, -1
                                            ;ends the program
;-------------------------------------------,------------------------------------
;Your new SEH service (xhandler)
;--------------------------------------------------------------------------------
xhandler:
        mov  eax, [esp+04]                  ;finds the exception number
        mov  ecx, [esp+0ch]                 ;reads the address of the beginning of the
                                            ;context
        inc  dword ptr [ecx+0b8h]           ;increases EIP by 1
        mov  eax, [eax]                     ;reads the exception number
        sub  eax, 80000003h
        jz   end                            ;if the exception number is the Exception
                                            ;Breakpoint the program will end
        inc  dword ptr [ecx+0b8h]           ;increases EIP by one
        dec  eax
        jnz  jump                           ;if it wasn't the Exception Access Violation
                                            ;then the program will end
        inc  mark                           ;SoftICE is active and the program will set
                                            ;the mark

end:
        xor  eax,eax
        ret                                 ;jump back into the program

ends
end Start
```

This is an excellent and little-known SoftICE detection method. This trick works only in Windows NT, 2000, and XP because the Int 1h instruction is incompatible with Windows 9x.

8

PROTECTING AGAINST BREAKPOINTS, TRACERS, AND DEBUGGERS

Now let's take a more in-depth look at ways to protect against crackers' attempts at using breakpoints, tracers, and debuggers against your programs.

Detecting Tracers Using the Trap Flag

This is one of my favorite tricks. It allows you to detect any tracer including SoftICE, TRW, FrogsICE, and ProcDump.

My friend EliCZ discovered this trick based on elegant idea. If the Trap flag is set in the Eflags, EXCEPTION SINGLE STEP will be launched. In short, this means that the SEH service will be called before the instruction is performed. We can use the fact that if a program is traced, the SEH service will not be called, and we can set a mark there to show whether it was called or not. If not, a tracer is active.

```
.386
.MODEL FLAT,STDCALL
locals
jumps
UNICODE=0
include w32.inc


;------------------------------------------------------------------------------
;While you do not need any API calls for detection, you will use them for printing out the result
;and for ending the program
;------------------------------------------------------------------------------


.DATA

message1    db "Tracer detection using the Trap flag",0
message3    db "Tracer found",0
message2    db "Tracer not found",0
DelayESP    dd 0                            ;the ESP register saves here
Previous    dd 0                            ;the ESP register saves the address of the
                                            ;previous SEH service here
mark        db 0                            ;sets a mark showing whether it went into the
                                            ;xhandler
.CODE
Start:

        call real_start                     ;jumps to the real start of the program

;------------------------------------------------------------------------------
;A new SEH service in case of an error (xhandler)
;------------------------------------------------------------------------------
        inc  mark                           ;increases the eax by one to show that it isn't
                                            ;being traced
        sub  eax,eax                        ;nulls the eax because of the future setting of
                                            ;the original SEH service
        ret                                 ;returns to the program
;------------------------------------------------------------------------------
real_start:
        xor  eax,eax                        ;nulls the eax register
        push dword ptr fs:[eax]             ;saves the original SEH service
        mov  fs:[eax], esp                  ;sets your new SEH service. Because you jumped
                                            ;by means of CALL, the following return address
                                            ;is saved into the stack. This will be your new
                                            ;SEH service.
```

```
            pushfd                          ;saves the flag registers
            or   byte ptr [esp+1], 1        ;sets the Trap flag in Eflags, which means that
                                            ;the program will launch EXCEPTION SINGLE STEP,
                                            ;and your new SEH service will be called
            popfd                           ;restores the flag registers with the previously
                                            ;set Trap flag. The whole process runs
            nop                             ;and xhandler is called
            pop  dword ptr fs: [eax]
            pop  ebx                        ;sets the previous SEH service and clears the
                                            ;stack
            dec  mark                       ;decreases the mark by 1. If it is -1
                                            ;(0FFFFFFFFh) after the decrease, then a tracer
                                            ;is active in memory because the xhandler hasn't
                                            ;been called
            js   jump                       ;and the program jumps

continue:
            call MessageBoxA,0, offset message2,\
            offset message1,0
            call ExitProcess, -1

jump:
            call MessageBoxA,0, offset message3,\
            offset message1,0
            call ExitProcess, -1

ends
end Start
```

This is a great detection method that is almost impossible for crackers to discover (when it is well hidden), especially because tracers seem to have a problem emulating it correctly.

To make it more difficult for the cracker to discover this trick, be sure that the protected application doesn't print out messages or warnings. The best response is to simply end the application incorrectly and punish the cracker that way, though you might use your imagination to come up with other responses.

This trick works in all Windows versions.

Detecting Breakpoints by Searching for Int 3h

To make debugging more difficult, it is very important to test for the presence of breakpoints. If a breakpoint is set in a debugger, there will be an Int 3h instruction at a particular place in memory.

The following example program first searches its code in memory for the value 0CCh, which is the prefix of the Int 3h instruction. There is one problem, though, which the program doesn't take into account: It is likely, in most applications, that the value 0CCh will exist somewhere in the code. In such a case, the testing routine should save these locations somewhere. Then, if it finds the value 0CCh, it will first test to see if it is where it was found before.

Once the program finishes this test, it tests to see if a breakpoint was set on an API call used by the program. It searches addresses for imported functions one by one in the IAT table, found after the program code. These are pointers to the beginnings of the API functions, and the 0CCh value would be found there if a breakpoint was set to this API function.

Another way to find the addresses of the API function routines would be to find them in the file's PE header, where this information is saved.

30

```
.386
.MODEL FLAT,STDCALL
locals
jumps
UNICODE=0
include w32.inc


Extrn SetUnhandledExceptionFilter : PROC


.DATA
message1        db "Breakpoint detection by searching for Int 3h",0
message3        db "Breakpoint found",0
message2        db "Breakpoint not found",0
delayESP        dd 0                      ;the ESP register saves here
previous        dd 0                      ;the ESP register will save the address of the
                                          ;previous SEH service here
current_import  dd 0                      ;the address of the imported function currently
                                          ;being tested is saved here


.code
Start:


;-----------------------------------------------------------------------------
;Sets SEH in case of an error
;-----------------------------------------------------------------------------
                mov  [delayESP], esp
                push offset error
                call SetUnhandledExceptionFilter
                mov  [previous], eax
;-----------------------------------------------------------------------------
```

```
        lea    edi, Start                 ;the starting address of the program will be put
                                           ;into the edi
        mov    ecx, End-Start+1           ;the length of the program, that is, the number
                                           ;of tested bytes, will be put into the ecx
        mov    eax,0BCh
        add    eax, 10h                    ;puts 0CCh into the eax (this is the prefix of
                                           ;the INT 3h instruction). Note! Do not use
                                           ;mov  eax,0CCh or you will find this value in
                                           ;the program and think that it is a breakpoint.
        repnz scasb                        ;searches for a breakpoint in the program
        test   ecx,ecx                     ;tests to see if ecx=0; if not, it has found a
                                           ;breakpoint
        jne    found                       ;and the program jumps
        lea    eax, Imports+2              ;puts the IAT (first function) into the eax
                                           ;register
        mov    dword ptr [current import], eax

start_searching:
        mov    eax,                        ;puts the imported function to be
        dword ptr [current_import]         ;tested into the eax
        cmp    dword ptr [eax], 0          ;tests to see if it is 0; if so, then this is
                                           ;the end of the Import table (the table of the
                                           ;imported functions)
        je     notfound                    ;the program jumps if it hasn't found any
                                           ;breakpoints
        mov    ecx, [eax]                  ;this reads the address where the imported
                                           ;function is located; that is the address of the
                                           ;beginning of its routine
        mov    ecx, [ecx]                  ;reads the address of the beginning of the
                                           ;routine of the imported function
        mov    eax, 0BCh
        add    eax, 10h                    ;puts 0CCh into the eax (the prefix of the INT
                                           ;3h instruction). Note! Do not use mov  eax,
                                           ;0CCh or you will find this value in the program
                                           ;and think that it is a breakpoint.
        cmp    byte ptr [ecx], al          ;tests for the breakpoint's presence in the
                                           ;tested imported function
                                           ;the program will search for 0CCh (actually Int
                                           ;3h) at the beginning of its routine
        je     found                       ;and if a breakpoint is found it will end
        add    [current_import], 6         ;sets to another imported function in the IAT

jmp start_searching                        ;jumps to search for a breakpoint in the next
                                           ;imported function
```

```
found:
                mov  eax, 1                         ;sets eax to 1 to show that the program has
                                                    ;found a breakpoint
                jmp  farther

notfound:
                xor  eax, eax                       ;sets eax to 0 to show that it hasn't found a
                                                    ;breakpoint

farther:
                push eax                            ;saves the return value
;------------------------------------------------------------------------------------
;Sets the previous SEH service
;------------------------------------------------------------------------------------
                push dword ptr [previous]
                call SetUnhandledExceptionFilter
;------------------------------------------------------------------------------------
                pop  eax                            ;restores the return value
                test eax, eax
                jnz  jump

continue:
                call MessageBoxA,0, offset message2,\
                offset message1,0
                call ExitProcess, -1

jump:
                call MessageBoxA,0, offset message3,\
                offset message1,0
                call ExitProcess, -1
error:                                              ;sets a new SEH service in case of an error
                mov  esp, [delayESP]
                push offset continue
                ret
End:
Imports:                                            ;this label must be at the very end of the
                                                    ;program, since the IAT begins there

ends
end Start
```

This trick is limited by the fact that it cannot find debug breakpoints that do not change the program code. Therefore, it is good to combine this trick with a way to detect debug breakpoints.

This trick works in all Windows versions.

Detecting Breakpoints by CRC

This example shows a different method of breakpoint detection that I think is even better than the previous one. It's based on the CRC calculation for the particular program and the checks that run during the course of the program. A program's current CRC is found at the CRC label. The CRC label changes with alterations in the program, and is therefore adjusted after each alteration. This method is even effective against changes performed in memory.

This trick is simple: First, you run the debugger, and once it returns from the CRC32 routine, the EAX register will contain the current CRC of the program code in the memory. Next, you put this value into the CRC label, and when a protected application is launched, the program calculates the CRC of the code in the memory. If the CRC isn't the same as the value at the CRC label, the program has been changed, which tells you that either there were changes performed in the program code or there is a breakpoint set in the code.

31

```
.386
.MODEL FLAT,STDCALL
locals
jumps
UNICODE=0
include w32.inc

Extrn SetUnhandledExceptionFilter : PROC

.data
message1    db "Breakpoint detection by CRC",0
message3    db "Breakpoint or a change in the program found",0
message2    db "Breakpoint not found",0
delayESP    dd 0                                 ;the ESP register saves here
previous    dd 0                                 ;the ESP register will save the address of the
                                                 ;previous SEH service here
;-------------------------------------------------------------------------------
;Following is a table of the values necessary for the program's CRC calculation.
;-------------------------------------------------------------------------------
CRCTable dd  00000000h,  77073096h,  0EE0E612Ch,  990951BAh
         dd  076DC419h,  706AF48Fh,  0E963A535h,  9E6495A3h
         dd  0EDB8832h,  79DCB8A4h,  0E0D5E91Eh,  97D2D988h
         dd  09B64C2Bh,  7EB17CBDh,  0E7882D07h,  90BF1D91h
         dd  1DB71064h,  6AB020F2h,  0F3B97148h,  84BE41DEh
         dd  1ADAD47Dh,  6DDDE4EBh,  0F4D4B551h,  83D385C7h
         dd  136C9856h,  646BA8C0h,  0FD62F97Ah,  8A65C9ECh
         dd  14015C4Fh,  63066CD9h,  0FA0F3D63h,  8D080DF5h
         dd  3B6E20C8h,  4C69105Eh,  0D56041E4h,  0A2677172h
         dd  3C03E4D1h,  4B04D447h,  0D20D85FDh,  0A50AB56Bh
```

```
dd    35B5A8FAh,    4282986Ch,    0DBBBC9D6h,    0AC8CF940h
dd    32D86CE3h,    45DF5C75h,    0DCD60DCFh,    0ABD13D59h
dd    26D930ACh,    51DE003Ah,    0C8D75180h,    0BFD06116h
dd    21B4F485h,    56B3C423h,    0CFBA9599h,    0B8BDA50Fh
dd    2802B89Eh,    5F058808h,    0C60CD9B2h,    0B10BE924h
dd    2F6F7C87h,    58684C11h,    0C1611DABh,    0B6662D3Dh
dd    76DC4190h,    01DB7106h,    98D220BCh,     0EFD5102Ah
dd    71B18589h,    06B6B51Fh,    9FBFE4A5h,     0E8B8D433h
dd    7807C9A2h,    0F00F934h,    9609A88Eh,     0E10E9818h
dd    7F6A0DBBh,    086D3D2Dh,    91646C97h,     0E6635C01h
dd    6B6B51F4h,    1C6C6162h,    856530D8h,     0F262004Eh
dd    6C0695EDh,    1B01A57Bh,    8208F4C1h,     0F50FC457h
dd    65B0D9C6h,    12B7E950h,    8BBEB8EAh,     0FCB9887Ch
dd    62DD1DDFh,    15DA2D49h,    8CD37CF3h,     0FBD44C65h
dd    4DB26158h,    3AB551CEh,    0A3BC0074h,    0D4BB30E2h
dd    4ADFA541h,    3DD895D7h,    0A4D1C46Dh,    0D3D6F4FBh
dd    4369E96Ah,    346ED9FCh,    0AD678846h,    0DA60B8D0h
dd    44042D73h,    33031DE5h,    0AA0A4C5Fh,    0DD0D7CC9h
dd    5005713Ch,    270241AAh,    0BE0B1010h,    0C90C2086h
dd    5768B525h,    206F85B3h,    0B966D409h,    0CE61E49Fh
dd    5EDEF90Eh,    29D9C998h,    0B0D09822h,    0C7D7A8B4h
dd    59B33D17h,    2EB40D81h,    0B7BD5C3Bh,    0C0BA6CADh
dd    0EDB88320h,   9ABFB3B6h,    03B6E20Ch,     74B1D29Ah
dd    0EAD54739h,   9DD277AFh,    04DB2615h,     73DC1683h
dd    0E3630B12h,   94643B84h,    0D6D6A3Eh,     7A6A5AA8h
dd    0E40ECF0Bh,   9309FF9Dh,    0A00AE27h,     7D079EB1h
dd    0F00F9344h,   8708A3D2h,    1E01F268h,     6906C2FEh
dd    0F762575Dh,   806567CBh,    196C3671h,     6E6B06E7h
dd    0FED41B76h,   89D32BE0h,    10DA7A5Ah,     67DD4ACCh
dd    0F9B9DF6Fh,   BEBEEFF9h,    17B7BE43h,     60B08ED5h
dd    0D6D6A3E8h,   0A1D1937Eh,   38D8C2C4h,     4FDFF252h
dd    0D1BB67F1h,   0A6BC5767h,   3FB506DDh,     48B2364Bh
dd    0D80D2BDAh,   0AF0A1B4Ch,   36034AF6h,     41047A60h
dd    0DF60EFC3h,   0A867DF55h,   316E8EEFh,     4669BE79h
dd    0CB61B38Ch,   0BC66831Ah,   256FD2A0h,     5268E236h
dd    0CC0C7795h,   0BB0B4703h,   220216B9h,     5505262Fh
dd    0C5BA3B8Eh,   0B2BD0B28h,   2BB45A92h,     5CB36A04h
dd    0C2D7FFA7h,   0B5D0CF31h,   2CD99E8Bh,     5BDEAE1Dh
dd    9B64C2B0h,    0EC63F226h,   756AA39Ch,     026D930Ah
dd    9C0906A9h,    0EB0E363Fh,   72076785h,     05005713h
dd    95BF4A82h,    0E2B87A14h,   7BB12BAEh,     0CB61B38h
dd    92D28E9Bh,    0E5D5BE0Dh,   7CDCEFB7h,     0BDBDF21h
dd    86D3D2D4h,    0F1D4E242h,   68DDB3F8h,     1FDA836Eh
dd    81BE16CDh,    0F6B9265Bh,   6FB077E1h,     18B74777h
dd    88085AE6h,    0FF0F6A70h,   66063BCAh,     11010B5Ch
```

```
          dd  8F659EFFh,   0F862AE69h,   616BFFD3h,    166CCF45h
          dd  0A00AE278h,   0D70DD2EEh,   4E048354h,    3903B3C2h
          dd  0A7672661h,   0D06016F7h,   4969474Dh,    3E6E77DBh
          dd  0AED16A4Ah,   009D65ADCh,   40DF0B66h,    37D83BF0h
          dd  0A9BCAE53h,   0DEBB9EC5h,   47B2CF7Fh,    30B5FFE9h
          dd  0BDBDF21Ch,   0CABAC28Ah,   53B39330h,    24B4A3A6h
          dd  0BAD03605h,   0CDD70693h,   54DE5729h,    23D967BFh
          dd  0B3667A2Eh,   0C4614AB8h,   5D681B02h,    2A6F2B94h
          dd  0B40BBE37h,   0C30C8EA1h,   5A05DF1Bh,    2D02EF8Dh
CRC       dd  1325596Eh,    ;CRC for a demo program


.code

Start:

;-----------------------------------------------------------------------------------
;Sets SEH in case of an error
;-----------------------------------------------------------------------------------
          mov  [delayESP],esp
          push offset error
          call SetUnhandledExceptionFilter
          mov  [previous], eax
;-----------------------------------------------------------------------------------
          lea  esi, CRCTable              ;address of the CRC table needed for the
                                          ;calculation
          lea  edi, Start                 ;beginning of data for which the CRC will be
                                          ;calculated (beginning of your program)
          mov  ecx, End-Start+1           ;length of the data in bytes (length of your
                                          ;program)
          call CRC32                      ;jump to calculate the CRC
          push eax                        ;saves the calculated CRC
;-----------------------------------------------------------------------------------
;Sets the previous SEH service
;-----------------------------------------------------------------------------------
          push dword ptr [previous]
          call SetUnhandledExceptionFilter
;-----------------------------------------------------------------------------------
          pop  eax                        ;restores the calculated CRC
          cmp  dword ptr, CRC, eax        ;compares the calculated CRC with the saved one
          jnz  jump                       ;if the CRCs do not match, the program was
                                          ;either changed or a breakpoint was set
```

```
continue:
            call MessageBoxA,0, offset message2,
            offset message1,0
            call ExitProcess, -1

jump:
            call MessageBoxA,0, offset message3,
            offset message1,0
            call ExitProcess, -1
error:                                          ;sets a new SEH service in case of an error
            mov  esp, [delayESP]
            push offset continue
            ret


;----------------------------------------------------------------------------------------
;The routine for the CRC calculation
;----------------------------------------------------------------------------------------
;input:
;
;ESI = CRCTable address
;EDI = beginning of the data address
;ECX = number of bytes for the calculation
;
;output
;
;EAX = 32-bit CRC result
;----------------------------------------------------------------------------------------


CRC32:
            mov  eax, 0FFFFFFFFh               ;initializes the eax and the edx
            mov  edx,eax                       ;saves the ecx into 0FFFFFFFFh
CRC32_1:    push ecx                           ;the number of bytes for the calculation
            xor  ebx,ebx
            mov  bl,byte ptr [edi]             ;reads 1 byte from the data
            inc  edi                           ;and moves to the next
            xor  bl,al
            shl  bx,1
            shl  bx,1
            add  ebx,esi                       ;sets according to the read byte in the CRC
                                               ;table
            mov  cx,word ptr [ebx+2]           ;reads a 32-bit
            mov  bx,word ptr [ebx]             ;the value from the CRC table
            mov  al,ah                         ;moves DX:AX to the right by 8 bytes
            mov  ah,dl
            mov  dl,dh
```

```
        xor   dh,dh
        xor   ax,bx                         ;XOR  CX:BX into DX:AX
        xor   dx,cx

        pop   ecx                           ;restores the number of the non-calculated data
                                            ;in bytes

        loop CRC32_1                        ;jumps if not all has been calculated yet, and
                                            ;decreases the number of bytes in the ecx by 1

        not   ax                            ;the final calculation of the CRC
        not   dx

        push dx                             ;saves the 16-bit values
        push ax                             ;into the stack

        pop   eax                           ;and after it has been read back, the complete
                                            ;32-bit CRC will be in the eax register

        ret                                 ;return

End:

ends
end Start
```

Checking changes in a program through the CRC is one of the best ways to protect software against changes in the code. It isn't a bad idea to use the trick in more places too, to prevent the simple removal of protection. The program will also be well protected against viruses and breakpoints.

NOTE *I will not discuss the mathematics of the CRC calculation here because it is easy to find detailed documentation about it. You can find several examples on the CD with this book, including some for the C language.*

This trick cannot be used to control breakpoints at the API calls, or at least not in such a way that the CRC results for the API functions would be saved somewhere in the program. (Their code is different for various Windows versions.) The only way to do this is to calculate the CRC of the API functions that the program uses right at the start of the program, and to check this CRC when the functions are called. (Doing so may slow the program significantly, though.)

The previous example tests the CRC for the code section of the program, but it doesn't check the data. It's a good idea to have an application check even its own data.

This trick works in all Windows versions.

Detecting Debug Breakpoints

In Chapter 7, in the "Finding an Active Debugger Through the DR7 Debug Register" section, I demonstrated how to use the DR7 debug register to determine whether a debugger is active in memory. X86 processors have other registers besides DR7, though, so we'll take a look at the DR0 through DR3 registers here, which contain debug breakpoints.

Unfortunately, it is only possible to work with these registers in ring0. As such, we can use the same trick for switching over into ring0 that I used in previous examples in Chapter 7.

32

```
.386
.MODEL FLAT,STDCALL
locals
jumps
UNICODE=0
include w32.inc

Extrn SetUnhandledExceptionFilter : PROC
Interrupt   equ 5                          ;the interrupt numbers 1 or 3 will make
                                           ;debugging more difficult
.DATA
message1    db "Debug breakpoint detection",0
message2    db "Debug breakpoint not found",0
message3    db "Debug breakpoint found",0
delayESP    dd 0                           ;the ESP register saves here
previous    dd 0                           ;the ESP register will save the address of the
                                           ;previous SEH service here

.CODE
Start:
;-------------------------------------------------------------------------------
;Sets SEH in case of an error
;-------------------------------------------------------------------------------
            mov  [delayESP], esp
            push offset error
            call SetUnhandledExceptionFilter
            mov  [previous], eax
;-------------------------------------------------------------------------------
            push edx
            sidt [delayesp-2]              ;reads IDT into the stack
            pop  edx
            add  edx, (Interrupt*8)+4      ;reads the vector of the required interrupt
            mov  ebx,[edx]
            mov  bx,word ptr [edx-4]       ;reads the address of the old service of the
                                           ;required interrupt

            lea  edi,InterruptHandler
            mov  [edx-4],di
            ror  edi,16                    ;sets the new interrupt service
            mov  [edx+2],di
```

```
        push ds                                    ;saves registers for security
        push es
        int  Interrupt                             ;jumps into Ring0 (a newly defined INT 5h
                                                   ;service)
        pop  es                                    ;restores the registers
        pop  ds
        mov  [edx-4],bx                            ;sets the original INT 5h interrupt service
        ror  ebx,16
        mov  [edx+2],bx
        push eax                                   ;saves the return value
;---------------------------------------------------------------------------------------
;Sets the previous SEH service
;---------------------------------------------------------------------------------------
        push dword ptr [previous]
        call SetUnhandledExceptionFilter
;---------------------------------------------------------------------------------------

        pop  eax                                   ;restores the return value
        test eax,eax                               ;tests to see if eax=0
        jnz  jump                                  ;if not, the program has found a debug
                                                   ;breakpoint and it ends

continue:
        call MessageBoxA,0, offset message2,\
        offset message1,0
        call ExitProcess, -1

jump:
        call MessageBoxA,0, offset message3,\
        offset message1,0
        call ExitProcess, -1
error:                                             ;sets a new SEH service if there is an error
        mov  esp, [delayESP]
        push offset continue
        ret


;---------------------------------------------------------------------------------------
;Your new service INT 5h (runs in Ring0)
;---------------------------------------------------------------------------------------


InterruptHandler:
        mov  eax, dr0                              ;reads a value from the DR0 debug register
        test ax,ax                                 ;tests to see if a breakpoint was set
        jnz  Debug_Breakpoint                      ;if so, the program jumps
        mov  eax,dr1                               ;reads a value from the DR1 debug register
```

```
        test ax,ax                          ;tests to see if a breakpoint was set
        jnz  Debug_Breakpoint               ;if so, the program jumps
        mov  eax,dr2                         ;reads a value from the DR2 debug register
        test ax,ax                          ;tests to see if a breakpoint was set
        jnz  Debug_Breakpoint               ;if so, the program jumps
        mov  eax,dr3                         ;reads a value from the DR3 debug register
        test ax,ax                          ;tests to see if a breakpoint was set
        jnz  Debug_Breakpoint               ;if so, the program jumps
        iretd                               ;if a breakpoint was not set the program will
                                            ;return 0 into the eax register

Debug_Breakpoint:
        mov  eax,1                          ;sets the value 1 into the eax register to show
                                            ;that breakpoints are active
        iretd                               ;jump back into Ring3

ends
end Start
```

This technique is one of the few ways to discover debug breakpoints, and it makes it possible to delete them without stopping the application in the debugger. However, rather than delete them, I recommend going to an incorrect end of the application.

Unfortunately, the trick works only in Windows 9x because of the need to switch over into ring0. One way to use it in Windows NT, Windows 2000, and Windows XP is to place it into a Sys driver running in ring0. The same is true for all tricks that exploit ring0.

Detecting User Debuggers

The following trick will only discover a *user debugger*—mostly older types of debuggers that work on a different principle than SoftICE and TRW. It will, for example, find a debugger that is located in WinDasm.

33

```
.386
.MODEL FLAT,STDCALL
locals
jumps
UNICODE=0
include w32.inc

Extrn SetUnhandledExceptionFilter : PROC

.data
message1    db "User debugger detection",0
message3    db "Debugger found",0
message2    db "Debugger not found",0
```

```
delayESP    dd 0                                    ;the ESP register saves here
previous    dd 0                                    ;the ESP register will save the address of the
                                                    ;previous SEH service here
.code
Start:


;-------------------------------------------------------------------------------------------
;Sets SEH in case of an error
;-------------------------------------------------------------------------------------------
            mov  [delayESP], esp
            push offset error
            call SetUnhandledExceptionFilter
            mov  [previous], eax
;-------------------------------------------------------------------------------------------
            xor  eax,eax                            ;nulls the eax register
            mov  al, fs:[20h]                       ;reads a value. If the value is other than 0, a
                                                    ;debugger is active
            push eax                                ;saves the value
;-------------------------------------------------------------------------------------------
;Sets the previous SEH service
;-------------------------------------------------------------------------------------------
            push dword ptr [previous]
            call SetUnhandledExceptionFilter
;-------------------------------------------------------------------------------------------
            pop  eax                                ;restores the value
            test eax,eax                            ;tests to see if the read value was 0
            jnz  jump                               ;if not, then a debugger is active in memory and
                                                    ;the program jumps

continue:
            call MessageBoxA,0, offset message2,\
            offset message1,0
            call ExitProcess, -1

jump:
            call MessageBoxA,0, offset message3,\
            offset message1,0
            call ExitProcess, -1
error:                                              ;sets a new SEH service in case of an error
            mov  esp, [delayESP]
            push offset continue
            ret

ends
end Start
```

While this trick will not find either TRW or SoftICE, it works reliably with older debuggers.

Detecting User Debuggers Using the API Function IsDebuggerPresent

You can use the API function IsDebuggerPresent to find a debugger that is active in memory. You needn't enter any parameters for calling this function. If a debugger was found, the EAX register will contain something other than 0.

34

```
.386
.MODEL FLAT,STDCALL
locals
jumps
UNICODE=0
include w32.inc


Extrn SetUnhandledExceptionFilter : PROC
Extrn IsDebuggerPresent           : PROC


.data
message1    db "User debugger detection with the API IsDebuggerPresent function",0
message3    db "Debugger found",0
message2    db "Debugger not found",0
delayESP    dd 0                              ;the ESP register saves here
previous    dd 0                              ;the ESP register saves the address of the
                                              ;previous SEH service here


.code
Start:


;-------------------------------------------------------------------------------
;Sets SEH in case of an error
;-------------------------------------------------------------------------------
            mov  [delayESP], esp
            push offset error
            call SetUnhandledExceptionFilter
            mov  [previous], eax
;-------------------------------------------------------------------------------
            call IsDebuggerPresent
            push eax                          ;saves the return value
;-------------------------------------------------------------------------------
;Sets the previous SEH service
;-------------------------------------------------------------------------------
            push dword ptr [previous]
            call SetUnhandledExceptionFilter
;-------------------------------------------------------------------------------
```

```
        pop  eax                               ;restores the return value
        test eax,eax                           ;tests to see if the return value was 0
        jnz  jump                              ;if not, a debugger is active in memory and the
                                               ;program jumps

continue:
        call MessageBoxA,0, offset message2,\
        offset message1,0
        call ExitProcess, -1

jump:
        call MessageBoxA,0, offset message3,\
        offset message1,0
        call ExitProcess, -1
error:                                         ;sets a new SEH service in case of an error
        mov  esp, [delayESP]
        push offset continue
        ret


ends
end Start
```

This trick will not find either SoftICE or TRW, but it will certainly find user debuggers such as the one in WinDasm.

9

OTHER PROTECTION TRICKS

Here are some other protection tricks.

API Hook Detection

An *API hook* is an exchange of an API function for some other code. For example, if your program calls the API function MessageBoxA, and some other program has placed an API hook on this function, your program will first perform a routine to replace this particular API function. Only once that routine has completed can the program call the original API function, though it doesn't have to. Thus, the program secures the API function and it may, for example, check the values by which the function was called, as well as the return values. API hooks may endanger the security of your programs, so I'll show you how to protect against them.

This trick takes advantage of the two functions VirtualQuery and GetModuleHandleA. The former is used to find the current address of the user of the API function that you are testing, which in this case is MessageBoxA. Next, the program finds the address of the real API function's user by means of GetModuleHandleA. (If the address is MessageBoxA, the user is the USER32.DLL library.) The program then compares the values it finds, and if they are different, there is an API hook on the function.

```
.386
.MODEL FLAT,STDCALL
locals
jumps
UNICODE=0
include w32.inc


Extrn SetUnhandledExceptionFilter : PROC
Extrn VirtualQuery                : PROC


.data

message1          db "Detection of an API hook on the MessageBoxA function",0
message3          db "API hook found",0
message2          db "API hook not found",0
delayESP          dd 0                      ;the ESP register saves here
previous          dd 0                      ;saves the address of the previous SEH here
Memory_structure:                           ;saves the return values of the API function
                                            ;VirtualQuery here

pvBaseAddress     dd 0
pvAllocBase       dd 0
dwAllocProt       dd 0
dwRegionSize      dd 0
dwState           dd 0
dwProtect         dd 0
dwType            dd 0


User              db "USER32.DLL",0         ;enter the source DLL for the tested API
                                            ;function here
.code
Start:


;-------------------------------------------------------------------------------------------
;Sets the SEH in case of an error
;-------------------------------------------------------------------------------------------
                  mov  [delayESP], esp
                  push offset error
                  call SetUnhandledExceptionFilter
                  mov  [previous], eax
;-------------------------------------------------------------------------------------------
                  mov  eax, dword ptr [Detection+1]
                                            ;searches for the IAT. This will put the offset
                                            ;of the jump to the API function MessageBoxA
                                            ;from the call MessageBoxA instruction into the
                                            ;eax call MessageBoxA= (E8xxxxxxxx). You will
                                            ;actually read the xxxxxxxx value.
```

```
                add eax, offset Detection+5+2
                                        ;adds the offset of the beginning of the jump
                                        ;table +5=call MessageBoxA= (E8xxxxxxxx)+2= jmp
                                        ;first_API_function (FF25xxxxxxxx)
                mov  eax, [eax]         ;reads the offset of the jump jmp
                                        ;first_API_function (FF25xxxxxxxx); you will
                                        ;actually read the xxxxxxxx value.
                mov  eax, [eax]         ;the program will eventually read the final real
                                        ;address of the API function routine,
                                        ;MessageBoxA, in the memory from the Import
                                        ;table
                call VirtualQuery, eax, offset Memory_structure, 4*7
                                        ;calls the API function VirtualQuery with the
                                        ;following parameters:
                                        ;eax = the address of the MessageBoxA routine in
                                        ;the memory offset
                                        ;Memory_structure = the buffer offset for the
                                        ;return values
                                        ;4*7 = the buffer size in dword (words). The
                                        ;program will use this call to find the address
                                        ;of the API function MessageBoxA user. The
                                        ;address will be in the buffer at the
                                        ;pvAllocBase offset.
                call GetModuleHandleA, offset User
                                        ;finds the DLL address that is supposed to use
                                        ;the API function (USER32.DLL)
                push eax                ;saves the return value
;------------------------------------------------------------------------------------------
;Sets the previous SEH service
;------------------------------------------------------------------------------------------
                push dword ptr [previous]
                call SetUnhandledExceptionFilter
;------------------------------------------------------------------------------------------
                pop  eax                ;restores the return value
                test eax,eax
                jz   continue           ;the program will jump if there was an error
                                        ;and eax=0
                cmp  eax, [pvAllocBase]  ;compares the addresses to see if the right
                                        ;module is really the user
                jnz  jump               ;if the addresses aren't equal, the program will
                                        ;jump because it has found an API hook of the
                                        ;particular function.
```

```
continue:
                call MessageBoxA,0, offset message2,
                offset message1,0
                call ExitProcess, -1

jump:
                call MessageBoxA,0, offset message3,
                offset message1,0
                call ExitProcess, -1
error:                                          ;sets a new SEH service in case of an error.
                mov  esp, [delayESP]
                push offset continue
                ret
Detection:                                      ;this label may be anywhere that the called API
                                                ;function MessageBoxA can be.
                call MessageBoxA


ends
end Start
```

This trick isn't limited to searching for an API hook on the MessageBoxA function; it is easily modified for any API function. When using this method, it is important to correctly set the library that uses the particular function.

The program can test to see if there is an API hook before calling any API function, but if you test too much, you may make the program terribly slow. The testing routine can be modified to get the information about the imported functions directly from the Import table of the file's PE header.

This trick works only in Windows 9x.

Anti-ProcDump Trick

This trick tries to prevent ProcDump from dumping a program. It's a good idea to consider using this trick in your application because ProcDump is currently the most frequently used decompressor, able to decompress almost all known compression and encoding programs (see Figure 9.1). If you use this trick, it will be impossible for a cracker to use ProcDump to decode your program.

You implement this trick by changing the program's PE header in memory. Once the program has been loaded, you increase its size in the PE header, which prevents the program from being saved correctly. ProcDump will then try to read the unallocated sections of the memory, and an error will occur.

You must use different routines for Windows 9x and Windows NT, because the process is different for each operating system. ANAKiN was the first person to use this method of fighting ProcDump in PE-SHiELD.

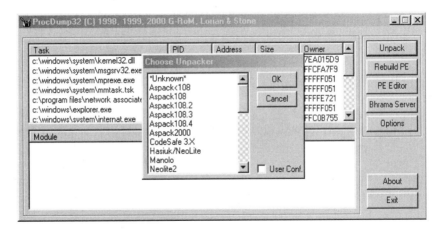

Figure 9.1: Besides decoding, ProcDump is able to do other useful things that any normal programmer can use

---

36

```
.386
.MODEL FLAT,STDCALL
locals
jumps
UNICODE=0
include w32.inc
Extrn SetUnhandledExceptionFilter : PROC


.data

message1    db "Anti-ProcDump trick",0
message2    db "Increased the file size in its PE header",0
delayESP    dd 0                          ;the ESP register saves here.
previous    dd 0                          ;the ESP register will save the address of the
                                          ;previous SEH service here.


.code
Start:

;-------------------------------------------------------------------------------------------
;Sets SEH in case of an error
;-------------------------------------------------------------------------------------------
            mov  [delayESP], esp
            push offset error
            call SetUnhandledExceptionFilter
            mov  [previous], eax
;-------------------------------------------------------------------------------------------
```

```
        mov  eax, fs:[30h]                    ;reads the Windows version
        test eax,eax                          ;tests the Windows version
        js   found_win9x                      ;the program will jump if Windows 9x is running

found_winNT:                                  ;the procedure for Windows NT
        mov  eax,[eax+0ch]
        mov  eax,[eax+0ch]
        add  dword ptr [eax+20h], 3000h       ;increases the program's size
        jmp  end                              ;jump, finished

found_win9x:                                  ;the procedure for Windows 9x
        push 0
        call GetModuleHandleA                 ;finds the module handle
        test edx,edx
        jns  end                              ;the program jumps if there was an error
        cmp  dword ptr [edx+08], -1           ;tests for the value -1
        jne  end                              ;if the value is not -1, there was an error, and
                                              ;the program jumps
        mov  edx, [edx+4]                     ;finds the address of the file's PE header
        add  dword ptr [edx+50h],3000         ;increases the size in such a way that it will
                                              ;change the item SizeOfImage in the PE header
end:

;--------------------------------------------------------------------------------------------
;Sets the previous SEH service
;--------------------------------------------------------------------------------------------

        push dword ptr [previous]
        call SetUnhandledExceptionFilter
;--------------------------------------------------------------------------------------------

continue:
        call MessageBoxA,0, offset message2,
        offset message1,0
        call ExitProcess, -1
error:                                        ;sets a new SEH service in case of an error.
        mov  esp, [delayESP]
        push offset continue
        ret


ends
end Start
```

Unfortunately, it isn't enough to add this trick into an application that has been encoded or compressed by a program that may be decompressed by

ProcDump because, once added, the code won't run at all. In such a case, this trick must be placed directly into the decoding routine.

There are only two ways to place the code into the decoding routine: Change the code of the compression program, or create your own compression program. The first method is easier, because you can find the code for compression programs on the Internet, at which point it isn't hard to modify the code and compile it. The best way, of course, is to program your own compression program, but that's a lot more difficult.

Switching a Running Program from Ring3 to Ring0

Most programs run in ring3, where you cannot make certain calls, like reading debug registers or performing VxD calls. Some programs, however, run directly in ring0, such as VxD files in Windows 9x, and Sys files in Windows NT, 2000 and XP.

I'm aware of three ways to switch a normal program running in ring3 into ring0, but only in Windows 9x. Windows NT, 2000, and XP systems were secured against these methods because of the prevalence of viruses that take advantage of them. (Older Windows NT versions did allow this switch, but after it was misused a few times, the possibility was removed from the system.)

As such, it is very important to test for the type of operating system before you use this call, or the program will end with an error in Windows NT, 2000 and XP.

Switching into Ring0 Using the LDT (Locale Descriptor Table)

This is the oldest method of switching into ring0. It isn't used much anymore because the other two methods are better. This method of switching over into ring0 using the LDT was often used by viruses, but not often used with normal applications. Here's an example, anyway, because you may encounter it.

37a

```
.386
.MODEL FLAT,STDCALL
locals
jumps
UNICODE=0
include w32.inc


Extrn SetUnhandledExceptionFilter : PROC


.data
message1    db "An example of switching into Ring0 using the LDT",0
message2    db "An error occurred",0
message3    db "Ring0 was successfully activated",0
delayESP    dd 0                            ;the ESP register saves here
previous    dd 0                            ;the address of the previous SEH service will
                                            ;be saved here.
```

```asm
gdt_        df 0
call_       dd 00
            dw 0Fh
o_gate      dw 0
            dw 028h                         ;a segment for RING0
            dw 0EC00h
dw 0

.code
Start:
;-------------------------------------------------------------------------------
;Sets SEH in case of an error
;-------------------------------------------------------------------------------
            mov  [delayESP], esp
            push offset error
            call SetUnhandledExceptionFilter
            mov  [previous], eax
;-------------------------------------------------------------------------------

            mov  eax, offset ring0          ;puts the offset of your service for RING0 into
                                            ;the eax.
            mov  [o_gate],ax                ;sets the address of your new RING0 service into
                                            ;the "callgate"

            shr  eax,16
            mov  [o_gate+6],ax
            xor  eax, eax
            sgdt fword ptr gdt_             ;saves the GDT
            mov  ebx, dword ptr [gdt_+2]    ;gets the GDT base address
            sldt ax
            add  ebx,eax                    ;gets the descriptor address
            mov  al, [ebx+4]
            mov  ah [ebx+7]
            shl  eax,16                     ;gets the LDT address in the eax register.
            mov  ax,[ebx+2]                 ;if you add into the eax, you will get the
                                            ;descriptor callgate address

            add  eax,8
            mov  edi,eax                    ;sets a location in the callgate where you will
                                            ;start making changes

            mov  esi,offset o_gate          ;puts the address of your "callgate" into the
                                            ;esi register
            movsd                           ;and moves it into the real callgate
            movsd                           ;which will prepare a jump into ring0
            call fword ptr [call_]          ;jumps your service into RING0
            xor  eax, eax
            sub  edi,8                      ;nulls your changes in the callgate
```

```
          stosd
          stosd
;------------------------------------------------------------------------------
;Sets the previous SEH service
;------------------------------------------------------------------------------
          push dword ptr [previous]
          call SetUnhandledExceptionFilter
;------------------------------------------------------------------------------

          jmp  jump                          ;jumps if the switch into RING0 was successful

continue:
          call  MessageBoxA,0, offset message2,\
          offset message1,0
          call  ExitProcess, -1

jump:
          call  MessageBoxA,0, offset message3,\
          offset message1,0
          call  ExitProcess, -1
error:                                       ;sets a new SEH service in case of an error.
          mov   esp, [delayESP]
          push  offset continue
          ret
;------------------------------------------------------------------------------
;Your new RING0 service
;------------------------------------------------------------------------------
ring0:
          mov  eax, dr7                       ;this instruction works only in RING0
          retf                                ;returns to RING3
ends
end Start
```

Switching into Ring0 Using the IDT (EliCZ's Method)

The following method is called the *IDT* (Interrupt Descriptor Table) method, and was used for the first time by the wonderful Czech system programmer EliCZ. It was then fully used a few days later by the well-known CIH virus. This method was really revolutionary at the time, and thus the virus spread very widely and caused an awful lot of damage.

Of course, you are good guys, so you will use this method for something good. Still, I wanted to point out how good things can be misused.

```
        .386
        .MODEL FLAT,STDCALL
        locals
        jumps
        UNICODE=0
        include w32.inc

        Extrn SetUnhandledExceptionFilter : PROC
        Interrupt   equ 5                           ;the interrupt number. The numbers 1 or 3 will
                                                    ;make debugging more difficult.
        .data
        message1    db "An example of switching into RING0 by using the IDT (EliCZ's method)",0
        message2    db "An error occurred",0
        message3    db "Ring0 was successfully activated",0
        delayESP    dd 0                            ;the ESP register saves the address of the
        previous    dd 0                            ;previous SEH service here

        .CODE
        Start:

;-----------------------------------------------------------------------------------
;Sets SEH in case of an error
;-----------------------------------------------------------------------------------
        mov   [delayESP], esp
        push offset error
        call SetUnhandledExceptionFilter
        mov   [previous], eax
;-----------------------------------------------------------------------------------

        push edx
        sidt [esp-2]                        ;reads the IDT into the stack
        pop   edx
        add   edx,(Interrupt*8)+4           ;reads the vector of the required interrupt
        mov   ebx,[edx]
        mov   bx,word ptr [edx-4]           ;reads the address of the old service of the
                                            ;required interrupt

        lea   edi,InterruptHandler
        mov   [edx-4],di
        ror   edi,16                        ;sets a new interrupt service
        mov   [edx+2],di
        push ds                             ;saves the register for security
        push es
        int   Interrupt                     ;jumps into RING0 (the newly defined INT 5h
                                            ;service)
        pop   es                            ;restores registers
        pop   ds
        mov   [edx-4],bx                    ;sets the original interrupt service (INT 5h)
```

```
            ror   ebx,16
            mov   [edx+2],bx
;-----------------------------------------------------------------------------
;Sets the previous SEH service
;-----------------------------------------------------------------------------
            push dword ptr [previous]
            call SetUnhandledExceptionFilter
;-----------------------------------------------------------------------------


            jmp  jump                        ;jumps if the switch into RING0 was successful

continue:
            call MessageBoxA,0, offset message2,\
            offset message1,0
            call ExitProcess, -1


jump:
            call MessageBoxA,0, offset message3,\
            offset message1,0
            call ExitProcess, -1
error:                                       ;sets a new SEH service in case of an error
            mov  esp, [delayESP]
            push offset continue
            ret


;-----------------------------------------------------------------------------
;Your new INT 5h service (runs in Ring0)
;-----------------------------------------------------------------------------


InterruptHandler:
            mov  eax,dr7                     ;this instruction is functional only in RING0
            iretd                            ;jumps back into RING3

ends
end Start
```

The IDT method is the one most frequently used for switching over into ring0. It has been used in many common applications that need to use ring0 for their special tasks, especially compression and encoding programs that want to prevent debugging. I have used this method in all the examples where I have taken advantage of ring0 because it's the easiest to understand.

When using this method, the program first reads the IDT using the SIDT instruction, after which it reads the address of the beginning of the interrupt vectors. Next, the program calculates the interrupt vector address to be used — Int 5h in this case.

The new service address is saved to its vector in its 16-bit DOS form — the offset first, and then the segment part of the address. Once the Int 5h interrupt is called in the following part of the code, the operating system calls the new service, which runs in ring0 like all interrupt services. Here is where you can take advantage of all the possibilities of ring0.

The service must be finished by the IRET instruction. The operating system switches the program back into ring3, and the program continues following the Int 5h instruction. Finally, you set the original Int 5h interrupt service to prevent problems.

Unfortunately, because this method needs to change the interrupt vectors and call the interrupt later, some programs, like FrogsICE, can discover it.

Switching into Ring0 Using the SEH (The Owl's Method)

The last, and probably the best, method for switching into ring0 is to use the SEH. I haven't seen this method used in any program yet, which is surprising because it has clear advantages over the preceding two methods.

The advantage of this method is that it's difficult to discover. While you can use other methods to call the SEH service and the Int 3h instruction, this solution is perfect when used with something like the previous example.

At the beginning of the program, you set a new SEH service that you then call with the Int 3h instruction, which causes an exception. The service tries to determine which exception caused it. Instruction Int 3h always causes the exception EXCEPTION_BREAKPOINT, so we can test it with our SEH service.

The program finds the address of the Context array. The Context array checks the register values in the CS and SS of the program before causing the exception, and it saves them in the Context field in the ECX and EDX registers right after the switch into ring0. (This is important for the eventual return into ring3.) The program also sets new values for the CS and SS registers in the Context field: 28h for CS and for 30h for SS, to ensure that the program will run in ring0 after the return. It also sets the flag for the CLI in the EFLAGS register, which prevents any interrupt calls.

While the program is running in ring0, it returns all the values necessary for running in ring3 to the registers. Finally, it sets an address from which the program will run, and it switches back into ring3 by means of the IRETD function.

Because this method is almost completely unknown, even programs like FrogsICE have problems detecting it.

```
.386
.MODEL FLAT,STDCALL
locals
jumps
UNICODE=0
include w32.inc
```

```
Extrn SetUnhandledExceptionFilter : PROC

.data
message1    db "An example of switching into Ring0 by means of the SEH (The Owl's method)",0
message2    db "RING0 was successfully activated",0

.code
Start:

        xor   eax,eax                       ;nulls the eax register because the new SEH
                                            ;service is set
        push offset xhandler                ;address for your new SEH service (xhandler)
        push dword ptr fs:[eax]             ;saves the address of the original SEH service
        mov  dword ptr fs:[eax], esp        ;sets the new SEH service
        pushfd                              ;saves the EFLAGS
        mov  eax,esp                        ;saves the ESP register (stack address)
        int  3h                             ;causes an error and will also call your new SEH
                                            ;service (xhandler)
;-------------------------------------------------------------------------------------------
;From here the program runs in RING0
;-------------------------------------------------------------------------------------------

        mov  ebx,dr7                        ;tests to see if you are really in RING0, and
                                            ;restores the original register values for RING3
        push edx                            ; GS
        push edx                            ; FS
        push edx                            ; ES
        push edx                            ; DS
        push edx                            ; SS
        push eax                            ; ESP
        push dword ptr [eax]                ; EFLAGS
        push ecx                            ; CS
        push offset ring3                   ; EIP = address where it will jump back
                                            ;into RING3
        iretd                               ;jump back into RING3


;-------------------------------------------------------------------------------------------
;From here the program runs again in RING3
;-------------------------------------------------------------------------------------------

ring3:
        popfd                               ;restores EFLAGS
        pop  dword ptr fs:[0]               ;sets the original SEH service
        add  esp,4                          ;clears the stack
        call MessageBoxA,0, offset message2,\
```

```
                offset message1,0
                call ExitProcess, -1              ;ends the program


;-----------------------------------------------------------------------------
;Your new SEH service (xhandler)
;-----------------------------------------------------------------------------


xhandler:
        push ebp                                  ;sets the stack
        mov  ebp,esp                              ;and finds its address
        push ebx
        push ecx

        mov  ebx,[ebp+8]                          ;reads the address containing the information
                                                  ;about the error, which is the exception
                                                  ;location or address.

        cmp  dword ptr [ebx], 80000003h           ;tests to see if EXCEPTION_BREAKPOINT was the
                                                  ;error caused by INT 3h

        jne  end                                  ;if not the program jumps

        mov  eax,[ebp+10h]                        ;reads the address of the beginning of the
                                                  ;context

        movzx ecx, word ptr [eax+0bch]            ;reads Seg.Cs from the Context

        mov  [eax+0ach],ecx                       ;saves .ECX into the Context (this value will
                                                  ;be in the ECX after switching into RING0)

        mov  dword ptr [eax+0bch],28h             ;saves Seg.Cs into the Context (this value will
                                                  ;be in the CS register). This will secure switch
                                                  ;over into RING0.

        movzx ecx, word ptr [eax+0c8h]            ;reads Seg.SS from the Context

        mov  [eax+0a8h],ecx                       ;saves .EDX into the Context (this value will be
                                                  ;in the EDX after switching into the RING3)

        mov  dword ptr [eax+0c8h],30h             ;saves Seg.SS into the Context (this value will
                                                  ;be in the SS register). This will secure a
                                                  ;switch over into RING0.

        or   dword ptr [eax+0c0h],0200h           ;sets CLI into the Context.EFLAGS (this value
                                                  ;will be in the EFLAGS register)

        mov  eax,0                                ;nulls EAX


end:
        pop  ecx                                  ;clears the stack
        pop  ebx
        mov  esp,ebp
        pop  ebp
        retn                                      ;jumps back into the program, but the example
                                                  ;program will continue running in RING0


ends
end Start
```

Anti-Disassembling Macros

To make debugging and disassembling more difficult, you can use short codes that repeat often and that are inserted between the program instructions. It is really unpleasant to debug code that contains something like this, and some disassemblers don't like these short codes. For example, WinDasm will often end with an error.

IDA, on the other hand, is much better off, and if you can check the translation there, you can also disassemble most of the anti-debugging macros, and the program will be much easier to understand. Fortunately, there are several methods for making disassembly in IDA much more tiresome.

The Simplest Method

```
push offset jump
ret
```

After the RET instruction, the program will jump to the jump label. When properly used, it may make the code hard to understand. For example:

```
push offset jump2
push offset jump

                    ;...this can include any code, but it mustn't
                    change the stack or, if it does, it must clear
                    it at the end of the code.
ret


jump:
                    ;...this can include any code, but it mustn't
                    change the stack or, if it does, it must clear
                    it at the end of the code.
ret                 ;jumps to the jump2 label


jump2:
                    ;...this can include any code, but it mustn't
                    change the stack or, if it does, it must clear
                    it at the end of the code.
```

This is a very simple method that will surprise hardly anyone. To make the code harder to read, use a more complicated way to calculate the address saved by the PUSH instructions, and save it as register values rather than as offsets.

A Similar Method

Here is a slightly more complicated example.

```
        mov  eax, offset jump
        push eax
                          ;...this can include any code, but it mustn't
                          change the stack or, if it does, it must clear it.
        pop  eax
        jmp  eax
jump:
                          ;...any code.
```

Making It Even Better

```
.data
address_    dd offset jump
for_a_jump

.code
        mov  eax, offset address_for_a_jump
        push eax
                          ;...this can include any code, but it mustn't
                          change the stack or, if it does, it must clear it.
        pop  eax
        jmp  [eax]
jump:
                          ;... any code.
```

Fantasy Is Unlimited

```
.data
address_
for_a_jump dd offset jump
.code
        mov  eax, offset address_for_a_jump
        push eax
                          ;...any code, but it mustn't change the stack or,
                          if it does, it must clear it.
        pop  eax
        call [eax]
jump:
                          ;... any code
```

Jumping into the Middle of Instructions and Making the Code Harder to Understand

You should put as little code as possible between these anti-disassembling macros to prevent the cracker from fully understanding them, because this makes their job more time consuming. Naturally, adding these macros makes the code itself longer, which may slow down the application. Therefore, think carefully about where you put the disassembling macros, and insert them only into those parts of the code where they are important.

NOTE *You can find more macros on the CD enclosed with this book. I didn't list them here because you will understand them best during debugging itself.*

Address	Instruction Code	Instruction	Explanation
00000000			;... any code (in this case 8 bytes long)
0000000B	60	pushad	;saves registers because of changes
0000000C	E803000000	call 00000014	;jumps to this address
00000011	D2EB	shr bl,cl	;this code is wrong
00000013	0B58EB	or ebx, [eax-15h]	
00000016	014840	add [eax+40h], ecx	
...			

;--
;after the jump the code will change:
;--

Address	Instruction Code	Instruction	Explanation
00000014	58	pop eax	;puts the return value into the eax ;(necessary for cleaning the stack)
00000015	EB01	jmp 00000018	
00000017	48	dec eax	;this instruction will jump over the ;dec eax instruction
00000018	40	inc eax	;increases the return value by 1 so the ;return address will be 00000012
00000019	EB01	jmp 0000001C	
0000001B	35FFE0E761	xor eax, 61E7E0FFh	;this code is wrong
...			

;--
;after the jump the code will change:
;--

Address	Instruction Code	Instruction	Explanation
0000001C	FFE0	jmp eax	;jump to 00000012

after the jump the code will change:

Address	Instruction Code	Instruction	Explanation
00000012	EB0B	jmp 0000001F	;another jump

after the jump the code will change:

```
0000001F    61                      popad
```

...	;insert any code here
...	;repeat

Detecting Attempts to Decompress Programs Prior to Decoding

Most programs compiled by Visual C++, Delphi, and similar compilers have an entry point at the 401000 address. If the entry point is somewhere else, it's easy enough to find using a debugger or another program for finding important information about the EXE files (like ProcDump).

Once a compression or encoding program for executable files has been used, this entry point will be changed. Your application then only has to test whether the program's entry point is different from the one that was there before the compressor was used. If the original entry point is still there (usually 401000), a decompression attempt has been made. The best solution in that case is to end the program incorrectly, or have it perform an error that may confuse the attacker because he cannot be sure that he decompressed the application correctly.

Testing a File's Checksum with the API Function MapFileAndCheckSumA

The API function MapFileAndCheckSumA offers a very simple way to test a file's checksum. It is part of the IMAGEHLP.DLL library that is part of the Windows installation.

MapFileAndCheckSumA calculates the current checksum of a file like this:

```
push offset new_checksum
push offset old_checksum
push offset file_name
call MapFileAndCheckSumA
```

Once the routine has been performed, the new_checksum address will contain the current checksum of the file. The old_checksum address will contain the original checksum, which is located in the file's PE header. The file_name address is the name of the file for which the checksum was calculated.

You could detect changes in the file by comparing the values of the old_checksum and the new_checksum, but this method would be correct only if the attacker didn't restore the checksum in the PE header. It is much better to locate the correct checksum somewhere else (such as in the Windows Registry or in the file), and then to compare this value with the value in the new_checksum.

Changes in Characteristics for the .code Section of the PE File

If the characteristics of the .code section of the PE file have been changed to the value C0000040, the program will be fully functional and will run without problems. Nevertheless, if the program is disassembled with WinDasm, the resulting code will not be correct. Also, when such a program has been loaded into memory using the Symbol Loader for SoftICE, it will not stop at its beginning but will continue running. Most compression and encoding programs use this trick.

If a cracker wants to remove this trick, he has to change the PE header, and you can detect his attempts using a CRC calculation. You can also directly test the characteristics in the file's PE header for changes.

Finding Monitoring Programs

Crackers often use various monitoring programs to help them determine which files the application works with, which API functions it uses, where it saves values in registers, and where it reads them. It is very important to protect against the use of monitoring programs because they allow a cracker to easily find information that should remain hidden.

There are several ways to find out if such a program is active in memory. One way is to search for a program window by its name. Another method is to use the API call CreateFileA to determine whether a VxD (a Sys file in Windows NT and 2000) for a particular program is active. While not all of these programs use their own VxDs, many use VxDs to get into ring0 because they want to use its possibilities. (There are other methods, such as searching for a process; you just have to experiment a bit.)

You can use the following code to search for the window name of a monitoring program.

```
.data

WindowName  db "Enter the name of the window here",0

.code
        xor  eax,eax                          ;nulls eax
        call FindWindowExA, eax,eax, eax, offset WindowName
                                              ;searches for the window
        test eax,eax
        jnz  jump_program                     ;jumps if it has found the window of the
                                              ;monitoring program
```

To search for an active VxD or Sys driver, you can use the same routine you would use to search for SoftICE drivers, as discussed in Chapter 7 in the "Detecting SoftICE by Opening Its Drivers and Calling the CreateFileA API Function (SICE, NTICE)" section and others. Naturally, you can use any other function (such as _lopen, _lcreat, or CreateFileW) instead of the API function CreateFileA, as shown in Chapter 7.

```
.data
name        db "\\.\driver name",0                 ;driver to be searched for

.code
        call CreateFileA, OFFSET name,\
        FILE_FLAG_WRITE_THROUGH, FILE_SHARE_READ,\
        NULL, OPEN_EXISTING, FILE_ATTRIBUTE_NORMAL,\
        NULL
        cmp  eax, -1                                ;tests to see if the driver is active
        jnz  found                                  ;if so, the program will jump
```

The following table lists the most famous monitoring programs and ways of detecting them. Of course, this list doesn't contain all the programs crackers use. These are the most frequently used programs. It is therefore suggested you follow new monitoring applications and then react fast.

Monitoring Program	Window Name	Name
ADUMP v1.0	db "Advanced Dumper v1.0",0	
ATM		db "\\.\ATM",0
C.u.Dilla rl final	db "C.u.Dilla rl final",0	
Debug Print Viewer	db "Debug Print viewer",0	db "\\.\DBGDD",0 (Windows 9x)
	db "\\.\DBGV",0 (Windows NT and 2000)	
DllView	db "DllView - System Internals: http://www.sysinternals.com",0	
ExeSpy98	db "ExeSpy98",0	db "\\.\FXVXD",0
File Monitor	db "File Monitor - System Internals: http://www.sysinternals.com",0	
	db " \\.\FILEVXD",0 (Windows 9x)	
	db " \\.\FILEM ",0 (Windows NT)	
OpenTrap	db " \\.\FUNCTRAP",0	
OpenList	db " OpenList",0	
Port Monitor	db " Port Monitor - System Internals: http://www.sysinternals.com",0	
	db "\\.\PORTMVXD",0 (Windows 9x)	
	db "\\.\PORTM",0 (Windows NT)	
ProcDump	db "ProcDump32 (C) 1998, 1999, 2000 G-RoM, Lorian & Stone",0 or for the Bhrama Server which is a part of the ProcDump	

	db "ProcDump32 - Dumper Server",0	
Registry Monitor	db "Registry Monitor - System Internals: http://www.sysinternals.com ",0	
	db "\\.\REGVXD",0 (Windows 9x)	
	db "\\.\REGSYS",0 (Windows NT)	
Registry Monitor 2000		db "\\.\FHNTVDD",0 (Windows NT)
Registry Monitor 98	db "Regmon98",0	db "\\.\FHVXD",0
ResSpy 98	db "Resspy",0	db "\\.\FHVXD",0
Setup Monitor 98	db "SetupMonitor98",0	db "\\.\FHVXD",0
Setup Monitor 2000		db "\\.\FHNTVDD",0 (Windows NT)
SMU Winspector	db "SMU Winspector",0	
Spy & Capture	db "Spy Window",0	
Microsoft Spy++	db "Microsoft Spy++ - Window 1",0	
TCP View	db "TCPView",0	
VxD Monitor	db "VxD Monitor",0	db "\\.\VXDMON",0
Win-Expose-I/O		db "\\.\WXIMONTR",0
Win-Expose-Registry		db "\\.\WXRMONTR",0

A Trick for Punishing a Cracker

Windows offers several possibilities for punishing crackers or users who want to illegally use your application. If your application discovers an illegal attempt to use it, or an attack against it, it can perform several unassuming changes without warning the user.

The user could, for example, be punished with several changes to the Windows Registry. For example, here's how to block RegEdit from accessing the Windows Registry:

```
[HKEY_CURRENT_USER\Software\Microsoft\Windows\CurrentVersion\Policies\system]
"DisableRegistryTools"=dword:00000001
```

Unblocking is possible only after replacing the 0s with 1s. It is a good idea to combine this trick with the following one, which causes a window with your message to appear after starting Windows.

```
[HKEY_LOCAL_MACHINE\Software\Microsoft\Windows\CurrentVersion\Winlogon]
"LegalNoticeCaption"="Illegal usage attempt."
"LegalNoticeText"= "A user is attempting illegal software usage at this location."
```

With access blocked to the registry, the user will be unable to remove the message.

There are also other methods of punishment. For example, a program that has discovered an attempt at illegal use doesn't have to work correctly. It may, for example, "freeze" after some time, save files incorrectly, or delete itself. It's up to the application's creator to choose the punishment.

An application may also surprise a cracker by deleting the debugger from his hard drive, though not as soon as it finds it, of course. It should first ask nicely for its removal from the memory, but if following tests discover the debugger in memory again, it is clear that this is an attack.

10

IMPORTANT STRUCTURES IN WINDOWS

There are important structures in Windows, without which the operating system cannot function. Standard file types (such as BMB, EXE, and DOC) are such structures, but there are also special structures in memory that contain important information about processes, threads, and so on. These structures can be very useful and sometimes absolutely necessary.

Context Structure

Context structure is a very important Windows structure, and every running thread contains it. You can find critically important information about every program in the context structure; information that may help you discover a debugger or better manage the program.

Two API functions are used for managing the context structure. GetThreadContext reads the context structure of a thread. Calling GetThreadContext in C looks like this:

```
BOOL GetThreadContext (
    HANDLE hThread,                      //handle to the thread with the context
    LPCONTEXT lpContext                  //address where the context structure will be saved
);
```

The other function, SetThreadContext, writes the new context structure for the thread. Naturally, you can also use it for your own purposes.

```
BOOL  SetThreadContext (
    HANDLE hThread,                      //handle to the thread with the context
CONST CONTEXT * lpContext                //address where the context structure is located
                                         //which will be set for the thread
);
```

The SEH service also allows you to read and change information in the context structure, and I have used it several times in anti-debugging tricks. SEH's advantage lies in the fact that you needn't call any API functions. The context structure looks like this:

```
include winnt.h
#if !defined (RC_INVOKED)
#define CONTEXT_i386      0x00010000                    //i386 and i486 structures
#define CONTEXT_I486      XX00010000                    //contain the same context entry
#define CONTEXT_CONTROL           (CONTEXT_i386|0x00000001L)
//if this flag has been set the context will contain values of the SS:SP, CS:IP, FLAGS, BP
//registers

#define CONTEXT_INTEGER           (CONTEXT_i386|0x00000002L)
//if this flag has been set the context will contain values of the AX, BX, CX, DX, SI, DI registers

#define CONTEXT_SEGMENTS          (CONTEXT_i386|0x00000004L)
//if this flag has been set the context will contain values of the DS, ES, FS, GS registers

#define CONTEXT_FLOATING_POINT     (CONTEXT_i386|0x00000008L)
//if this flag has been set, the context will contain the 387 status

#define CONTEXT_DEBUG_REGISTERS    (CONTEXT_i386|0x00000010L)
//if this flag has been set, the context will contain values of the DR 0-3, 6, 7 debug registers

#define CONTEXT_FULL              (CONTEXT_CONTROL | CONTEXT_INTEGER |\ CONTEXT_SEGMENTS)
//Be careful with these settings because they will not set the context flags for the
//CONTEXT_FLOATING_POINT and CONTEXT_DEBUG_REGISTERS

#endif
```

```
//A structure for the 387 state

#define SIZE_OF_80387_REGISTERS                          80
typedef struct FLOATINGSAVE_AREA {                       //the length is 70h bytes
    DWORD           ControlWord;                          //offset 0
    DWORD           StatusWord;                           //offset 04h
    DWORD           TagWord;                              //offset 08h
    DWORD           ErrorOffset;                          //offset 0Ch
    DWORD           ErrorSelector;                        //offset 10h
    DWORD           DataOffset;                           //offset 14h
    DWORD           DataSelector;                         //offset 18h
    BYTE            RegisterArea[SIZE_OF_80387_REGISTERS]; //offset 1Ch
    DWORD           Cr0NpxState;                          //offset 6Ch
} FLOATING_SAVE_AREA;

typedef FLOATING_SAVE_AREA * PFLOATING_SAVE_AREA;

typedef struct _CONTEXT {
    DWORD           ContextFlags;                         //offset 00
                                                         //offset saves the flags here


//DEBUG REGISTRY
//
//This section will be returned/set only when the context flag for the CONTEXT_DEBUG_REGISTERS has
been set.

    DWORD           Dr0;                                  //offset 04
    DWORD           Dr1;                                  //offset 08
    DWORD           Dr2;                                  //offset 0Ch
    DWORD           Dr3;                                  //offset 10h
    DWORD           Dr6;                                  //offset 14h
    DWORD           Dr7;                                  //offset 18h

//387 STATUS
//
//This section will be returned/set only when the context flag for the CONTEXT_FLOATING_POINT has
//been set.

    FLOATING_SAVE_AREA FloatSave;                         // offset 1Ch
```

```
//SEGMENT REGISTRY
//
//This section will be returned/set only when the context flag for CONTEXT_SEGMENTS has been set.

    DWORD           SegGs;                              //offset 8Ch
    DWORD           SegFs;                              //offset 90h
    DWORD           SegEs;                              //offset 94h
    DWORD           SegDs;                              //offset 98h

//BASIC REGISTERS
//
//This section will be returned/set only when the context flag for CONTEXT_INTEGER has been set.

    DWORD           Edi;                                //offset 9Ch
    DWORD           Esi;                                //offset A0h
    DWORD           Ebx;                                //offset A4h
    DWORD           Edx;                                //offset A8h
    DWORD           Ecx;                                //offset ACh
    DWORD           Eax;                                //offset B0h

//CONTROL REGISTERS
//
//This section will be returned/set only when the context flag for the CONTEXT_CONTROL has been
set.

    DWORD           Ebp;                                //offset B4h
    DWORD           Eip;                                //offset B8h
    DWORD           SegCs;                              //offset BCh MUST BE SANITIZED
    DWORD           EFlags;                             //offset C0h MUST BE SANITIZED
    DWORD           Esp;                                //offset C4h
    DWORD           SegSs;                              //offset C8h

} CONTEXT;
typedef CONTEXT *PCONTEXT;
```

The context structure is ubiquitous, and it is vital when working with Windows NT and 2000, where access to certain critical information is very difficult and sometimes nearly impossible. The situation is rather different in Windows 9x, where you can switch your program over to ring0 and get the highest authorization, yet even there the context structure has its place, and it can be used in many ways.

Windows NT Executable Files (PE Files)

Windows NT executables, also referred to as *Portable Executable* (PE) files because they are not architecture-specific, are probably one of the most important and most frequently used Windows file formats. The PE file is the native file format for Win32, and all 32-bit Windows executable files (such as EXE and VxD files) contain this structure.

It is definitely good to know the PE header structure. You can use it when creating tricks against various memory dumpers. When a development team writing protection decides to create their own encoding program for executable files, they will not be able to avoid it.

The PE file structure looks like this:

DOS MZ header
DOS stub
PE header
Section table
Section 1
Section 2
Section n

All PE files must start with a classic *DOS MZ header* to ensure that when the PE file is launched in DOS, the *DOS stub* (an MS-DOS executable, stored next to the MZ header) will be launched, too. This header is a short routine that typically displays the well-known message: "This program cannot be run in DOS mode," or it may display additional information, too, if necessary.

The *PE header*, which follows the DOS stub, is of great interest to us. Its structure is called by the IMAGE_NT_HEADER, and it contains many essential fields that are used by the PE loader. When a program is launched in an operating system that knows the program's structure, the PE file loader will read important information from the header and will prepare the file for launching. Thus, the PE loader can find the starting offset of the PE header from the DOS MZ header, skip the DOS stub, and go directly to the PE header (which is the real file header).

The PE header determines where a particular section begins and where it ends. *Sections* are blocks of data with common attributes that follow the PE header and that contain the PE file's real content.

The *section table* is an array of structures with information about each section in the PE file.

You can find the beginning of the PE header in the 3Ch offset of the DOS MZ header. It's important to know its location when setting up a jump over the DOS stub in order to correctly load the PE file.

This is a PE header's structure:

00	SIGNATURE BYTES	CPU TYPE	n OBJECTS
08	TIME/DATE STAMP	RESERVED	
16	RESERVED	NT HDR SIZE	FLAGS
24	RESERVED | LMAJOR | LMINOR	RESERVED	
32	RESERVED	RESERVED	
40	ENTRYPOINT RVA	RESERVED	
48	RESERVED	IMAGE BASE	
56	OBJECT ALIGN	FILE ALIGN	
64	OS MAJOR | OS MINOR | USER MAJOR | USER MINOR		
72	SUBSYS MAJOR | SUBSYS MINOR	RESERVED	
80	IMAGE SIZE	HEADER SIZE	
88	FILE CHECKSUM	SUBSYSTEM | DLL FLAGS	
96	STACK RESERVE SIZE	STACK COMMIT SIZE	
104	HEAP RESERVE SIZE	HEAP COMMIT SIZE	
112	RESERVED	#INTERESTING RVA/SIZES	
120	EXPORT TABLE RVA	TOTAL EXPORT DATA SIZE	
128	IMPORT TABLE RVA	TOTAL IMPORT DATA SIZE	
136	RESOURCE TABLE RVA	TOTAL RESOURCE DATA SIZE	
144	EXCEPTION TABLE RVA	TOTAL EXCEPTION DATA SIZE	
152	SECURITY TABLE RVA	TOTAL SECURITY DATA SIZE	
160	FIXUP TABLE RVA	TOTAL FIXUP DATA SIZE	
168	DEBUG TABLE RVA	TOTAL DEBUG DIRECTORIES	
176	IMAGE DESCRIPTION RVA	TOTAL DESCRIPTION SIZE	
184	MACHINE SPECIFIC RVA	MACHINE SPECIFIC SIZE	
192	THREAD LOCAL STORAGE RVA	TOTAL TLS SIZE	

Offset 00 — SIGNATURE BYTES — size DWORD

A mark that shows whether the file is an executable. It changes with the type of the executable file into the following bytes:

```
"P", "E", 0, 0
"M", "Z", 0, 0
"N", "E", 0, 0
"L", "E", 0, 0
```

Offset 04 — CPU TYPE — size WORD

Specifies the minimum processor necessary to launch the file.

Value	Explanation
0000h	Unknown
014Ch	80386
014Dh	80486

014Eh	80586
0162h	MIPS MARK I (R2000, R3000)
0163h	MIPS MARK II (R6000)
0166h	MIPS MARK III (R4000)

Offset 06 — n OBJECTS — size WORD
Specifies the number of entries (objects) in the object table.

Offset 08 — TIME/DATE STAMP — size DWORD
Stores the date and time when the file was created or modified by the linker.

Offset 12 — RESERVED — size DWORD
A reserved area of the PE header.

Offset 16 — RESERVED — size DWORD
A reserved area of the PE header.

Offset 20 — NT HDR SIZE — size WORD
Determines the size of the PE header in bytes.

Offset 22 — FLAGS — size WORD
Flag bits for the image. The possible values are as follows:

Value	Explanation
0000h	Program image.
0002h	Image is executable. If this byte isn't set, errors were detected at link time or the image cannot be loaded.
0200h	Indicates that if the image can't be loaded at the image base, then do not load it.
2000h	Set if this is a library image (DLL).

Offset 24 — RESERVED — size WORD
A reserved area of the PE header.

Offset 26 — LMAJOR — size BYTE
Specifies where the main part of the linker version is located.

Offset 27 — LMINOR — size BYTE
Specifies where the second part of the linker version is located.

Offset 28 — RESERVED — size DWORD
A reserved area of the PE header.

Offset 32 — RESERVED — size DWORD
A reserved area of the PE header.

Offset 36 — RESERVED — size DWORD
A reserved area of the PE header.

Offset 40 — ENTRYPOINT RVA — size DWORD

This address is relative to the image base. It is a starting address for program images and for libraries (DLLs). It is an initializing and ending address for library images.

Offset 44 — RESERVED — size DWORD

A reserved area of the PE header.

Offset 48 — RESERVED — size DWORD

A reserved area of the PE header.

Offset 52 — IMAGE BASE — size DWORD

The virtual base of the image. This will be the virtual address of the first byte of the file (DOS MZ header). It must be divisible by 64 and it is usually 400000h for EXE files.

Offset 56 — OBJECT ALIGN — size DWORD

Determines the alignment of the object and is the same for all objects. In practice, this means that if this value is, for example, 1000h, then each section will have to start with a multiple of 1000h bytes. If the first section (object) is at 401000h and its size is 10h bytes, then the following section must start at 402000h, even if the remaining space will not be used.

Offset 60 — FILE ALIGN — size DWORD

Determines the alignment of pages in the file and is the same for all pages. In practice, this means that if this value is, for example, 200h, then each page will have to start with a multiple of 200h bytes. If the first page is at the 200h file offset, and its size is 10h bytes, then the following section must start at 400h, even if the remaining space will not be used.

Offset 64h — OS MAJOR and OS MINOR — size DWORD

The type of operating system necessary for launching the file.

Offset 68 — USER MAJOR and USER MINOR — size DWORD

You can find the user's number here.

Offset 72 — SUBSYS MAJOR and SUBSYS MINOR — size DWORD

The number of the subsystem. If the PE file was created for Win32, there should be version 4.0 because otherwise the dialog box will not be displayed in 3D.

Offset 76 — RESERVED — size DWORD

A reserved area of the PE header.

Offset 80 — IMAGE SIZE — size DWORD

The virtual size (in bytes) of the image is set here. This offset is a part of all headers and sections. For the value to be correct, it must be divisible by the object align setting.

Offset 84 — HEADER SIZE — size DWORD
The total header size, which is the sum of the DOS MZ header, PE header, and object table sizes.

Offset 88 — FILE CHECKSUM — size DWORD
Checksum of the entire file.

Offset 92 — SUBSYSTEM — size WORD
The value that determines which NT subsystem is necessary to run the file.

Value	Explanation
0000h	Unknown
0001h	Native
0002h	Windows GUI
0003h	Windows character
0005h	OS/2 character
0007h	POSIX character

Offset 94 — DLL FLAGS — size WORD
Indicates special loader requirements. This flag has the following bit values. All other bits are reserved and should be set to zero.

Value	Explanation
0001h	Per-process library initialization
0002h	Per-process library termination
0004h	Per-thread library initialization
0008h	Per-thread library termination

Offset 96 — STACK RESERVE SIZE — size DWORD
The stack size needed for the file. The memory is reserved, but only the STACK COMMIT SIZE has been used. The following stack page is the guarded page. If an application uses the guarded page, the guarded page becomes a normal page, and the next page becomes a guarded page. This continues until the reserve size is reached.

Offset 100 — STACK COMMIT SIZE — size DWORD
Determines how much reserved memory will be used for the stack.

Offset 104 — HEAP RESERVE SIZE — size DWORD
Size of the local heap reserved.

Offset 108 — HEAP COMMIT SIZE — size DWORD
The amount of the local heap that is actually used.

Offset 112 — RESERVED — size DWORD
A reserved area of the PE header.

Offset 116 — # INTERESTING RVA/SIZES — size DWORD
Size of the RVA/SIZE file that follows.

Offset 120 — EXPORT TABLE RVA — size DWORD
Relative virtual address (RVA) of the export table. This address is relative to the image base.

Offset 124 — TOTAL EXPORT DATA SIZE — size DWORD
Size of the export table.

Offset 128 — IMPORT TABLE RVA — size DWORD
RVA of the import table. This address is relative to the image base.

Offset 132 — TOTAL IMPORT DATA SIZE — size DWORD
Size of the import table.

Offset 136 — RESOURCE TABLE RVA — size DWORD
Relative virtual address of the resource table. This address is relative to the image base.

Offset 140 — TOTAL RESOURCE DATA SIZE — size DWORD
Size of the resource table.

Offset 144 — EXCEPTION TABLE RVA — size DWORD
Relative virtual address of the exception table. This address is relative to the image base.

Offset 148 — TOTAL EXCEPTION DATA SIZE — size DWORD
Size of the exception table.

Offset 152 — SECURITY TABLE RVA — size DWORD
Relative virtual address of the security table. This address is relative to the image base.

Offset 156 — TOTAL SECURITY DATA SIZE — size DWORD
Size of the security table.

Offset 160 — FIXUP TABLE RVA — size DWORD
Relative virtual address of the fix-up table. This address is relative to the image base.

Offset 164 — TOTAL FIXUP DATA SIZE — size DWORD
Size of the fix-up table.

Offset 168 — DEBUG TABLE RVA — size DWORD
Relative virtual address of the debug table. This address is relative to the image base.

Offset 172 — TOTAL DEBUG DIRECTORIES — size DWORD
Size of the debug table.

Offset 176 — IMAGE DESCRIPTION RVA — size DWORD
Relative virtual address of the description string specified in the module definition file.

Offset 180 — TOTAL DESCRIPTION SIZE — size DWORD
Size of the reference data.

Offset 184 — MACHINE SPECIFIC RVA — size DWORD
Relative virtual address of a machine-specific value. This address is relative to the image base.

Offset 188 — MACHINE SPECIFIC SIZE — size DWORD
Size of the machine-specific value.

Offset 192 — THREAD LOCAL STORAGE RVA — size DWORD
Relative virtual address of the thread local storage. This address is relative to the image base.

Offset 196 — TOTAL THREAD LOCAL STORAGE — size DWORD
Size of the thread local storage.

Object Table

The object table follows the PE header. The number of fields that it contains is determined by the NumberOfSections field in the PE header. The structure of the object table is called the IMAGE_SECTION_HEADER.

Offset 0 — IMAGE SIZE OF SHORT NAME — size 8 bytes
The name of the section in ASCII. Because the name doesn't end in 0, all 8 bytes will be used. Typical names are .data or .code. The name of the section doesn't mean that it must contain only code though; it may easily contain both code and data.

Offset 8 — PHYSICAL ADDRESS — size DWORD
The file address. This item isn't much used. There are linkers that set an address here, but it is usually 0.

Offset 12 — VIRTUAL SIZE — size DWORD
The size of the contents when loaded into memory (in bytes). This item isn't much used. There are linkers that set an address here, but it is usually 0.

Offset 16 — VIRTUAL ADDRESS — size DWORD
Address of the first byte of the data section when loaded into memory, relative to the image base.

Offset 20 — SIZE OF RAW DATA — size DWORD
Size of the initialized data on disk, rounded to the next multiple of the FileAlignment.

Offset 24 — POINTER TO RAW DATA — size DWORD
An offset to the beginning of the section from the start of the file. If it is 0, then the section doesn't contain any data.

Offset 28 — POINTER TO RELOCATIONS — size DWORD
Only object files use this item, or it occurs only under special circumstances.

Offset 32 — POINTER TO LINENUMBERS — size DWORD
Only object files use this item, or it occurs only under special circumstances.

Offset 36 — NUMBER OF RELOCATIONS — size DWORD
Only object files use this item, or it occurs only under special circumstances.

Offset 38 — NUMBER OF LINENUMBERS — size DWORD
Only object files use this item, or it occurs only under special circumstances.

Offset 40 — CHARACTERISTICS — size DWORD
Flags that determine whether the section is data or code and whether it can be written to or read from.

Bit 5	(IMAGE_SCN_CNT_CODE) Set if the section contains executable code.
Bit 6	(IMAGE_SCN_CNT_INITIALIZED_DATA) Set if the section contains data that will become real values (initialized) before the file has been launched.
Bit 7	(IMAGE_SCN_CNT_UNINITIALIZED_DATA) Set if the section contains uninitialized data, and all of the data will be initialized as 0-byte values before the file is launched. This is usually the BSS section.
Bit 9	(IMAGE_SCN_LNK_INFO) Set if the section doesn't contain image data but rather commentary, description, or other documentation. This information is part of the object file and it may, for example, contain information for the linker telling it which libraries will be necessary.
Bit 11	(IMAGE_SCN_LNK_REMOVE) Set if the section will be removed from the object file after linking. It is often used with bit 9.
Bit 12	(IMAGE_SCN_LNK_COMDAT) Set if the section contains the common block data (COMDAT).
Bit 15	(IMAGE_SCN_MEM_FARDATA) Set if there is distant data. (I haven't determined the exact meaning of this bit.)
Bit 17	(IMAGE_SCN_MEM_PURGEABLE) I don't know the meaning of this bit.
Bit 18	(IMAGE_SCN_MEM_LOCKED) I don't know the meaning of this bit.
Bit 19	(IMAGE_SCN_MEM_PRELOAD) I don't know the meaning of this bit.
Bits 20–23	I don't know the meanings of these bits.
Bit 24	(IMAGE_SCN_LNK_NRELOC_OVFL) Set if the section contains extended relocations.
Bit 25	(IMAGE_SCN_MEM_DISCARDABLE) Set if the data sections will not be necessary after the file is launched (such as the starting routine of a driver that will be launched only once).
Bit 26	(IMAGE_SCN_MEM_NOT_CACHED) Set when the data sections will not be preserved.

Bit 27	(IMAGE_SCN_MEM_NOT_PAGED) Set when the data sections will not be paged. This is relevant to drivers.
Bit 28	(IMAGE_SCN_MEM_SHARED) Set when the data sections can be shared.
Bit 29	(IMAGE_SCN_MEM_EXECUTE) Set if the section can be executed as code.
Bit 30	(IMAGE_SCN_MEM_READ) Set if the section can be read.
Bit 31	(IMAGE_SCN_MEM_WRITE) Set if the section can be written to.

Section Types

The various section types include code, data, BBS, and exported and imported symbols. The characteristics of each section are described below.

Code Section

This section usually contains only the program code, and each file contains only one code section, though that doesn't have to be the rule. *Text, code,* and *AUTO* are some of the typical names for this section.

Characteristic bits:
'IMAGE_SCN_CNT_CODE', 'IMAGE_SCN_MEM_EXECUTE', and 'IMAGE_SCN_MEM_READ'
The AddressOfEntryPoint points to an offset in this section where the first function to be launched is located.

Data Section

This section contains initialized static values (for example, int x 3D 10;)

Characteristic bits:
'IMAGE_SCN_CNT_INITIALIZED_DATA', 'IMAGE_SCN_MEM_READ', and 'IMAGE_SCN_MEM_WRITE'
Some linkers for this section do not set the bit for writing. *Data, idata,* and *DATA* are typical names for this section, among others.

BSS Section

This section contains the uninitialized data (int x;), and it is very similar to the data section. The 'IMAGE_SCN_CNT_UNINITIALIZED_DATA' bit set is found here instead of 'IMAGE_SCN_CNT_INITIALIZED_DATA'. Such a file will contain only the section header but not the section itself. The section, itself, will be created only by the loader, and it will be filled in with zero bits. *Bss* and *BSS* are typical names for this section, among others.

Exported Symbols

This section contains the exported functions, mostly found in DLL files. (Normal executable files usually don't contain exported symbols.)

'.edata'

---

is the most frequent name for this section.

The structure of the export directory table is as follows:

Offset 0 — CHARACTERISTICS — size DWORD
This item isn't much used; it is set to zero.

Offset 4 — TIME DATE STAMP — size DWORD
This item contains the time when the data was created, and it is in the time_t-format. However, it isn't frequently set, and many compilers set it to 0.

Offset 8 — MAJOR VERSION — size WORD
This is the user-settable major version number, and it is typically set to zero. If it is not zero, it contains information about the version.

Offset 10 — MINOR VERSION — size WORD
This is the user-settable minor version number, and it is typically set to zero. If it is not zero, it contains information about the version.

Offset 12 — NAME RVA — size DWORD
The RVA of the DLL ASCII name. This is an ASCII string ending in 0.

Offset 16 — BASE or ORDINAL BASE — size DWORD
The first valid exported ordinal. This field specifies the starting ordinal number for the export address table for this image, and is normally set to 1. (The export address table contains the address of exported entry points and exported data and absolutes.)

Offset 20 — NUMBER OF FUNCTIONS — size DWORD
The number of the exported items.

Offset 24 — NUMBER OF NAMES or NUMBER OF ORDINALS — size DWORD
The number of the exported names. While each exported item usually has only one name, one item may have more names or even none, in which case it is only possible to call the exported function by means of the "ordinal number."

Offset 28 — ADDRESS OF FUNCTIONS — size DWORD
The relative virtual address to the export address table, relative to the image base. Here are the 32-bit values that are the RVA to the exported function. If the RVA in the list is 0, the exported function hasn't been used. The RVA may point into the section containing the export directory, and this is called a *forwarded export*. A forwarded export is a pointer to an export in another binary file.

Offset 32 — ADDRESS OF NAMES — size DWORD

The relative virtual address of the export name table pointers, relative to the beginning of the image base.

Offset 36 — ADDRESS OF NAME ORDINALS or ADDRESS OF ORDINALS — size DWORD

Relative virtual address of the export ordinals table entry, relative to the image base.

Imported Symbols

This section contains all the imported functions. If the program calls an API function, the information for the call will be located in this section. When the file is being loaded into memory, the loader reads the import information and modifies the file in memory. "idata" is the most common name for this section.

This section starts with a field containing the IMAGE_IMPORT_DESCRIPTOR. It contains an array of import direct entries — one for each DLL library that the file references. The last directory entry is empty (null), and you can find the end of the directory table by finding the IMAGE_IMPORT_DESCRIPTOR that contains zero bits.

IMAGE_IMPORT_DESCRIPTOR Structure

The IMAGE_IMPORT_DESCRIPTOR structure is special because it contains two parallel fields with pointers to the IMAGE_THUNK_DATA. The first field, called by the ORIGINAL FIRST THUNK, is always the same. The second field, called by the IMAGE_IMPORT_DESCRIPTOR, is rewritten every time the PE loader launches it. The loader searches for the address of each function and rewrites the IMAGE_THUNK_DATA with the address of each imported function.

The IMAGE_IMPORT_DESCRIPTOR structure is as follows:

Offset 0 — ORIGINAL FIRST THUNK or characteristics — size DWORD

This item contains the RVA to the IMAGE_THUNK_DATA.

Offset 4 — TIME DATE STAMP — size DWORD

Time when the file was created; usually zero.

Offset 8 — FORWARDER CHAIN — size DWORD

This item contains a pointer to the first redirected function. It is sometimes used when other functions have been redirected into another DLL.

Offset 12 — NAME — size DWORD

This item contains the RVA to an ASCII string ending in 0. It is the name of the imported DLL library.

Offset 16 — FIRST THUNK — size DWORD

This item is an RVA to a field ending in a zero bit containing the RVA to the IMAGE_THUNK_DATA. Each RVA is for one imported function, and it is often called the pointer to the IMAGE_IMPORT_BY_NAME structure.

NOTE *The import may only be an ordinal number.*

IMAGE_THUNK_DATA

Each structure of the IMAGE_THUNK_DATA corresponds to one imported function. If a function was imported by the ordinal value, the upper bit in the IMAGE_THUNK_DATA will be set. For example, 0x80000010 from the field for the KERNEL32.DLL means that every tenth function of this DLL will be imported. This method isn't recommended, though, because if there is a change in the DLL version, the tenth function may be different than it was originally.

If the function was imported by name, the IMAGE_THUNK_DATA will contain an RVA for the IMAGE_IMPORT_BY_NAME structure.

IMAGE_IMPORT_BY_NAME Structure

The structure of IMAGE_IMPORT_BY_NAME is as follows:

Offset 0 — HINT — size WORD

This is the best estimate of what the export ordinal for the exported function is like. This value doesn't have to be correct; the loader uses it as a recommended value for searching for the exported function. It is often zero.

Offset 2 — BYTE — size ?

This is an ASCII string with the name of the imported function. When loading the file, the PE loader uses the initialization information from the IMAGE_THUNK_DATA for finding the imported function's address. The loader will rewrite the IMAGE_THUNK_DATA with the address of the imported function.

Resources

The PE file's resources (menu, dialog boxes, and so on) are located in this section. Resources are located in the main directory, which contains subdirectories. These subdirectories may contain further subdirectories.

The main directory and the subdirectories have a common structure, IMAGE_RESOURCE_DIRECTORY, which has the following format:

Offset 0 — CHARACTERISTICS — size DWORD

Theoretically, the flag for resources should be here, but actually it isn't used. Therefore, this is only zero.

Offset 4 — TIME DATE STAMP — size DWORD

The time when the resource was created.

Offset 8 — MAJOR VERSION — size WORD

The resource version should be located here, but usually it is zero.

Offset 10 — MINOR VERSION — size WORD

The resource version should be located here, but usually it is zero.

Offset 12 — NUMBER OF NAMED ENTRIES — size WORD

Number of field items using names. (To understand this, you must study the structure of the directory entries field.)

Offset 14 — NUMBER OF ID ENTRIES — size WORD

Number of field items using an identification number. (To understand this, you must study the structure of the directory entries field.)

Offset 16 — IMAGE RESOURCE DIRECTORY ENTRY — size NUMBER_OF_NAMED_ENTRIES + NUMBER_OF_ID_ENTRIES

While not actually an item of the IMAGE_RESOURCE_DIRECTORY structure, this immediately follows it. The sum of the NUMBER_OF_NAMED_ENTRIES and the NUMBER_OF_ID_ENTRIES is the size of the field. Items in the field may point to other subdirectories or to the IMAGE_RESOURCE_DATA_ENTRY, which describes where the resources are located in the file.

You will usually need to go down at least three levels to get to the IMAGE_RESOURCE_DATA_ENTRY. The first directory is located at the highest level, and you can find it at the beginning of the resource section. Other subdirectories are divided in accordance with the resource type (dialog box, menu, and so on). Each of these type-divided subdirectories has one identification subdirectory, which is always marked with a text string (the name of the menu) or by an identification number.

IMAGE_RESOURCE_DIRECTORY_ENTRY Structure

The structure of the IMAGE_RESOURCE_DIRECTORY_ENTRY is as follows:

Offset 0 — NAME — size DWORD

If the upper bit (0x80000000) is set to zero, this field will contain the ID number item for the resource identification. If the upper bit is set to 1, the field will contain the offset item (relative to the beginning of the resource section) to the IMAGE_RESOURCE_DIR_STRING_U structure. This structure contains a WORD value representing the length, and, right behind it, a Unicode string with the name of the file.

Offset 4 — OFFSET TO DATA — size DWORD

If the upper bit is set (0x80000000), this item will contain an offset to the following IMAGE_RESOURCE_DIRECTORY. If the upper bit isn't set, this field will contain an offset to the IMAGE_RESOURCE_DATA_ENTRY structure.

This structure determines where resource data is located in the file, its size, and code page.

IMAGE_RESOURCE_DATA_ENTRY Structure

The structure of the IMAGE_RESOURCE_DATA_ENTRY is as follows.

Offset 0 — OFFSET TO DATA — size DWORD
RVA address of the resource data.

Offset 4 — SIZE — size DWORD
Size of the data.

Offset 8 — CODEPAGE — size DWORD
The code page.

Offset 12 — RESERVED — size DWORD
A reserved area.

11

SUGGESTIONS FOR BETTER SOFTWARE PROTECTION

Protecting software against illegal copying has both advantages and disadvantages.

It frequently happens that developers underestimate the testing process, and the protection that they add causes problems for users. For example, tricks that protect against CD copying don't always work correctly on all CD-ROM drives. I have seen programs where it wasn't possible to enter the correct registration number.

Therefore, it is important to test as thoroughly as possible. Testing should also be performed with all operating systems for which the application is designed. If something works correctly with Windows 9x, it might not work correctly with Windows NT, 2000, or XP. Anti-debugging tricks also should not be used too much, and only those that work extremely well should be used at all. However, this doesn't mean that you should be afraid to try new methods.

Remember that crackers are often better informed than you are. The best of them are also excellent programmers, and they cannot be surprised easily. It is, for example, more and more common to use RSA encrypting methods for registration numbers. Only a few people understand that even if you use a 128-bit encrypting key, or even the 512-bit key, it is still possible to break the protection and create a registration number generator. It is impossible to break the RSA protection with a 1024-bit key. There are many examples like this.

The best way to protect your software is to keep your eyes open for the latest developments. The situation changes incredibly quickly. If someone breaks through your protection, don't surrender, but fight even harder, because there is always a way to make the protection better.

You can find so-called "crackme" programs on the Internet, mostly created by crackers. You can find new ideas and methods there, some of which are excellently programmed and hard to overcome. Study them and you may discover something new.

Rules for Writing Good Software Protection

It is difficult but not impossible to program good software protection. But remember: If you use typical programming methods when writing a new protection program, you make the cracker's job easier. Most crackers use several well-tested methods to crack particular types of protection and, as such, are able to remove 80 to 90 percent of protection programs. The key is to use less-common methods, which will slow the cracker down or even stop him.

Therefore, I present these rules for writing good software protection.

1. **Never give a testing routine a self-describing name.** For example, if you use the function name TestRegistration in a DLL library, the cracker will immediately know where in the code to focus his effort.

2. **Avoid unnecessary error messages.** If the program gives an error message after an incorrect registration number has been entered, the cracker can simply search the program code for the error message to track down the procedure that called it. When error messages are unavoidable, hide them as much as possible, and create them (dynamically) in real time rather than use resources for them. It's also a good idea to encode the data and the procedure that creates an error message, which makes it much more difficult for the cracker to find in the disassembled code.

3. **Use very good encoding for the registration files and other protections.** If this doesn't stop the cracker, it will at least slow him down considerably. I recommend RSA 1024, which is unbreakable.

4. **Use random tests for the registration.** There is a good chance that this protection will succeed, especially if you use a testing method that differs from the original one. These random tests should start several days or hours after registration. Crackers really hate them because it usually takes a lot of time to remove them.

5. **Don't start the registration number test for several seconds or even minutes after the registration.** This will make it much more difficult for the cracker to trace the application in a debugger. Better still, require the program to restart before testing begins.

6. **Use checksums in your application.** If you test your EXE and DLL files, and even other files, for changes, crackers will be unable to modify them with patches. However, they will still be able to modify the code directly in memory, so it is a good idea to test for changes to the application code in memory, as well. It is also a good idea to perform checksums for smaller sections of your program, because a cracker may change the checksum to the correct value after he changes the program. When you perform checksums on smaller sections of the program, you make the cracker's job very difficult.

7. **Use more checking routines to make it harder to remove the protection.** Any one routine should test only a part of the correctness of the registration, not the whole of it, to prevent the registration being understood when a cracker discovers it. By using more than one checking routine, the cracking of the program will often be incorrect because the cracker may miss one or more of the checking routines.

8. **Have the program change while running.** By having the program change as it runs, you make its code more difficult to understand. You can also use this technique to create false testing routines that will confuse the cracker while they are disassembling your program.

9. **Put your registration information in a non-obvious place.** If you keep the registration information in the Windows registry, it can be easily discovered. Instead, keep it in a file that nobody would suspect would contain the registration, like a DLL. By placing such a DLL into the Windows system directory, you will make the registration situation very confusing for the cracker. Even if a cracker uses a monitor to follow access to files, it may take a long time before he understands that the registration is in such a file. Better still, locate the registration in more than one place to make it likely that the protection will be removed incorrectly.

10. **Encrypt the registration.** Encrypt your registration using a technique that is dependent on the particular computer's hardware to make it impossible to use the file to register the program on another computer. (It's a good idea to use the serial number of the hard drive.)

11. **Don't be afraid of long registrations.** The longer the registration file or number, the longer it takes to understand it. If the registration file or number is sufficiently long, it may contain important information that the program needs, and if such a program is patched, it will not run correctly.

12. **Test several current bits of data when using time-limit protection, such as file date, system.dat, and bootlog.txt.** If the current date or time is the same or smaller than when the program was run previously, it will be clear that the time was adjusted. Also, you can save the date and time after each

launch of the program, and then test the current date and time during a new launch.

13. **Testing routines may be unbelievably long.** Something that takes only a few seconds when a program is running may take an extremely long time to run while disassembling or debugging. Nevertheless, make sure that it isn't possible for the cracker to tell whether this is important or useless code, or they will know whether they can jump right over it. Your testing routine should run anywhere from 10 to 30 seconds in length.

14. **If you limit your program's functionality, make sure that the program doesn't contain the code for the limited function.** Many developers make the mistake of including in the unregistered program the code for a function that is only to be available after registration (the ability to save files, for example). In such a case, the cracker can modify the code so that the function will work.

    A better approach is to include parts of the code (a sufficiently long bit) together with the registration, such as an EXE file. Under the best protection strategies, the user receives the code upon registration, and the program will use this code after it checks the registration. With such a protection scheme, it's virtually impossible for the cracker to remove the protection without the correct registration.

    Also, consider encrypting sections of the code that are not supposed to function in an unregistered version, to be decoded only after registration. The decoding key must then contain the registration, so that the program cannot be decoded without it.

15. **If your program has been cracked, release a new version.** Frequent updates to your program may put off crackers, especially when the protection was removed by changing the code, because the patch will not work in the new version.

16. **Use the best, current compression or encoding programs to encode your software.** Keep an ear to the ground to find out which is currently the best compression or encoding program, and which have decoders. A good compressor will be difficult for a cracker to remove.

17. **If your application uses a registration number, that number should never be visible in memory.** This means that it should be impossible to find your program's registration number when the program is being debugged.

    When programming a method that checks to see whether the correct registration number was entered, do something other than just comparing two strings. The best way is to encode the entered registration number and the correct registration in the same way. In this way, the two numbers can be compared without risk of the cracker discovering the code.

    You might also compare a checksum of the entered registration number with the checksum of the correct registration number, though if you do so, you will have to use more checking methods to really make sure that the correct registration number was entered, rather than modified in accordance with the checksum that the cracker had seen in his debugger.

18. **Consider requiring online registration.** The Internet has greatly increased the feasibility of online registration. When a program is registered online, its registration data is sent to a particular server. In its most basic form, this server then sends back information to the program telling it whether the registration was successful or not. However, the server can also be used to send data that the program needs in order to launch the registered application. This data may range from important parts of the code to a key needed to decode parts of the program.

19. **Remember the anti-debugging tricks and various anti-disassembling methods that have been described in this book.** Be sure that the innovations you learn about and choose to implement are functional. If you cannot debug or disassemble something, you cannot remove it either.

20. **Test your software's protection.** Test your software's protection for all operating systems under which it will run. Often, protection that works with Windows 9x doesn't work correctly with Windows NT, 2000, or XP.

Keep Current

Finally, visit these web sites to stay abreast of the latest developments.

w3.to/protools/	A page focusing on new tools for programmers. You can find compression, encoding, monitoring, and decoding programs here.
win32asm.cjb.net	A great page devoted to the assembler programming language. It is especially good for beginners, but even more experienced people can learn something new here.
www.egroups.com/list/exelist	A discussion list about compression and encoding programs.
elicz.cjb.net	A page about system programming with excellent source code.
www.anticracking.sk	My page, focused on software protection against illegal copying.

GLOSSARY

Algorithm   A detailed sequence of actions to perform in order to accomplish some task.

API (application programming interface)   The interface by which an application accesses operating system and other services. An API is defined at source code level and provides a level of abstraction between the application and the kernel to ensure the portability of code.

API calls   Functions included in the Microsoft Windows DLL libraries. They should make the programmers' job easier.

API hook   Replacement of a library function with another code, without a program being aware of it.

Application code   The program code for an application.

Assembler   A program that converts assembly language into machine code.

Assembly   A programming language.

Breakpoint   A point in a program that, when reached, causes some special behavior. It is usually associated with debugging. During an interactive debugging session, when the breakpoint is reached, program execution halts, at which point the cracker can examine the contents of both the memory (and variables).

Brute force attack   An attempt to decrypt a specific encrypted text by trying every possible key.

Checksum   A computed value that depends on the contents of a block of data. A checksum is transmitted or stored along with the data in order to detect corruption of the data.

Compiler   A program that converts another program from a programming language to machine language (*object code*). Some compilers output assembly language, which is then converted to machine language by a separate assembler. Each programming language must have its specific compiler. Most compilers for higher programming languages can also work with assembly. A compiler differs from an assembler in that each input statement does not, in general, correspond to a single machine instruction.

Compression   A mathematic method for "decreasing" the size of the compressed data and the resulting decrease in their volume.

Compressor   An application compressing data or files.

Coprocessor   Any computer processor that assists the main processor by performing certain special functions, usually much faster than the main processor could perform them in software. The coprocessor often decodes instructions in parallel with the main processor and executes only those instructions intended for it.

Crack   A program that removes software protection from an application after it has been launched. When a person removes software protection, they are said to be *cracking*.

Cracker   A person who removes protection from software.

CRC (cyclic redundancy code)   A number derived from, and stored or transmitted with, a block of data in order to detect corruption. By recalculating the CRC and comparing it to the value originally transmitted, the receiver can detect certain errors or the validity of a file.

Debug   To tune an application and search for errors in the program code. For crackers, it means to search the application code for protection schemes.

Debugger   A tool that can step through execution of a program and examine variables and memory. Debuggers can also set breakpoints at which program execution will stop when the program is running in the debugger. Crackers often use a debugger when cracking.

Decoder   An application decoding data or a file into the original form that existed before encoding.

Decompiler   An application that can translate an executable file back into the programming language in which it was created. You can use a decompiler only for an application that was created in a programming language supported by the particular decompiler.

Delphi   A programming language from Borland.

Disassembler   An application that can translate an executable file back into the original programming language, most frequently assembler. This term is sometimes used to describe decompilers.

DLL (dynamically linked library)   A library that is linked to applications when they are loaded or run.

Encode   To convert data into a given format.

Encoder   Any program or algorithm that can encode data or a file by means of a selected encryption.

EPROM (erasable programmable read-only memory)   Programmable read-only memory (programmable ROM) that can be erased and reused. EPROM keeps data even after disconnecting from the power source.

EXE file   An executable binary file.

EXE protector   An application that tries to protect EXE files and other executables from debugging, decompiling, disassembling, and cracking.

Freeware   An application that may be used without paying for it.

Key   A value used to identify a record in a database.

Linker   A program that combines one or more files prepared by a compiler into a single file containing loadable or executable code (such as EXE, COM, or DLL files). Each operating system has its own type of linker because their executable files are different.

Machine code   The representation of a computer program that is actually read and interpreted by the computer.

Object code   The machine code generated by a source code language processor, such as an assembler or compiler.

Patch   To change the program code in memory or directly in the file.

P-Code   A type of software compilation in Visual Basic.

Pirate   A person who illegally spreads software.

Pirate group   A group of people who illegally spread software.

Processor   A functional unit in a computer that performs the program's execution.

Program release   To release an application into circulation, or the released program itself.

Register   One of a small number of high-speed memory locations in the processor.

Source code   The form in which a computer program is written by the programmer. Also *source*.

Trace   Tracing application code in a debugger.

VxD (virtual device driver) A device driver under Windows 3.x/Windows 95 running as part of the kernel, and thus having access to the memory of the kernel and all running processes, as well as raw access to the hardware. VxD's usually have the filename extension .386 under Windows 3.x and .vxd under Windows 95.

XOR Encoding of program code using the XOR instruction.

INDEX

C

M

N

O

P

U

UnhandledExceptionFilter, 163–64
unSafeDisc (program), 47
Update Time & Date Stamp
    function, 58
UPX (compression program), 72
Use Quick Compression Method
    function, 58
user debuggers, detecting, 180–82
USER MAJOR and USER MINOR -
    size DWORD, 214
user's number, of PE file, 214
Use Windows DLL Loader
    function, 56

V

VB40016.dll library, 20
VB40032.dll library, 21
vboxpxx.PreviewExecGate_By_Weiju
    nLi call, 88
Vbox (software protection
    program), 86–89
Vboxt4xx.dll, 88
VCOM's Sourcer (disassembler), 10
versions, releasing new if program
    cracked, 228
VIRTUAL ADDRESS - size
    DWORD, 217
VIRTUAL SIZE - size DWORD, 217
VirtualQuery function, 185
Virus Heuristic function, 67
Visual Basic programs
    registration-number (serial-
        number) protection in, 19–23
    and time-limited programs, 28
VMMCall Get_DDB, 129
VMM_GetDDBList call, 160
VOB (CD protection software), 48

VWIN32_Int41Dispatch function
    4fh, 135
VxD call VMM_GetDDBList, 160
VxD file, searching for/determining
    whether active, 203
VxD Monitor (monitoring
    program), *205*
VxD SIWVID, 122–26
VxD (Virtual Device Driver), 103
VxDCall, SoftICE detection with,
    129–32, 135–39

W

w3.to/protools/ (website), 229
websites
    of crackers, 2–3
    software protection resources,
        229
wf command, 14
win32asm.cjb.net (website), 229
WinDasm (disassembler), 9–10
Windows API calls. *See* API functions
Windows DLL loader, 56
Windows NT executable files (PE
    Files), 211–17
    .code section of, 203
    header, 170
        changing, 188
        checksum in, 202
        deleting, 67
        detecting attempts change,
            203
        structure of, 211–17
    loader, 211
    section table, 211
Windows (operating system)
    registry
        changes to for punishing
            cracker, 205–6

STEAL THIS COMPUTER BOOK 2
What They Won't Tell You About the Internet

by WALLACE WANG

This bestseller will open your eyes to the Internet underground, with coverage of everything from viruses and password theft to Trojan Horse programs and encryption. The cd-rom includes over 200 anti-hacker and security tools.

"An engaging look at the darker side of the information superhighway."
— Amazon.com

2000, 462 PP. W/CD-ROM, $24.95 ($38.95 CDN)
ISBN 1-886411-42-5

THE LINUX COOKBOOK
Tips and Techniques for Everyday Use

by MICHAEL STUTZ

Over 1,500 step-by-step Linux "recipes" cover hundreds of day-to-day issues, including printing; managing files; editing and formatting text; working with digital audio; creating and manipulating graphics; and connecting to the Internet.

2001, 402 PP., $29.95 ($44.95 CDN)
ISBN 1-886411-48-4

JIN SATO'S LEGO MINDSTORMS
The Master's Technique

BY JIN SATO

LEGO legend Jin Sato shares his way of thinking about designing MINDSTORMS robots like his famous robotic dog, MIBO, in this landmark book.

"Every LEGO Mindstorms enthusiast should have this book next to their LEGO storage bin." — Slashdot

2002, 364 PP., $24.95 ($37.95 CDN)
ISBN 1-886411-56-5

THE BOOK OF OVERCLOCKING
Tweak Your PC to Unleash Its Power

BY SCOTT WAINNER AND ROBERT RICHMOND

If you don't mind voiding the manufacturer's warranty on your CPU, overclocking is for you. Learn how not to fry your system while souping up everything from the Pentium II to the latest Athlon XP and Pentium 4. Sections on cooling, troubleshooting, and benchmarking make sure you get the most out of your machine.

2002, 304 PP., $29.95 ($44.95 CDN)
ISBN 1-886411-76-X

LINUX IN THE WORKPLACE
How to Use Linux in Your Office

BY SSC, PUBLISHERS OF LINUX JOURNAL

Linux in the Workplace introduces Linux users to the desktop capabilities of Linux and the K Desktop Environment (KDE) graphical user interface, a powerful Open Source graphical desktop environment for UNIX workstations. Includes information on how to use email and surf the Internet; perform general office-related tasks; work with the command line; and much more.

2002, 400 PP., $29.95 ($44.95 CDN)
ISBN 1-886411-86-7

Phone:

1 (800) 420-7240 OR
(415) 863-9900
MONDAY THROUGH FRIDAY,
9 A.M. TO 5 P.M. (PST)

Fax:

(415) 863-9950
24 HOURS A DAY,
7 DAYS A WEEK

Email:

SALES@NOSTARCH.COM

Web:

HTTP://WWW.NOSTARCH.COM

Mail:

NO STARCH PRESS
555 DE HARO STREET, SUITE 250
SAN FRANCISCO, CA 94107
USA

Distributed in the U.S. by Publishers Group West

ABOUT THE CD

Here's what you'll find on this CD:

"Compression and Protection Programs" Directory

1. aPLib v0.36: The best (32 bit) compression library
2. Armadillo 2.60c: One of the best commercial protection programs
3. ASPack v2.1: The compression program with the best compression ratio
3. AsProtect v1.2: One of the best commercial protection programs
4. CodeCrypt v0.164: A simple protection program
5. Crunch v1.0: Commercial protection software
6. Ding Boy's PE-lock v1.2: A simple commercial protection program
7. JCALG1 RELEASE 5.21 SOURCE CODE: Source code for one of the best compression libraries from PE Compact
8. NeoLite v2.0: A good compression program
9. NFO 1.0: A simple protection program
10. PC Shrink v0.29: An older compression program with source code
11. PC Shrink v0.71: Compression program
12. PE Compact 1.76: A very good compression program
13. PE Diminisher v0.1: A simple compression program
14. PE Protect v0.9b: An older, but still good protection program
15. PECRYPT32 1.02: This was the best protection program until the release of

PE-SHiELD

16. PE-Encrypter 2.0: A simple protection program with source code

17. PELOCKnt v2.04: One of the best protection programs

18. PE-SHiELD v0.25: One of the best protection programs available today (in a special registered version for this book!)

19. Petite v2.2: A good compression program

20. Shrinker v3.4: Formerly one of the best protection programs

21. SVK Protector v1.11: My own protection program

21. tElock 0.98: One of the best protection programs

22. ucl-0.91: Very good compression library, with source code

23. UPX 1.23: One of the best compression programs, with source code

24. VGCrypt PE Encryptor v0.75 Beta: An older protection program with source code

25. WWPack32 v1.20: A good compression program

"Examples" Directory

Complete programming examples and their executables keyed to this book by number

"Text" Directory

1. debug registers: A description of debug registers

2. ImpByOrd: Example from EliCZ about how to implement direct ordinals

3. Intel Pentium Instruction Set Reference: A description of instructions for Assembler

4. Constants for API functions in Assembler: Values for API functions

5. Structured Exception Handling (SEH): File which inludes constants for working with SEH

"Tools" Directory

1. ApiHooks 2.2, 3.0, and 5.6: A very good program from EliCZ which makes it easier to use API Hooking in your application

2. FrogsICE v1.08.5: A program for hidding a debugger against anti-debuggin tricks. You can try it with examples from this book.

3. icedump 6.018 and nticedump 1.9: A very good application, which is a plugin for SoftICE.

4. ProcDump 1.6.2: A very good program which can help the coder to understand the PE structure

5. Resource Hacker v3.4.0: A very good program for working with resources

6. TRW2000 for Win9x v1.22: A high quality debugger for Windows9x with some interesting functions

UPDATES

Visit **http://www.nostarch.com/crackproof_updates.htm** for updates, errata, and other information.